AN ARTLESS ART

THE ZEN AESTHETIC
OF SHIGA NAOYA

AN ARTLESS ART

THE ZEN AESTHETIC
OF SHIGA NAOYA

A Critical Study with Selected Translations

Roy Starrs

JAPAN
LIBRARY

AN ARTLESS ART
THE ZEN AESTHETIC OF SHIGA NAOYA
A Critical Study with Selected Translations

First published 1998 by
JAPAN LIBRARY

Japan Library is an imprint of Curzon Press Ltd
15 The Quadrant, Richmond, Surrey TW9 1BP

© Roy Starrs 1998

British Library Cataloguing in Publication Data
A CIP catalogue entry for this book is
available from the British Library

ISBN 1–873410–64–6

Typeset in Plantin 11 on 12pt by LaserScript, Mitcham, Surrey
Printed and bound in England by Bookcraft, Avon

CONTENTS

In Memory of
Yamaguchi Toshiko
(1926–1994)
Mamesue no mame na obaasan.

Shiga Naoya at a tea ceremony at Tōdaiji Temple, Nara, in 1946

PART ONE

AN ARTLESS ART
The Zen Aesthetic of Shiga Naoya

INTRODUCTION

THE IMPORTANCE OF SHIGA NAOYA

1

For Japanese readers throughout most of this century, there would have been no need to explain the importance of Shiga Naoya (1883–1971). He was long seen as the leading practitioner of a genre regarded as central to twentieth-century Japanese literature, the *shi-shōsetsu*[1]. Indeed, he was even popularly anointed as 'the god of the *shōsetsu* (*'shōsetsu no kamisama'*) or, in a less grandiose if more sentimental phrase, as 'the hometown of Japanese literature' (*nihon bungaku no kokyō*)[2]. From Western readers, however, he has received conspicuously less recognition. Though he lived to a ripe old age, very few of his works were translated into Western languages during his lifetime, and he received very little Western critical attention. To be more specific: although most of his major stories were written in the Taishō period (1912–1926) and his single novel-length work appeared in 1937, it was not until the 1970s that any substantial translation and criticism of his work was undertaken in English. Not until 1987 was there published a book-length collection of his short stories (though earlier in French[3]). Until then a mere handful of them were scattered throughout various anthologies – this in spite of the fact that Shiga had long been recognized as one of the great masters of the form in Japan. His one novel-length work, *A Dark Night's Passing (An'ya kōro*, 1937) was finally translated by Edwin McClellan in 1976.

As for critical studies, the first to be published in book form was Francis Mathy's *Shiga Naoya* (1975). As I intend to show, this is a rather narrow and unsympathetic treatment. William Sibley's *The Shiga Hero*, a revision of his 1971 doctoral dissertation, appeared in 1979. Though more sympathetic to his subject than Mathy, Sibley nevertheless takes a markedly Freudian approach that, in my view, results in an almost

5

equally distorted image of Shiga's art. Perhaps the most helpful and perceptive study published in English during the 1970s was the chapter Ueda Makoto devoted to Shiga in his *Modern Japanese Writers and the Nature of Literature* (1976), which began the process of placing Shiga's *shi-shōsetsu* within the context of its own culture. Ueda's initial efforts were taken a good deal further by two general studies of the *shi-shōsetsu* as a distinct literary genre which appeared in the 1980s: Irmela Hijiya-Kirschnereit's *Selbstentblössungsrituale* (1981), recently translated in a revised edition as *Rituals of Self-Revelation: Shishōsetsu as Literary Genre and Socio-Cultural Phenomenon* (1996) and Edward Fowler's *The Rhetoric of Confession: Shishōsetsu in Early Twentieth-Century Japanese Fiction* (1988). More recently, a salutary counter-argument, stressing the undeniable Western literary and philosophic influences on Shiga and other *shi-shōsetsu* writers, has been voiced by Tomi Suzuki in her *Narrating the Self: Fictions of Japanese Modernity* (1996). Although, as will be obvious from the present study, I do not agree that these Western influences were decisive or definitive – Shiga's goal of an 'impersonal self', for instance, is a far cry from Rousseau's romantic egoism – nevertheless it could be argued that, without the initial impetus he received from Western culture, including Christianity, Shiga might never have been inspired to rediscover his own literary and spiritual roots. Indeed, this was a common enough pattern among early twentieth-century Japanese writers, many of whom took a long 'parabolic route' through Western culture to a renewed understanding and appreciation of their own traditions.

Although some such academic attention has finally begun to be paid to Shiga since his death in 1971, acknowledging his central position in the Japanese literature of this century, the basic fact remains that, despite his high reputation in Japan, during his lifetime he was never accepted in the West as one of the great representative Japanese writers, a potential Nobel Prize candidate, and he never achieved anything like the popularity of writers such as Kawabata, Tanizaki or Mishima. Yet in Japan for much of this century the view persisted that he was perhaps the quintessential Japanese writer of the age. We might well ask, then, why there has existed such an extraordinary gap between native and foreign critical evaluations in this one case, whereas generally Japanese and Western readers have agreed on who are the most important modern Japanese writers?

We have here, it seems to me, a genuine and quite fascinating example of cultural difference, the ramifications of which extend far into Japanese culture and history – and, for that matter, into Western culture and history too. In this sense, Shiga is important not only for his high status in Japan or for his literary achievement in itself but also for what that status and achievement tell us about some of the mainstream values of the culture in which he writes. Conversely, of course, the long-standing neglect of his work in the West implies certain deeply ingrained Western literary and cultural values and prejudices, especially those which led to the perception of the 'difference' of his writings in purely negative terms: that is, as the lack of certain formal qualities which 'good fiction' was expected to possess. For it is equally possible to take a more positive view, not by some arbitrary trick of value-reversal or cross-cultural legerdemain but by recognizing that the 'different' character of Shiga's work issues from the very heart of Japanese culture – in fact, from that same 'Zen aesthetic' which Westerners have often admired and savored in the traditional Japanese arts.

For a long time, though, those few Westerners who were able to read Shiga's work in Japanese seem to have been discouraged by the fact that it lacked what they regarded as the usual and necessary attributes of 'fiction'. Since most of the events described are taken directly and in a seemingly random fashion from the author's own life, there is little in the way of conventional 'well-built' plot-structure; and, since the author himself, or his fictional persona, is almost invariably the protagonist of these self-absorbed works, there is no development of a wide range of 'well-rounded' characters. Edward Seidensticker typically expresses the negative Western view of Shiga's kind of *shi-shōsetsu* when he refers to them as 'unformed reminiscence' and as 'a form of autobiographical jotting that may scarcely seem to deserve the name fiction at all.'[4] At the same time, however, Seidensticker admits the significance of this genre, albeit reluctantly, in the overall context of modern Japanese fiction when he says that 'if there is any one characteristic distinguishing the modern Japanese novel from the modern novel elsewhere, it is the importance of undisguised and unshaped autobiography.'[5] Mishima Yukio also recognized the central place of this genre in the contemporary literature of his country, but he saw it in a more cosmopolitan and less belittling light:

> The 'I-novel' of modern Japanese literature is a
> complex creation of mixed ancestry, bred from the

> French naturalist novel, from the Japanese occa-
> sional essay style of the Middle Ages (called,
> revealingly, 'following one's thoughts') and from
> the self-worship of European romanticism. And,
> because of the peculiar characteristics of Japanese
> poetry which I have mentioned before, the 'I-novel'
> form was also made to serve the function of fulfilling
> poetic needs through the vehicle of prose.[6]

The issue, in fact, is even larger than that of the *shi-shōsetsu per se*, though this is a very widely practised genre. In his above-mentioned study of eight major Japanese novelists, for instance, Makoto Ueda has shown convincingly that the problematic relation between the writer's life and work or, in other words, between reality and fiction, has been a central concern of all of them – even those whose writings were not so obviously autobiographical.

On the other hand, a critic such as Francis Mathy, it seems to me, attempts to evade this central issue which inevitably arises in any consideration of Shiga, in this sense at least the most 'Japanese' of writers, by over-emphasizing the few more Western-style or more conventional (from a Western point of view) works of fiction he wrote. To do so is to present a distorted image both of Shiga's actual accomplishment as a writer and of his abiding influence on the literature of his country. The truth is that Shiga Naoya must stand or fall as a writer of *shi-shōsetsu*; to try to 'dress him up' in more acceptably conventional or Western garb is a futile exercise that only belies the true nature of the subject. Thus, in the critical section of the present work, I have chosen to concentrate exclusively on Shiga as a *shi-shōsetsu* writer, though, for the sake of variety, I include some of his more 'fictional' stories among those I translate.

On the one hand, I try to address the central critical problem which arises in connection with the *shi-shōsetsu*, a problem that Shiga himself came ultimately to deal with in his one novel-length work: the on-going dialectic between fiction and reality. On the other hand, I try to present this aspect of Shiga's work not merely as a 'critical problem' but in a more positive light, as a remarkably successful expression, in modern form, of certain aesthetic and spiritual values which have a long history in Japanese and East Asian culture.

When I speak of Shiga's 'Zen aesthetic' I am to some extent, of course, using a term of convenience, and may well provoke protest from scholars who insist on a stricter terminological precision. In some respects their objections would be well founded. They might point out, for instance, that Shiga was not a 'Zen artist' in the same sense as were the great Zen writers or painters of the past, men like Sesshū, Zeami, Ikkyū, Bashō and Hakuin, who were actual Zen practitioners and even monks, or like the great modern Zen poet, Takahashi Shinkichi. In fact, Shiga expressed his contempt for institutional Zen as it existed in the Japan of his day. And not only ideologically but aesthetically, too, he may not seem to have subscribed to the full range of Zen values or ideals. One of the best-known contemporary Japanese writers on Zen aesthetics, Hisamatsu Shin'ichi, lists 'seven characteristics' of Zen art, and claims that true Zen art must possess all seven.[7] Whether Shiga's work hits the Zen jackpot with all lucky seven – including even such quaint and imponderable ones as 'austere sublimity' – is certainly open to question. Then again, it might also be objected that his aesthetic/ethical/spiritual credo of 'following nature' does not even necessarily derive from Zen: there are many other possible sources for it, including Japanese folk culture, Shintō, Daoism, the many other forms of Buddhism – or, indeed, European Romanticism. Thinking along similar lines but using a more *au courant* terminology, contemporary cultural theorists may also accuse me of 'essentializing' Japanese culture in the manner of many a *nihonjinron*[8] writer, both Japanese and Western, by presenting Shiga as a modern Japanese artist who embodies 'Japanese tradition' with his 'Zen aesthetic'.

These various objections would all be instructive, but not, it seems to me, conclusive. I would continue to use my term of convenience, not merely for its convenience but – generally speaking and with all provisos duly taken into account – for its ultimate legitimacy.

First of all, to speak of Shiga's 'Zen aesthetic' is a short-hand way of pointing out, especially to Western readers, that his 'artless art' is a modern expression of a very ancient aesthetic tradition, one that includes not only writers but every other kind of artist and artisan in the 'Zen tradition'. It seems to me entirely appropriate – and enlightening – to link Shiga in this way with, for instance, Sesshū, the fifteenth-century Zen monk and painter whose 'Broken-ink Landscape' (*Haboku sansuizu*), reproduced on the cover of this book, is a perfect embodiment, traditional but timeless, of the ideal of an 'artless art'. What is expressed so clearly in the visual language of this great painting, but what is so hard to define satisfactorily in words, is an extreme form of the age-old tension between aesthetic order and creative chaos. In this sense it may be compared with the Apollonian/Dionysian dialectic which Nietzsche discovered at the heart of Greek tragedy. Up close, Sesshū's brush-strokes seem almost wildly spontaneous, irregular, 'artless', but when we step back and see the work as a whole its composition immediately appears flawless, especially in its mastery of what is regarded as the most difficult and important aspect of Zen ink painting: the articulation of empty space. Only the greatest artists can take these kind of risks: if their mastery is lacking, as it is in the work of countless imitators, the end product is merely crude and 'artless' in the worst sense of the word.

Of course, this paradoxical aesthetic ideal is not unknown to the West – one finds it brilliantly expressed, for instance, in the quick, calligraphic sketches of some of our greatest artists, from Rembrandt to Picasso. But, at least until the twentieth century, it was never part of mainstream Western aesthetics: the finished, studied work of art always took precedence over the 'mere sketch', the novel over the notebook, the philosophical treatise over the random essay, and so forth. In Japan, at least since the late middle ages, the philosophical support of Zen Buddhism was certainly one of the main factors which kept the aesthetic of an 'artless' art central to the tradition. And ultimately, I would argue, Shiga is related to this tradition not merely in his aesthetics but also in his philosophy.

It is hardly surprising that Shiga, as a twentieth-century Japanese intellectual, rejected the authority of institutional Zen. For him as for many others, the official Zen world was part of a corrupt, complacent and reactionary establishment whose power any independent-minded person should resist. But when I speak of his 'Zen aesthetic' I am not speaking of his official allegiances in this sense. Although he was not a Zen practitioner like many of the great Zen artists of the past, what ultimately links him to them on a deeper level is not only his aesthetic but also the manner in which that aesthetic relates to the moral, psychological and spiritual dimensions of his work. In short, one realizes ultimately that his 'artless art' is based on the traditional ideal of a 'selfless self' – which is also, however, something more than an ideal in both Zen and in Shiga, being grounded on the 'mystical' experience of the dissolution of the personal ego in an ecstatic union with nature. As we shall see, the clearest and most powerful expression of this comes in the climactic scene of Shiga's *magnum opus*, *A Dark Night's Passing*. In other words, what places Shiga squarely within the long tradition of 'Zen art' in Japan – by whatever name we call it – are two factors working closely together: his presentation of a monistic or mystical world view as the core ontology of his work, and his expression of this through the aesthetic of an 'artless art'.

In answer to the charge that I am in danger of 'essentializing' or stereotyping Japanese culture, I would advance the following simple argument. Though I would not contend, as do some of the *nihonjinron* writers, that there is any such thing as a fundamental 'Japanese cultural style' which survived through all ages, nevertheless it does seem undeniable to me that, since the late middle ages, there has been a dominant style in Japanese high culture, and that this style has been influenced, to a remarkable extent, by the aesthetics and philosophy of a single Buddhist sect: Rinzai Zen. This is why, for instance, the leading Western authority on Japanese literature, Donald Keene, in his essay on 'Japanese Aesthetics', recognizes, first of all, that, in Japan more than in most other countries, enough uniformity in aesthetic taste exists to talk of such a phenomenon as a single, characteristically Japanese aesthetics, and, secondly, defines the phenomenon in terms almost identical to those used by the Japanese Zen scholar, Hisamatsu, to define what he calls 'Zen aesthetics'?[9] To point out Shiga's links to this mainstream tradition may do nothing to endear him to Western readers, but at least it should help solve for them the mystery of his great popularity in Japan.

2

Shiga Naoya was born in 1883 at the village of Ishimaki in Miyagi Prefecture on the northeast coast of Japan, where his father was posted as an employee of the Dai-ichi Bank. The family did not remain long in this remote provincial outpost, however; the father was an ambitious and successful businessman, a graduate of the new, prestigious Keiō University, and soon he returned to Tokyo, quit his job at the bank and set out to make a name for himself in the world of high finance. Eventually he became the director of both a railway and an insurance company.

Long before his father's generation, too, the Shiga family had enjoyed high status as upper-level *samurai*, leading retainers of the Sōma clan of Mutsu Province (now the northeastern corner of Fukushima Prefecture), entrusted with handling the clan's finances. The first significant fact about Shiga's early biography, then, is that he was born into a 'good' family, both in terms of wealth and of social status. As many critics have noted, this undoubtedly had its effect on his general world view, giving him an attitude of aristocratic detachment and even, at times, disdain – which often made him the object of attack by critics of a Marxist persuasion. But it also gave him an easy familiarity with the world of Japanese high culture, especially the classical tradition of court poetry, poetic diaries and lyrical essays – and, of course, the *shi-shōsetsu* as Shiga came to write it is essentially a continuation of this lyrical tradition in modern prose form.

More specifically, Shiga's 'high birth' enabled him to attend the Gakushūin or 'Peers' School', where he first came into contact with other upper-class boys who were also aspiring writers, some of whom would become his lifelong friends and supporters – most notably, Mushanokōji Saneatsu, who would become not only Shiga's best friend but one of the most popular authors of the day. When this group of young men had advanced together to Tokyo Imperial University, they published a literary magazine called *Shirakaba* (*White Birch*). Remaining in circulation from 1910 to 1923, the magazine not only published works by members of the group itself but also attempted to introduce contemporary Western literature and art to Japanese readers. By serving both of these functions it became a cultural influence of considerable importance in Taishō Japan (1912–26). At any rate, this was the vehicle through which Shiga's stories first became widely known. And Shiga himself is still identified as the leading member of the 'Shirakaba' group, which is now regarded as one of the key 'writers' groups' of the Taishō period. Nonetheless, although Japanese scholars have a strong tendency to analyze their own literary history as an ongoing power struggle between opposing groups of this kind, one must be wary of any facile categorizations of Shiga as a member of this or any other group. The importance of the Shirakaba group to him lay far more in the friendship and support it provided than in any direct influence of its literary theories on his work. As I intend to show, Shiga the writer was very much his own man.

Although Shiga attended one of the best schools and, later, the best university in the country, he profited from this mainly in the friends he made. He was not a particularly good student.

In fact, he had to repeat two years at Gakushūin and he dropped out of Tokyo Imperial University before completing his course of studies (in English literature). This is significant in view of his later reputation as a 'primitive', a man who valued instinct and emotion above intellect.

Perhaps the most important consequence of Shiga's upper-class background was the financial independence bequeathed him by his father's business acumen. This enabled him, throughout the rest of his life, to concentrate exclusively on his writing, turning out works at a leisurely pace without the necessity of making a living. What gives this a somewhat ironic twist is another fact which must be mentioned about his early biography: his stormy relationship with his father. Needless to say, as a hard-headed businessman the father was none too pleased with his son's choice of vocation, particularly since it meant that he would remain financially dependent for much of his life. There were other sources of friction too: Naoya's protests over the pollution caused by a copper mine his family was associated with; his affair with one of the family maids and his determination to marry her; and, finally, his marriage in 1914 without his father's consent to a cousin of Mushanokōji. During the years 1913 to 1915, however, Shiga's state of mind underwent a significant change, a change reflected, as we shall see, in his stories *At Kinosaki* and *Bonfire*. His close brush with death on the one hand (he was hit by a streetcar in Tokyo in the summer of 1913) and his increasing sense of union with nature on the other (in 1915 he went with his new bride to live amid the beautiful mountain scenery of Akagi in central Japan) changed his attitude of confrontation and self-assertion into one of longing for harmony and peace of mind. With this new attitude he was soon able to effect a reconciliation with his father, an event which is movingly described in one of his most celebrated *shi-shōsetsu*, *Wakai* (*Reconciliation*, 1917), translated in the second part of this book. With this reconciliation the principal drama of Shiga's life came to an end, and he was able to spend the rest of his days (until his death at the age of eighty-eight in 1971) in the quiet enjoyment of his family, of the world of nature and of the traditional Far Eastern arts. With time, in fact, Shiga became an almost archetypal figure on the Japanese cultural scene, seeming more and more like the reincarnation of some enlightened sage of old.

But, as a writer, one final great struggle awaited him after his reconciliation with his father: he had still to finish his *magnum opus, A Dark Night's Passing.* This was a long and tortuous process: the first part of the work was published in 1921, and it was not until 1937 that the last instalment appeared, a full twenty-five years after the work was begun. After the publication of this one great novel-length work Shiga wrote little of any consequence, though he lived another thirty-four years. This fact alone seems to tell us much about the special relationship between a writer of *shi-shōsetsu* and his work. Having poured all of the agony and the hard-earned wisdom of his life into this one work, it seems that Shiga now felt he had best maintain a dignified silence.

CHAPTER ONE

THE LOGIC OF EVERYDAY LIFE

Shiga Naoya may be regarded as first and foremost a writer of short stories and short-story-length *shi-shōsetsu*. This is not to deny the importance of his one novel-length work, *A Dark Night's Passing*, upon which much of his high reputation in Japan rests. Nor is it to deny the wide appeal of his most famous novella-length work, *Reconciliation*, that *shi-shōsetsu par excellence* which has moved critics to such effusive heights (or depths) in describing its emotional impact. But the fact remains that Shiga was far more prolific as a writer of shorter pieces than as a 'novelist' and, more significantly, that his shorter *shi-shōsetsu* such as *Bonfire* and *At Kinosaki* seem to embody, to a greater extent than any of his other works, those qualities which most critics, I think, would regard as 'quintessentially Shiga'. Furthermore, even his great novel-length work is rather episodic in character – although, I hasten to add, there is no value judgement implied here but merely a different structural principle than that embodied by the conventional 'well-made' Western novel. Indeed, despite its eventual length, the work was originally planned as a series of loosely related 'short stories'.[1] One might add that Shiga took the major part of his working life (about twenty-five years) to write his one novel-length work – which, needless to say, seems to imply that large-scale writing did not come easy to him.

Although Shiga wrote some sixty-odd short works, the problem of which to single out as representative is not a particularly vexing one. What he is renowned for, above all, is his style (and, as we shall see, he himself considered style to be the quintessence of the writer's art) but, unlike his most famous contemporaries, Tanizaki and Akutagawa, he did not possess a facile command of a variety of styles. This already tells us much about the kind of writer he was. In his case in particular, the 'style is the man'. Shiga's own view, which we shall explore in more depth presently, was that a writer's style arose spontaneously from the depths of his being; it was the man's own basic 'rhythm' that, in the case of a great writer, communicated itself forcefully to the reader through the written word. Because style, then, was such a deeply personal thing, it could not be changed at will like a suit of clothes. In keeping with this view Shiga left his characteristic stamp on everything he wrote. This is not to say that all his works are masterpieces, but they do all manifest, to some extent, that unmistakable 'Shiga style'. As a result, almost any one of them would serve to represent this primary aspect of his art.

As for content, the stories may be divided into two broad categories: those that are more or less 'autobiographical' (the *shi-shōsetsu*), comprising by far the majority, and those that are more invented or 'fictional'. With this classification, there already appears the fiction/non-fiction or fiction/reality dialectic which will be a recurring theme in my study of Shiga. But again I hasten to add that there is no value judgement implied here either. It seems to me that Francis Mathy, for instance, is swayed too much by Western preconceptions about what constitutes 'good literature' when he ranks the 'fictional' stories above the 'autobiographical'.[2] In his book, the first full-length study of Shiga in English, Mathy gives 'star coverage' to the fictional stories in a chapter called 'A Golden Ten' and laments that Shiga was unable to write more because he was 'hampered by an impossible theory of prose fiction',[3] i.e., he generally preferred to write in 'such a defective genre as the autobiographical novel'.[4] Furthermore, it seems to me that by over-emphasizing the fictional stories at the expense of the autobiographical, Mathy distorts our view of Shiga's achievement as a writer, since the great majority of his stories are *shi-shōsetsu* and since he is known in Japan mainly as the master of this genre (and it is as such that he exercised his enormous influence on modern Japanese literature). With this in mind, in the present study I view Shiga primarily as a *shi-shōsetsu* writer.

As I have said, there is a remarkable unity to Shiga's entire *opus*. Even in his first published story, *One Morning* (*Aru asa*, 1908), there already appear many of the characteristic features of his style and some foreshadowings, at least, of his major thematic motifs. In fact, it would be only a slight exaggeration to say that this five-page product of Shiga's early manhood already contains the greater portion of his later work in microcosm.

One Morning is the simple story of a young man, Shintarō, who has trouble getting out of bed one morning. The night before he had persisted in reading a novel until very late, despite the protestations of his grandmother, who is sharing the same bedroom. She had warned him that a Buddhist priest would be coming early the next morning to celebrate a memorial service for his dead grandfather, and that they would have to rise long before the priest arrived to get everything ready. But Shintarō had continued reading until the early hours of the morning. Now, whenever his grandmother comes to get him up, he falls back asleep again. She grows increasingly irritated, until finally she is not politely requesting but sternly commanding him to get up, and to be quick about it. This in turn brings out the rebel in Shintarō, who defiantly tells her that all her pestering has only made it more difficult for him to get up. Calling him a 'devil', his grandmother stalks angrily out of the room. Even though he is no longer really sleepy, Shintarō's stubborn pride now prevents him from getting up.

When his grandmother returns once more, she tries a bit of 'psychology' on him: she begins folding up her own heavy mattress and quilts, even though, at seventy-three, she should not be putting herself to such a strain. But the clever Shintarō sees through her strategy and still refuses to budge. Finally, his grandmother becomes angry and accuses him of having no sense of 'filial duty'. "'If filial duty means being at the beck and call of an old lady"', Shintarō answers rather spitefully, "'then I want no part of it."'[5] His grandmother rushes out in tears.

Now that he has enjoyed this cathartic release of animosity, Shintarō finally feels in the mood to get up. But he still has not exhausted all his resentment. While getting dressed, he entertains another spiteful thought: perhaps he will go skating on a lake where three students drowned recently – surely that would make his grandmother worry about him.

His grandmother now enters the room again. Relieved that Shintarō is finally up, she tries to make peace with him by asking his advice about which writing brushes to offer to the priest when he comes. She meekly obeys when he orders her to put two brushes back as not suitable. With this further salve to his ego, Shintarō is thoroughly appeased. Left alone again, he suddenly feels like laughing. He cancels the idea of the skating trip and begins to fold up his bedding neatly and put it away. Now completely 'reconciled', he even folds up his grandmother's bedding. While doing so, though, he is suddenly overcome, 'in the midst of laughter', by an uncontrollable urge to cry. The tears stream down his cheeks, so many that 'he could no longer see anything'. But when finally the tears stop, he feels 'refreshed, purified'.[6]

In the final scene of the story, Shintarō goes to his younger brother and sisters in the next room, where he joins in their playful joking. The story thus ends on an appropriately light note, signifying Shintarō's euphoria not just at having been purged of some negative emotions but, more importantly, at being able to rejoin the comfortable family circle, the all-important Japanese realm of *amae*.[7]

Although the style in which *One Morning* is written is not quite yet the mature 'Shiga style', we already can discern here some of its major features. Generally, there is a kind of strong, authoritative tone to the writing which comes, no doubt, from the almost staccato rhythm: short, clipped sentences in which no words are wasted and facts are stated simply and clearly. One is given the sense that the words have been chosen with extreme care, and these words are generally of a simple, basic kind. There is a very sparse use of adjectives; the language is not in any way 'decorative' but rather economical, efficient. It is, as Tanizaki Jun'ichirō once pointed out, an essentially 'masculine' style (and Tanizaki contrasted it with the 'feminine' style that descends from Lady Murasaki and finds its principal modern expression in his own works).[8] If one were to look for its equivalent in English, perhaps the closest would be the equally celebrated 'Hemingway style' – and there are, in fact, some remarkable similarities between the styles of these two writers, even in such details as their choice of words.[9]

Shiga is renowned above all for his style. It is used, for instance, as a model of an ideal prose style in Japanese schools. And style, as I have said, occupies an all-important position in his own view of literature. In a significant essay he wrote on the subject, which might be considered a personal manifesto of his 'way' as a writer (I mean 'way' in the Zen-influenced sense of *dō*, as in the 'ways' of calligraphy, *shodō*, tea, *chadō*, swordfighting, *kendō*, etc., for it becomes apparent that writing was as much a spiritual discipline to him as an art), Shiga uses the English word 'rhythm' to describe that quality which he considers to be the quintessence of good writing. This is not merely a matter of the skillful arrangement of words – it is, one might say, something communicated almost 'between the words', a kind of 'reverberation' from the author's 'mind and spirit' – somewhat akin, it seems, to the Shavian or Bergsonian concept of 'life-force'. Of necessity, then, the author must be not just a talented artist but also a highly developed, spiritually powerful human being. (Perhaps this view does much to explain the 'biographical fixation' of many Japanese Shiga critics – he was himself, by all accounts, an impressive, charismatic person.) According to Shiga: 'One can always tell from one's own reaction on reading a story how strongly (or feebly) the author's sensibility has pulsated with this rhythm while he wrote.'[10] And the medium used is almost irrelevant, since the rhythm is always basically the same: 'All encounters with the work of superior men, whether their deeds, their pronouncements or their writings, give us real pleasure .... Good words, good paintings, good books – all good works have this effect upon us.'[11] The true pleasure of reading, then, is the pleasure of a kind of spiritual communion with great men: 'Our eyes are opened to whatever qualities hidden within ourselves we might share with them. Our mind and spirit grow taut ....'[12] This quasi-mystical view of the function of literature is also highly relevant to what is probably the most recurrent theme of Shiga's works and a theme which, as we have seen, is already adumbrated in *One Morning*: the hero's struggle to overcome all sense of alienation by achieving total communion with his fellow human beings, particularly with other members of his family, and with nature at large. With his concrete sense of 'rhythm' as a kind of natural force that could be transmitted from person to person, Shiga obviously saw literature itself as a very practical means for achieving this communion.

Furthermore, according to Shiga 'rhythm' transcends both form and content in a work of literature. He makes this clear in his discussion of Ihara Saikaku, the writer he admired more than any other of the Japanese tradition: 'Saikaku's *Ogeba* and *Oridome* are written with a cool, clean detachment and a strong rhythm. Their subjects are various trivial occurrences in the "floating world"; and yet they have that effect upon the reader which I mentioned before: a tightening up of one's mind and spirit.'[13] Thus a writer is able to make great art even out of 'trivial' subject matter, providing he commands a masterful style.

Apparently, Francis Mathy does not see eye-to-eye with Shiga on this point. He finds the style of *One Morning* to be 'splendid' but does not feel that this sufficiently compensates for the 'triviality' of its contents.[14] In particular, he is irritated by the 'immature self-centeredness' of the hero, who is 'not a little boy, as his actions and words would seem to indicate, but a grown man of twenty-five.'[15] Surely this is too much like arguing *ad hominem*. After all, one does not necessarily have to morally approve of the protagonist's behaviour to appreciate a story as a story. If this were not so, it would be impossible for the 'cosmopolitan' reader to freely enjoy the literature of cultures with values very different to his own, and the discipline of 'comparative literature' could not aspire to even the minimum level of scientific objectivity. In the present case, for instance, it may seem implausible or even reprehensible to the Western reader of today that a twenty-five-year-old man should act so 'childishly' towards his grandmother. In the context of Meiji Japan, however, where family relations were often oppressively close and where young men lived at home until married, Shintarō's behaviour is far more understandable.

But there is a larger issue at stake here. It seems to me, in fact, that Mathy misses the very essence of Shiga's achievement. Here is a writer who has taken the small, seemingly insignificant events of everyday life and turned them into a significant work of literary art. Triviality, after all, is, like beauty, very much in the eye of the beholder. Ever since van Gogh did a splendid painting of a pair of old shoes, modern art has taught us this if nothing else. The point is that once Shiga has turned a 'trivial' incident into a short story, it no longer seems trivial. But one must not be misled by authorial pronouncements – Shiga accomplishes this Midas-like feat of alchemy not only by the force of his style or 'rhythm'. He also possesses considerable powers of insight into the human psyche, and this enables him to show us the disturbing forces at work beneath the calm, seemingly uneventful surface of everyday life.

On closer view, then, *One Morning* does not seem so 'trivial' after all. In fact, one of Shiga's major themes is prefigured in this short work: seen from a 'social' perspective, it is the conflict between the hero's needs as an individual and his needs as part of a social group. The whole issue of 'individualism' was very much in the air in the late Meiji period. This was the time, for instance, when Natsume Sōseki delivered his famous talk, *My Individualism* (*Watakushi no kojinshugi*), which, as Jay Rubin has noted, was in response to 'the remarkable upsurge in individualism that followed the Russo-Japanese War of 1904–05.'[16] In the realm of literature, 'naturalist fiction, with its emphasis on the liberation of the individual, was gaining in popularity'.[17] And Sōseki too, both in his public talk and in his novels, was concerned with the 'tension between a proud commitment to modern, rationalistic individualism and the longing for emotional submergence in the group.'[18] In his talk, for instance, he contrasts his own independent stance with the 'feudalistic' cliquishness of Japanese literary groups. But he also admits to suffering the 'loneliness of individualism'.[19] Such Meiji writers as Sōseki and Mori Ōgai saw 'individualism' as a necessary but problematical ingredient of the Western culture they themselves were helping to import into Japan.[20]

In his insistence on his own rights as an individual, Shiga too was very much a product of his time. But, unlike the older writers, he does not approach individualism as an intellectual problem. He is not concerned, for instance, with how it conflicts with traditional Japanese cultural values in the abstract; rather for him it is more a personal, emotional problem to be worked out in his day-to-day relations with his family. It is a matter of his will to act according to his own deepest instincts and feelings, as opposed to his family's will that he conform to their standards of behaviour. (In the same way he rejected the teachings of the Christian leader Uchimura Kanzō not so much on ideological as on personal grounds – when they threatened to interfere with what he considered to be the 'natural' free expression of his sexual instincts.[21]) Thus Shiga did not suffer from any vague, quasi-metaphysical sense of alienation such as his more intellectual contemporary, Akutagawa Ryūnosuke, gave as his reason for committing suicide;[22] and, since he was not concerned with any 'larger' political or philosophical issue, once he was completely 'reconciled' with his family, he was able to spend the rest of his long life in a relatively tranquil state of mind (and, ironically, writing very little).

Because of this almost exclusive focus on his personal emotional life, there are those who would accuse Shiga of having too 'narrow' a scope as a writer. In response one might quote some eloquent words of his greatest apologist, the 'dean of Japanese critics', Kobayashi Hideo:

> Empty thought can go anywhere, my own feet can tread only a small bit of ground. We think of eternal life, I must shortly die. I cannot have many friends, I cannot have many lovers. The things to which I can give assent from my very entrails add up to but a tiny sum, the people I can love and hate can number no more than the few immediately beside me. This is

> the state of life for me, and it is for everyone . . . . The
> fact that the writer does not depart from his own life
> means that he gives it his assent, and it alone.[23]

The distinguished scholar Nakamura Hajime has devoted a
good part of a lengthy volume to demonstrating the essential
'down-to-earthness' of the Japanese world-view, but it is
doubtful whether anyone has expressed it better than Kobayashi in this brief passage.[24] Shiga himself has put what we may
regard as his 'writer's credo' even more succinctly: 'A superficial experience of rare and sensational events is of little value
to the writer. It is more important for him to experience even
small things deeply.'[25]

Unfortunately, it seems that for some Western readers it is
difficult to accept Shiga's 'small things' for what they are. Even
those more sympathetic to his work than Mathy are forever
trying to make something out of it that it clearly is not. Edward
Seidensticker, for instance, would have us see the typical Shiga
story as a kind of modern-day version of the *utamonogatari* of
the Heian period, 'poem-tales' such as the *Ise Monogatari* (*Tales
of Ise*) in which:

> . . . a fictional or non-fictional ground was provided
> for a succession of lyrics. The ground itself was
> usually formless and of slight literary value. It but
> served to set off the lyrics . . . . So it is with Shiga.
> The triviality of the autobiographical background is
> to be forgiven to the extent that it offers a setting for
> the moments of lyrical awareness. The whole is to be
> judged as a unified work of fiction no more than is an
> *utamonogatari*.[26]

While this may be regarded as a valiant attempt on the part
of a sympathetic Western critic to rescue Shiga from the charge
of 'triviality', it is doubtful whether, at least in the eyes of his
Japanese admirers, Shiga is in need of such rescue. Triviality, as
I have said, is in the eye of the beholder. And, in dismissing
Shiga's 'trivial and annoying reminiscence' as merely the 'prosy
setting' for a few 'moments of poetry', it seems that Seidensticker would throw out the baby with the bathwater. The
'autobiographical background' is, after all, the substance of the
works. It is an absurd notion anyway that any author would
write long stretches of prose merely to set off a few 'moments of
poetry'. Many of Shiga's stories, in fact, including *One
Morning*, have no such distinguishable 'poetic moments'. If

Shiga's intentions had been so single-mindedly lyrical, surely he would have written poetry.

In his study of Shiga, William Sibley takes quite an opposite tack: he calls on the 'big ideas' of Freudian psychoanalysis to try to make Shiga's 'small things' seem larger than they are. To Sibley, for instance, *One Morning* is not simply the story of a willful young man who is reluctant to get out of bed one morning (surely not an unheard-of case!); the hero's irascibility towards his grandmother has deeply Oedipal origins that can be understood only in the total context of Shiga's life and work – and, of course, the life and work of Dr. Freud. Sibley concedes that, on its own, *One Morning* is a 'slight story' that 'represents Japanese personal fiction (*shi-shōsetsu*) at its most limited.'[27] In his view, we can begin to make sense of the 'seemingly pointless detail' of this story only after we have subjected the 'Shiga hero' as he appears throughout the author's entire *opus* to thorough psychoanalysis.[28] Sibley is not too clear about what we shall discover then, but it seems to have something to do with the hero's crying spell. It appears to me that he gives inordinate emphasis to Shintarō's tears:

> Is it, we wonder, a sudden grief for his dead grandfather that has elicited his tears? Remorse for his treatment of his grandmother? Or perhaps he has been upset by a brief reference to his father which she makes at one point, provoking at first a particularly ill-tempered outburst on the hero's part. Most of those who read *One Morning* when it was first published in *Shirakaba* did not, presumably, make much sense of it. Indeed, they could not, without some 'inside' knowledge of the author's life and personality on which they might draw to complete the story. And so they may well have felt justified in not, finally, caring too much what it is that makes the hero cry.[29]

To me this is a prime example of the kind of *reductio ad absurdum* that follows inevitably from the 'reductive' approach to literature: first Sibley assumes that Shiga has hidden some tidbits of psychoanalytical insight 'between the lines' and then he rebukes the author for having hid them too successfully. He would reduce *One Morning* to a kind of psychoanalytical detective story in which the main clue, the hero's tears, can be understood only in the total context of the hero's 'case history' (and this, of course, is playing an unfair trick on the reader).

Although it is true, as many critics have pointed out, that Shiga's *shi-shōsetsu*, if regarded as pure autobiography, are often incomplete or even distorted – that is, they delete or distort certain details of his actual life – if regarded in their proper light, as self-sufficient works of fiction, generally they divulge as much as is necessary to achieve their desired aesthetic effect. One does not, of course, have to accept the author's word on this point, but the fact is that Shiga himself seemed to regard the practice of withholding necessary information from the reader as a kind of intellectual trickery which compromised the story's 'sincerity' (which, however, is a different thing from saying that the author is obliged to divulge all, a practice which would violate Shiga's minimalist aesthetic). In one famous instance, he reprimanded Akutagawa for 'tricking the reader' in just this way in his story, *The Martyr*, wherein, in the manner of O. Henry, the 'surprise fact' that the 'hero' is actually a girl is not revealed until the very end.[30]

It seems to me that, in the present case too, there is no mystery at all about 'what it is that makes the hero cry'. In fact, it is perfectly transparent to anyone who is not too preoccupied with unearthing psychological profundities to notice what is actually happening in the story. If we look at the passage in which Shintarō's 'crying spell' is described, we see that Shiga does, in fact, give us a strong hint as to the cause of the young man's outburst: it comes over him 'spontaneously' while he is folding up his grandmother's bedding. Here, in Shiga's first story, we already have a characteristic example of the kind of concreteness or tactility for which he is famous – and which derives ultimately from his 'poetic' or even 'mystical' sense of the intimate communion of 'subjective' self with 'objective' world. Shintarō does not begin to cry until he actually touches something belonging to his grandmother – which, in Shiga's 'animistic' world, is filled with her 'presence'. It is this immediate physical contact with his 'grandmother' which awakens his intense though dormant love for her, thus obliterating all traces of the animosity he had felt towards her just a few moments before. What causes his tears is not so much remorse (the 'Shiga hero', as we shall see, does not waste time feeling guilty about 'doing what comes naturally') but a simple feeling of relief that an unpleasant negative emotion has been replaced by a powerful positive emotion – in other words, a simple release of tension. One does not need to be a trained psychoanalyst to see that the real 'message' of the hero's tears is simply that he loves his grandmother very deeply.

24

Shiga's stories may well be described, as they have been by Japanese literary historians, as *shinkyō shōsetsu* (psychological or, literally, 'state of mind' stories) but it is important to emphasize that the '*shinkyō*' is all in the '*shōsetsu*'. Nothing extraneous to the stories is necessary for our understanding of them. No doubt it is interesting to observe how later Shiga heroes are prefigured by the hero of his first story, but this should not prevent us from accepting *One Morning* as a story in its own right, however 'simple' or however much of a 'small thing' it is.

Long before it became a vogue in the West, the Japanese understood the beauty of 'minimal art'. The power of this beauty has been hauntingly evoked by Kobayashi Hideo in his lyrical essay on the *nō* play, *Taema*:

> Music and dance and song are reduced to the barest essentials. The music is like a cry, the dance is little more than a walk, and the song is like ordinary prayer. It is enough. What else is needed?[31]

Similarly Shiga's is an art of 'barest essentials'. His 'small things' are to be appreciated in all their simple, immediate reality, in their 'suchness', to use a Buddhist term, like the frog in Bashō's haiku, like the rocks in a Zen temple garden or, to take a more contemporary example, like the simple images of family life in the films of Ozu Yasujirō. As soon as the reader begins to analyze, to intellectualize, to look for deep symbolic or psychological meaning, he has immediately 'lost it', as the Zen masters say. Obviously this puts the critic or academic in a rather difficult position. Thus it is significant that Kobayashi Hideo, Shiga's most successful apologist, was more of an intuitive poet or philosopher than an 'orthodox' analytical critic in the Western sense – his impressionistic, oracular pronouncements, though highly suggestive, are often far more difficult to fathom than the writings they are meant to elucidate. Nevertheless, it is Kobayashi's understanding of the traditional Japanese aesthetic sensibility, as revealed in the essay just quoted, that enables him to appreciate Shiga's work so deeply.

One Morning, then, is the simple story of a young man's altercation and eventual reconciliation with his grandmother. But it is interesting to note that it anticipates in this, as we shall see, the basic pattern of the 'action' in many of Shiga's later stories, including his two major works (both in length and in quality): *Reconciliation* and *A Dark Night's Passing*. The cause of the rift between the Shiga hero and his family is not always so clear or so straightforward as in *One Morning*, though it generally has to do with his being more willful and 'self-oriented' than Japanese society permits. But, in all these stories, what Shiga emphasizes more than anything is that the hero must allow his feelings to run their 'natural' course before a 'reconciliation' is possible. In the present story, we observe that, once he has been angered by his grandmother's pestering, Shintarō's mood becomes conciliatory only after he has thrown a few insults her way and she has humbled herself by asking his advice. We may agree with Francis Mathy that this is 'childish' behaviour but, nevertheless, it is convincingly human and, therefore, 'natural'. As Makoto Ueda has pointed out in an excellent essay on Shiga's aesthetics, 'natural beauty' is a primary quality in Shiga's concept of the 'ideal novel'.[32] But this does not belong only to mountains and trees – it is, above all, a human beauty:

> An impression of natural beauty comes from observing a man who conducts himself honestly, in accordance with his inmost feelings. Such a man would not repress his true feelings in the interest of social convention .... He would follow the dictates of his innermost self even if that would lead to an explosive clash with his father or even to the death of his wife. A man fighting for his survival was beautiful, because he was, if nothing else, pure in his motives.[33]

Again, it is not necessary for the reader to morally approve of a hero in order to derive aesthetic enjoyment from his portrayal. And here, in *One Morning*, we have our first taste of Shiga's 'amorality': the 'natural' – raw gut feelings, intuitions, instincts – counts far more than the 'moral' – a mere intellectual abstraction.

But now, in seeming to come perilously close to confusing Shiga himself with the Shiga hero, we approach what is perhaps, at least from a Western viewpoint, the central critical problem of his work: its status as 'fiction'. In the case of *One Morning*, the author himself, at first, seemed to have doubts. In a diary entry of January 14, 1908, he notes that, having written during the morning about a quarrel he had had with his grandmother the previous day, he called the piece: *A Non-Story, Grandmother* (*Hi-shōsetsu, sobo*).[34] Significantly, though, Shiga later changed his mind about the status of this work as 'non-fiction'. In a commentary on it written in 1928, he describes it as his first 'short story' (*tanpen shōsetsu*).[35] One may speculate that, in the meantime, his view of what constitutes a work of fiction or a *shōsetsu* had broadened or, perhaps we might say, had become more traditionally Japanese.[36] The young Shiga was, after all, an avid reader of Chekhov, Tolstoy and Flaubert and was likely to be influenced by Western concepts of fiction. As he matured in his art he naturally developed the confidence to set his own aesthetic standards.

One Morning is the first in a long line of Shiga's *shi-shōsetsu*, stories closely based on the events of his own life and featuring a hero more or less identifiable as himself. Certain Western critics are hesitant or even refuse to accept such works as 'legitimate' fiction. Edward Seidensticker, as we have seen, describes the *shi-shōsetsu* as 'unformed reminiscence' and as a 'form of autobiographical jotting that may scarcely seem to deserve the name fiction at all'.[37] Francis Mathy makes the same point in regard to *One Morning*: 'The piece is hardly more than a sketch ....'[38] And he laments that the author was 'hampered by an impossible theory of prose fiction',[39] although occasionally 'Shiga was able to transcend the autobiographical mode and find objective fictional symbols to express his inner states'.[40] Even an eminent Japanese critic, Nakamura Mitsuo, has said that he was 'tempted' to describe Shiga's longest work, *A Dark Night's Passing*, as 'non-literature'.[41]

What these critics object to is not, of course, the presence in fiction of autobiography *per se*. Many of the most celebrated Western novels of this century are more or less autobiographical: Joyce's *Portrait of the Artist as a Young Man*, Proust's *A la Recherche du temps perdu*, Lawrence's *Sons and Lovers* – one could go on almost indefinitely. But it seems that, to the Western eye at least, these works appear more consciously structured for aesthetic effect, more finely shaped into 'works of fiction' than the Japanese *shi-shōsetsu* – which Seidensticker, for instance, calls 'the unshapen ones'.[42] But this sense of 'formal structure', it seems to me, is exactly what Shiga wished to avoid. His love of the 'natural' made him eschew anything that smacked of fabrication (*koshiraemono*, to use the word by which one of the fathers of the *shi-shōsetsu*, Tayama Katai, denounced a certain Western novel[43]) – including the formal plot-structure of conventional fiction. (We have already mentioned his aversion to some of Akutagawa's well-plotted stories.) Nor is he alone in this predilection for the 'storyless novel' (*hanashi no nai shōsetsu*, to use the term Akutagawa himself applied to Shiga's work).[44] In fact, he has a very substantial part of the Japanese literary tradition behind him. The contempt for 'popular' fiction that merely 'tells a story' in the conventional sense has a venerable lineage in both China and Japan – it is, in fact, embodied in the very word *shōsetsu*. As Herbert Franke points out in his introduction to a collection of Chinese stories:

> The Chinese term for novellas, *Hsiao-shuo* [*shōsetsu* in Japanese], 'little tales', contains a certain under-tone of disparagement. Narrative prose, and indeed every sort of light fiction, was not generally regarded as a branch of serious literature, and, unlike poetry or the formal essay, it was not a field in which literary ambition could lead on to fame and social prestige.[45]

The stern strictures of Confucius no doubt had much to do with this. Like Plato in a famous passage of the *Republic*,[46] the Chinese philosopher took a dim view of the fictive imagination, abjuring any talk of 'miracles, acts of violence, troubles, and ghosts.'[47] This strict Confucian attitude seems to have been imported, along with much else, into Japan. As is often pointed out, the greatest works of fiction of the Heian period were written by women, while the men were occupied with the more 'serious' business of writing poems and essays in Chinese or Japanese. Lady Murasaki is obviously responding to the charge of 'falsity' often leveled against prose fiction in her day when she puts her famous 'defense of fiction' into the mouth of Prince Genji:

> '*The Chronicles of Japan* and the rest are a mere fragment of the whole truth. It is your romances that fill in the details .... There are differences in the degree of seriousness. But to dismiss them as lies is itself to depart from the truth ....'
> He now seemed bent on establishing the uses of fiction.[48]

Unfortunately, though, it seems that Prince Genji's arguments failed to convince the male literary establishment. Until the arrival of the great critic Motoori Norinaga in the eighteenth century, even Murasaki's own masterpiece was rendered acceptable to Buddhists and Confucians, if at all, only by being contorted to fit various allegorical interpretations. Meanwhile, the 'mainstream' aristocratic tradition of Japanese literature continued to consist of *waka* poetry, *nikki* (diaries), *zuihitsu* (random essays), *renga* (linked verse) and so on – a literature, in other words, of the 'personal' or lyric rather than of the epic or dramatic mode. (Although, on a more popular level, a variety of anonymously composed narratives, including Buddhist parables and *samurai* war tales, did flourish in the medieval period.)

Fiction may seem to have enjoyed something of a renaissance with the arrival of Ihara Saikaku in the late seventeenth century. As Donald Keene remarks, 'it is not much of an exaggeration to say that he re-established prose fiction as an art after over four hundred years of anonymous writings.'[49] But, as Keene also points out, Saikaku is admired not so much for the content of his stories, which are, for the most part, light, comic tales of the pleasure quarters, the 'floating world'. What sets him apart from countless other writers of *ukiyo zōshi* is his masterful style. In the words of Howard Hibbett, Saikaku, like the great woodblock print artists, achieves his 'finest effects by sheer stylistic verve'.[50] Indeed, as already noted, Shiga himself, who admired Saikaku more than any other Japanese writer, shared this view of his works: 'Their subjects are various trivial occurrences in the "floating world"; and yet they have that effect upon the reader which I mentioned before: a tightening up of one's mind and spirit.'[51] This was because of the 'strong rhythm' of the author's style.

In other words, the great popularity of Saikaku did nothing to change the traditional view that well-plotted fiction *per se* was not an appropriate medium for 'serious' literary expression. And certainly no cause for a change in this view was provided by any of Saikaku's successors, writers of *ukiyo-zōshi* that, as Keene says, were 'devoted to trivial incidents of the licensed quarters or to the implausible doings of paper-thin heroes',[52] and that resemble Saikaku's works in style, if at all, only because they were directly plagiarized from him.[53] There were, of course, a few important exceptions over the centuries – most notably, Ueda Akinari and Takizawa Bakin. But Akinari himself considered his fictional works to be of 'small consequence' in comparison with his non-fiction,[54] and Bakin's novels, though heavily didactic, were lumped together with the *gesaku* fiction of his era (literally, the 'low works') – in Keene's terms, the 'playful compositions', a term that was 'originally intended to indicate that the author disclaimed responsibility for a frivolous work'.[55] The general trend of Japanese critical opinion is bluntly summarized by Ivan Morris: 'During the Tokugawa period, and indeed ever since the days of *The Tale of Genji*, scholars have looked down on prose fiction, which was widely regarded as being fit only for women, children, and the lesser breeds.'[56]

With this long tradition behind them of fiction having such an ambiguous status, it is little wonder that the 'men of Meiji' were somewhat startled to find that the novel was regarded so highly as an art form in the nineteenth-century West. As Morris says: 'One result of the introduction of Western literature was to enhance the position of prose fiction in Japan.'[57] Tsubouchi Shōyō's *The Essence of the Novel* (*Shōsetsu shinzui*), written in 1885, was the first Japanese work of theoretical criticism to reflect the influence of the nineteenth-century Western attitude of taking the novel seriously as an art form. Shōyō laments the low state of fiction in his country, and then expresses the pious hope that 'by dint of steady planning from now on for the improvement of our novels we may finally be able to surpass in quality the European novels, and permit our novels to take a glorious place along with painting, music, and poetry on the altar of the arts.'[58]

At first the Meiji writers tried to imitate their Western models as faithfully as they could, writing political novels à la Disraeli and novels of social concern à la Zola. But it did not take long for the native tradition to reassert itself, though under the guise of the very modern-sounding 'naturalism'. From the outset, as Morris points out, 'Japanese naturalism began to diverge from the movement in Europe that had inspired it. The publication in 1908 of *Futon* (*The Quilt*), a novel by Tayama Katai, one of the leading naturalists, served to establish the autobiographical approach as the standard for Japanese writers of the naturalist school.'[59] Whereas the French naturalists, aiming to give the portrait of a whole society, created highly structured novels featuring a broad range of characters, after Katai their Japanese counterparts tended to focus more on the everyday events of their own lives, especially their own sex lives, writing in a discursive, diary-like fashion. To these writers is usually traced the origin of the *shi-shōsetsu*, which achieved its full flowering only with the next, 'Taishō' generation, Shiga's generation. According to Morris:

> The main legacy of naturalism in Japan has been the belief of many writers that the only worthwhile and

'sincere' form of literature is that which takes its material directly from the facts of the author's physical and spiritual life. This trend affected several writers who were in other respects strongly opposed to the naturalists. Among them was Shiga Naoya.[60]

The foremost practitioner of the day of a more 'Western' form of novel-writing, Natsume Sōseki, was regarded by the naturalists as a rather superficial panderer to popular taste. According to one Japanese literary historian, they 'criticized Sōseki, saying that his works were all "fictions" with no descriptions of harsh realities, and that the writer should fully expose himself in his works.'[61] When Sōseki finally did write an autobiographical novel, *Grass by the Wayside* (*Michikusa*), it was:

> ... generally appreciated as the best of Sōseki's entire works, and as the only one worthy of the name of novel .... Sōseki too may have written an 'I' novel because he realized the persuasive power that that mode of writing had. As I have mentioned before, there exist in Japanese society solid grounds for a personal novel to win readers.[62]

The fact that the traditional 'anti-fiction' bias was still very much alive in Shiga's day is clearly shown in an essay written in 1925 by Kume Masao, perhaps the best-known apologist of the *shi-shōsetsu* during the 1920s. Kume regards the *shi-shōsetsu* as 'the essence of prose writing' and comes close to dismissing such Western classics as *War and Peace, Crime and Punishment* and *Madame Bovary* as 'great popular novels, and fabricated stories just for entertainment'.[63] Taking up the familiar Japanese theme of the 'artificiality' of conventional fiction, Kume resorts to a rather trite metaphor: 'I think that no matter how beautifully produced, an artificial flower falls too far short of one in wild nature.'[64]

As Edward Seidensticker has shown, at the basis of this 'anti-fiction' view is the peculiarly Japanese concept of 'pure literature' (*jun bungaku*), which has played an important part in indigenous theories of the novel since the Meiji period. It may seem paradoxical or even contradictory to Western readers, but in this context the 'pure' novel is not the one which is entirely a product of the writer's imagination (i.e., completely 'fictional') but the one which is intimately personal and self-revelatory (i.e., autobiographical) – in other words, works which some Western critics, as we have seen, would not even regard as 'literature' at all! What is seen by Japanese critics as standing at the opposite pole to the literarily 'pure' is *tsūzoku* or popular fiction. (And, as Seidensticker has pointed out elsewhere, Japanese popular writers 'often have a slick patness in their plotting that would be worthy of the most skillful science-fiction writer.'[65] Thus the tendency of critics to regard the 'well-plotted novel' as a 'popular' novel.) The above-mentioned Kume Masao, in his 1935 essay, *Pure Literature as Avocation (Jun bungaku yogisetsu)*, recommends to the financially straightened literatus 'writing pot-boilers for a living and producing "pure literature" in one's spare time'.[66] He offers Shiga's work as the 'highest peak' of the pure.

Kume's strictures setting up the *shi-shōsetsu* as 'pure literature' are, of course, every bit as narrow as those of Western critics who regard it as 'non-literature'. Needless to say, Shiga cannot be held accountable for the excesses of his apologists. As we have seen, he did attack one of Akutagawa's stories for its artificial 'surprise ending', but, on the other hand, he himself wrote some highly successful 'fictional' works when he chose to do so. In other words, his views on 'fiction' versus 'non-fiction' were not as exclusive or as doctrinaire as those of some of his apologists. His preference for the autobiographical mode was more an aesthetic than an ideological one.

Indeed, it is questionable whether Shiga was influenced by literary trends at all – whether by the naturalists, as Morris implies, by his fellow members of the *Shirakaba-ha*, or by anyone else. Shiga himself claimed to have read little Western literature and even less Japanese. But the important thing is that Japanese readers were well prepared by the long tradition we have just reviewed to accept his 'plotless' autobiographical stories as quite legitimate *shōsetsu*. And what of Western readers? Seidensticker makes the interesting claim that all would be well if only the *shi-shōsetsu* writers would change the genre designation of their works: 'Perhaps in the end one's chief complaint against Shiga and his colleagues and followers is that they chose to give their lyrics-with-setting the name *shōsetsu*, and so to arouse false expectations in the breasts of those accustomed to rendering *shōsetsu* as "short story" or "novel".'[67] We may overlook, for a moment, the strange suggestion that Shiga *et al.* must be held responsible for the 'false expectations' of Western readers (for, of course, Japanese readers would not have such expectations aroused by the word *shōsetsu*). But does the whole problem really boil down to a simple matter of the confusion of genres? Would not, to paraphrase the Bard, a *shi-shōsetsu* smell as bad (or as good) by any other name? Would a Western reader suddenly cease to find Shiga's stories 'weari-some', to use Seidensticker's word,[68] if he were told that they were not 'short stories' but 'lyrics-with-setting' or *utamonoga-tari*? It seems a rather doubtful proposition. One can change one's glasses easily enough but not one's eyes – and it is the culturally conditioned eyes that we are really talking about here.

We might say, for instance, that Shiga's autobiographical stories should be read in the same spirit as one reads, say, a literary diary or an autobiography in the West. But Western diaries and autobiographies, like Western novels, tend to be highly structured works bearing a strong imprint of the 'ordering intellect'. (One thinks, for instance, of the autobio-graphy of Rousseau or the journals of André Gide.) It seems, in fact, that we have come across a truly fundamental cultural difference here, not just in aesthetic values but in the whole way of perceiving and approaching the world – which is in turn reflected, of course, in the aesthetics. In commenting on the distinctive 'Japanese concept of structural unity', Makoto Ueda remarks:

> Japanese arts generally shun logic as the principle of unity and try to minimize the role of intellect in the structure of a work; this is true even of those arts that could admit into themselves a large measure of discursive reason if they wanted to .... When talking about the work of prose, which is supposedly more logical than poetic language, Japanese aestheticians never emphasize the importance of tight, logically coherent structure. Lady Murasaki speaks only of natural smoothness, the rhythm of life, which is never logical; *The Tale of Genji*, in fact, is almost a series of short stories loosely strung together. A tragedy could certainly make use of a logically constructed plot, but Chikamatsu seldom does so; his plays, especially his historical plays, present a series of incidents that are in themselves dramatic but loosely connected to one another .... Perhaps beneath all this lies a view of life that Norinaga says is traditionally Japanese: human life is essentially irrational and the universe is not logically con-structed. The work of art, if it aims to copy life and nature faithfully, cannot have a logical structure.[69]

This last sentence, it seems to me, is especially pertinent to Shiga's works. The only logic they possess is, as Kobayashi Hideo has said, the 'logic of everyday life'.[70] In other words, Shiga's narratives do not progress in the linear, syllogistic fashion of the classic Aristotelian plot-line,[71] with a 'logical' cause-and-effect relation between a clearly identifiable beginning, middle and end. Rather, the events in his stories are linked in a loosely associative manner reminiscent of Japanese linked verse (*renga*[72]) – or, indeed, of the 'randomness' of life itself. The total aesthetic effect of this technique is one of a quiet, relaxed naturalness. As Kobayashi has said of Shiga: 'His spirit does not know drama. His trials are those of a growing tree.'[73]

Already in *One Morning* we can see the results of this method of writing in which 'the logic of everyday life itself becomes the logic of literary creation.'[74] There is a delicate art involved here – it is certainly not, as one might expect, merely a matter of reporting 'things as they happen'. The writer must exercise great sensitivity in selecting details and in following the 'natural' course of events. As we have already seen, Shintarō must go through a rather complex series of mood-changes before he is finally able to feel 'reconciled' with his grandmother – and to get out of bed. Shiga conveys all this with admirable economy, in just a few short narrative sentences and a few snatches of dialogue. To quote again from Kobayashi: 'Since Tayama Katai learned from Maupassant the literary value of daily life as it is, no writer has succeeded as well as Shiga Naoya has in boldly, even violently, wresting from his own life a <u>work of art</u>.'[75] (Underlining my own.)

But to see Shiga's art of what has been called the 'natural plot'[76] in full flower, we must go on to some of his more mature works.

CHAPTER TWO

THE NATURAL WAY OF DEATH

*A*t *Kinosaki* (*Kinosaki nite*) was written in 1917, almost a decade after *One Morning*, and it has often been regarded as a prime example of the famous 'Shiga style' in its full maturity, and as an exemplary model of the *shi-shōsetsu* in its shorter form.[1]

The story is structured around three encounters which the narrator has with death as manifested in the natural world. A near-fatal accident that he has recently suffered has made him sensitive to the omnipresence of death, so that he notices things he would normally overlook and notices them with an abnormal clarity and intensity. The relationship between the three incidents described is thus not causal as in conventional narrative but associative as in poetry.

The story opens with a typically vigorous first sentence, no words wasted, which takes us immediately into the heart of the matter: '*Yamanote-sen no densha ni hanetobasarete kega o shita, sono ato yōsei ni, hitori de Tajima no Kinosaki onsen e dekaketa.*' ('To recover from injuries I suffered on being hit and sent flying by a train of the Yamanote line, I travelled by myself to the Kinosaki hot spring in Tajima.'[2]) This is a fine example of what Tanizaki calls the 'practicality' (*jitsuyō*) of Shiga's style – perhaps not so rare a quality in English as in Japanese prose, which generally tends to be more circumlocutory.[3]

In the first paragraph we are also told that the narrator has not yet completely escaped from under the shadow of death: according to his doctor, there is still a chance that he might develop tuberculosis of the spine, which could prove fatal. Thus he takes an understandable interest in even the smallest manifestations of death in the world around him.

The narrator's first 'encounter' is with a dead bee. He sees it one morning on the roof of the *genkan*, the entranceway to his hotel. The impact which this sight has on his death-oriented consciousness is made real to us in two ways: by a graphic description of the pathetic figure of the dead bee, its legs 'stuck tight to its underbelly' and its antennae 'drooping down sloppily over its face', and by a contrast of the dead bee with the many living bees swarming busily around it:

> These bees going so busily about their work gave one the sense of something intensely alive. And the one bee lying beside them – which, whenever one looked at it, morning, noon or night, was still curled up face-down and motionless in exactly the same spot – this gave one just as intensely the sense of something dead.[4]

We are then told explicitly of the narrator's emotional response:

> Whenever I looked at it I was overcome by a feeling of profound quietness. And of loneliness. It made me feel lonely to look at this one dead bee left alone on the cold roof tile when, after sunset, all the other bees had entered the hive. But it was also very quiet.[5]

This is a familiar pattern in Shiga's *shi-shōsetsu*: a graphic evocation of the natural world, or an equally vivid depiction of the world of human relations, followed by an extended analysis of the narrator's usually rather complex responses – in other words, a continual reciprocation between outer and inner worlds.

As is evident from the above quote, the narrator's response to his first encounter with death is generally a rather positive one. He is attracted to the peaceful quietude of death. After the dead bee has been washed away by the rains, he imagines it lying somewhere completely motionless: 'It seemed so quiet because the bee who had spent his whole life working so busily now could not move at all. I felt close to that quietness.'[6] He mentions that he has recently written a story called *Han's Crime* (*Han no hanzai*, one of Shiga's more 'fictional' stories), in which a Chinese juggler, Han, had murdered his wife. In his present mood he would like to rewrite the story from the wife's point of view: 'to write out of the feeling of quietness of his murdered wife lying in her grave.'[7] Without being overly facetious, one might remark here that Shiga (or his narrative *alter ego*) comes uncomfortably close to a writer usually considered his opposite in 'healthy-mindedness', Kawabata Yasunari, the 'necrophilic' author of *The House of Sleeping Beauties* (*Nemureru bijo*). But, perhaps fortunately, Shiga assures us that he never did write *The Murdered Wife of Han*, although 'I did feel the need to write it'.[8] He tells us further: 'And this depressed me, because it meant I had begun to think and feel in a way very different to the hero of *A Dark Night's Passing*, a novel I had been writing for some time.'[9] The reference is, of course, to Shiga's own novel or novel-length *shishōsetsu*, in which the hero, Kensaku, is almost desperately life-affirming and 'positivist'; the present narrator's mood of feeling 'close to the peace which followed death'[10] would no doubt seem abhorrent to Kensaku. This is true, at least, for those early portions of the work that Shiga was writing at the same time as *At Kinosaki* – though, as we shall see, it becomes less and less true as Kensaku moves towards his final, climactic experience of 'self-dissolution' and union with nature on Mount Daisen in the work's penultimate chapter.

The narrator's second encounter with death is a rather more violent and unpleasant one. Walking through the town one day, he notices a noisy crowd of people gathered along the bank of a small stream, making a lot of fuss about something. When he investigates, he finds that:

> It was a large rat which had been thrown into the water. The rat was swimming with all his might, desperate to escape. A seven-inch-long fish skewer had been run through his neck. It protruded about three inches above his head and three inches below his throat.[11]

Some of the bystanders are making sport of the unfortunate creature by throwing stones at it. It struggles to climb up the bank and into a hole, but the skewer catches on some rocks and it falls back into the stream: 'The rat tried with all his will to save himself. His facial expressions may not have been comprehensible to a human being, but one understood how determined he was from his actions.'[12] The narrator turns away from the scene: 'I didn't feel like watching the rat's last moments.'[13]

Whereas his first experience gave him an inviting sense of the ultimate peace of death, then, the sight of the tormented rat is far more disturbing:

> It was terrible that, before I could enjoy the quietness I longed for, I would have to endure that kind of suffering. Though I felt close to the peace which followed death, I feared the struggle which must precede it.[14]

And indeed he is reminded that, after his recent accident, his own instinct to survive had welled up as powerfully and irresistibly as the rat's:

> I had tried to do everything I could to survive at that moment. I had decided by myself which hospital I should be taken to. I had even specified which mode of transportation should be used. Concerned that, if the doctor was out, any necessary operation could not be performed the moment I arrived, I asked someone to phone ahead to warn the hospital I was coming. When I thought about it later, it seemed strange to me that, even in its half-conscious state, my mind dealt efficiently with those matters it considered of utmost importance.[15]

Strangely, though, he remembers that, at the same time: 'even though I had wondered whether my wounds would prove fatal, I had wondered this in a strangely detached way, without being overcome by any fear of dying.'[16]

The narrator's final encounter with death is even more disturbing, as he himself is the agent who brings it about. While out for an evening stroll, he comes across a water lizard sitting on a rock beside a stream. Wishing merely 'to scare the lizard into the water',[17] he absent-mindedly tosses a stone in its direction. By what seems to him like some perverse twist of fate, the stone scores a direct hit and the lizard is killed. Again, Shiga's descriptive powers are vividly evocative:

> The stone struck something with a sharp sound and then fell into the stream. At the same time as I heard the stone striking, the lizard seemed to fly about four inches sideways. He curled his tail and lifted it up high. I wondered what had happened. At first I didn't think the stone had hit him. His curled-up tail quietly and naturally uncurled again. He seemed to brace himself so as not to slide down the slope. But then he retracted the claws on both his forelegs and fell helplessly forward. His tail lay completely flat against the rock. He no longer moved. He was dead.[18]

There is no trace left now of the narrator's previous attraction to death. What especially troubles him is the way the lizard's death seems such a product of arbitrary chance. Indeed, long before Camus and Ionesco, Shiga here presents us with an acute sense of 'existential absurdity':

> Though I had often killed creatures of that sort, what gave me a strange and unpleasant feeling was that I had killed it without intending at all to do so.

> Although it had happened because of something I'd
> done, this made it seem all the more a matter of
> chance.[19]

Contemplating the lizard's death in this way, the narrator is
filled with a sense of 'the loneliness of all living creatures'.[20]
This is further intensified when he thinks now of what might
have become of the two other dead creatures, the bee 'washed
underground by the rain that swept him away',[21] and the rat:
'He'd probably been swept out to sea and by now his bloated
body might have been washed ashore with some garbage.'[22] His
thoughts then turn to himself:

> And now I, who had not died, was walking along like
> this. Such were my thoughts. I felt that I should be
> grateful. But in reality no feeling of joy arose within
> me. Living and dying were not polar opposites. I felt
> there was not so much difference between them.[23]

In this almost nihilistic mood, he stumbles back to his inn in
the growing darkness: 'Unable to see where I was stepping, I
walked forward uncertainly.'[24] We are thus left with the feeling
that the narrator has been somewhat devastated, albeit
'enlightened', by his final encounter with death. The work
ends with a kind of 'footnote' that is rather more positive in
tone: 'More than three years have passed since then. I have
been spared at least from getting spinal tuberculosis.'[25] Thus
the story is set in a sort of 'frame' by the opening and closing
paragraphs, in which the narrator reminisces about the events
'at Kinosaki' from a distance of three years.

As Tanikawa Tetsuzō has noted, Japanese writers, 'from
Akutagawa Ryūnosuke on, have lavished praise on this story.'[26]
What the critics have found to praise in it, above all, is the
excellence of its style. To illustrate what he considers to be the
source of this excellence, Tanikawa quotes from Shiga's
commentary on the story:

> This too is a story based on the events as they
> actually happened. The deaths of the rat, the bee
> and the water lizard all were really witnessed by me
> over a period of several days. And I intended to write
> directly and sincerely about the feelings that arose in
> me at the time.[27]

The very fact, then, that the writer is so close to the events of
which he writes gives his style an immediacy, a 'directness' and
'sincerity', that it might not otherwise attain. This idea is by no

means peculiar to the apologists of the *shi-shōsetsu*, despite
Francis Mathy's claim that the term 'sincerity' has 'but a low
place in the Western critical vocabulary.'[28] As a matter of fact, it
has a high place in the vocabulary of no less a writer than
Tolstoy, who maintained that art is 'infectious' (i.e., persuasive)
'in consequence of the sincerity of the artist, that is, of the
greater or lesser force with which the artist himself experiences
the sensation which he is conveying ....'[29] This sounds very
close indeed to Shiga's concept of *jikkan* ('felt realizations')
which, as Mathy himself points out, is central to his espousal of
a more or less 'autobiographical' art.[30] To take but one other
example, one of the leading English critics of this century, F.R.
Leavis, in an essay entitled, *Reality and Sincerity*, maintains that
'sincerity' is a term 'to which a critic must try and give some
useful force by appropriate and careful use ....'[31] And he goes
on to compare a poem by Emily Brontë unfavorably with one by
Thomas Hardy because Brontë is 'dramatizing herself in a
situation such as she has clearly not known in actual experience:
what she offers is betrayingly less real.'[32] And 'to say that
Hardy's poem has an advantage in reality is to say (it will turn
out) that it represents a profounder and completer sincerity.'[33]

Of course, this does not mean that there is unanimity on this
point in the West. As Leavis himself notes, one of the most
influential of English literary theorists, Samuel Taylor Coler-
idge, declared unequivocally that among the 'promises of
genius' is:

> .... the choice of subjects very remote from the
> private interests and circumstances of the writer
> himself. At least I have found that, where the subject
> is taken immediately from the author's personal
> sensations and experiences, the excellence of a
> particular poem is but an equivocal mark, and often
> a fallacious pledge, of genuine poetic power.[34]

And we might add to this Flaubert's dictum: 'toute oeuvre est
condamnable ou l'auteur se laisse deviner.'[35] Flaubert, says
William Barry, 'warned us against every work of art in which
the author's face seems to be reflected .... Such egotism, he
thinks, is unworthy of a supreme artist, and bears its
condemnation in itself.'[36] In other words, the debate between
the apologists of the 'fictional' in the sense of the 'purely
imaginary' and those who admire the 'sincerity' of more or less
autobiographical writings is an eternal one and has been
conducted as vigorously in the West as in Japan.

Nevertheless, it seems that, in the Japan of Shiga's day at least, it was the 'sincerity' of the *shi-shōsetsu* which won the most admirers – although the 'other side' was well represented by such consummate story-tellers as Akutagawa Ryūnosuke and Tanizaki Jun'ichirō. Again it is Kobayashi Hideo who, with a few memorable similes, best expresses the sense of immediacy and spontaneity in Shiga's style that Japanese readers find so appealing:

> His perceptions are direct indeed, like the cobra swaying to the sound of the flute, or the wings of the ptarmigan turning white with the advent of winter. The immediacy of the awareness does not permit of hesitation in the choice of words. They are found before the ripples have reached the edge of the pond.[37]

It is doubtful whether Shiga – or any other writer – could attain this miraculous degree of immediacy if he did not write directly out of his own experience. Nevertheless, there is a lot more involved here than the author's simple adherence to the 'facts' of his life – although, admittedly, some Japanese literary scholars do seem to believe that, if the author departs from the facts even slightly, he breaks a sacred trust.

A basic article of faith found widely throughout traditional East Asian culture is that one's moral character, in Confucian terms, or one's state of being or proximity to enlightenment, in Buddhist terms, is infallibly reflected in the way one breathes, walks, sits, holds oneself – and, of course, writes (in both the physical sense, the quality of one's calligraphy, and in the literary sense, the quality of one's style). One form this belief takes is what we might call the ethical/aesthetic equation. In more popular terms, this was interpreted to mean that only a strong, healthy, simple, 'sincere' person could write in a strong, healthy, simple, 'sincere' style – like Shiga's. These qualities were the natural, spontaneous outflow of an upright character and a 'pure heart'. Thus they could not be faked or turned into a mere 'rhetoric' which could be consciously mastered by anyone with a sufficient degree of literary talent. In aesthetic terms, this doctrine led inevitably to the high appreciation of a certain kind of 'artlessness'. Mere technical mastery, a dry academic perfection of form, was often held in contempt. The very 'artlessness' of calligraphy and ink painting by Zen masters such as Hakuin and Sengai was seen as a token of the freedom and 'sincerity' of the artist, whose spiritual power was conveyed all the more effectively by a strong, simple, unpretentious style, however amateurish or even childish the end product might appear. Nor was this aesthetic confined to the Zen world: it formed the basis of the art, for instance, of the eighteenth-century *bunjin*, the 'literary gentlemen' painters who prided themselves on their amateur status and style. And, needless to say, this aesthetic (and ethic) has continued to hold a great attraction for Japanese writers and artists down into the twentieth century.

That Shiga subscribed to his own version of this ethical/aesthetic equation may be seen clearly in many of his pronouncements on the art of writing – for instance, the passage already quoted which expresses his idea of 'rhythm': because of the powerful rhythm which emanates from a writer like Saikaku, even when he deals with 'trivial matters' his writing makes a profound impression on the reader's 'mind and spirit'.

As with the guiding doctrines or faiths of any culture, of course, a certain amount of exaggeration and over-simplification can easily be detected in this 'myth' of artlessness and sincerity. One could point, for instance, to the obvious fact that a certain minimum level of technical competence, consciously acquired if not consciously applied, is necessary for the practice of any art. Even the Buddha was not born wielding a pen or a paint brush. But, again as with many fundamental cultural assumptions, the basic kernel of conviction here – that the style is the man – is neither verifiable nor falsifiable by empirical means. Edward Fowler, in his impressive study of the *shishōsetsu*, *The Rhetoric of Confession*, seems to think that he has proved the case against Shiga's 'sincerity' by showing how he changed or deleted certain facts about, for instance, his quarrel with his father, and that it follows, therefore, that such 'sincerity' is a mere rhetorical device.[38] But I doubt whether a millennium or so of cultural tradition can be so easily dismissed. There is, as I have said, a lot more to the Japanese idea of 'sincerity' than mere fidelity to biographical detail. Thus Fowler's 'empirical approach' is fundamentally misguided – an ontological approach would have been more appropriate, given that 'sincerity' in this context is more than anything a state of being. One simply believes or disbelieves in the ethical/aesthetic equation and, obviously, if one were born into the Japan of Shiga's day, chances are that one would have believed. But, whether one accepts this as an article of faith or not, the fact remains that it was the 'cultural ground' which gave birth to Shiga's *shi-shōsetsu*, his 'artless art', and which sustained it as a major force in Japanese literature for much of this century. Indeed, even Fowler himself, in struggling to account for the 'extraordinary power' of Shiga's *magnum opus*, *A Dark Night's Passing*, admits that nearly 'every commentator has pointed to Shiga's inimitable ability to project his presence on paper'.[39]

To return now to the native viewpoint, Yoshida Sei-ichi also emphasizes Shiga's spontaneity, even going so far as to say that the selection of pertinent details, a process that most writers agonize over, comes to him simply and naturally. Furthermore:

> Shiga's sentences are alive because they do not describe too much, they select only the necessary details. Shiga himself once observed: 'When one looks at a particular thing and tries to think about using it as the material for one's writing, one's attention is all the more distracted to other, superfluous things – and this serves no purpose. When I do something I do it almost unconsciously, and usually I write down only whatever remains in my mind about it afterwards.' But these are the words of a man blessed with the true writer's temperament! To see the essential things naturally, without even trying to see them – this is indeed a born writer. The process of selection operates in him unconsciously.[40]

Yoshida goes on to say, though, that from the point of view of the 'science of rhetoric' Shiga's writing, looked at sentence by sentence, does not necessarily qualify as 'fine prose' (*meibun*). He notes, for instance, the many repetitions of words and phrases, quoting as an example the following passage from *At Kinosaki* (repeated words are underlined):

> *Su no deiri ni isogashiku sono waki o haimawaru ga mattaku kōdei suru yōsu wa nakatta. Isogashiku tachihataraite iru hachi wa ika ni mo ikite iru mono to iu kanji o ataeta. Sono waki ni ippiki, asa mo hiru mo yū mo, miru tabi ni hitotsu tokoro mattaku ugokazu ni utsumuki ni korogatte iru no o miru to, sore ga mata ika ni mo shinda mono to iu kanji o ataeru no da. Sore wa mikka hodo sono mama ni natte ita. Sore wa mite ite, ika ni mo shizuka na kanji o ataeta. Samishikatta. Hoka no hachi ga mina sue e haitte shimatta higure, tsumetai kawara ni hitotsu nokotta shigai o miru koto wa samishikatta. Shikashi, sore wa ika ni mo shizuka datta.*[41]

The following is a rather literal translation but it still cannot, of course, reproduce the exact effect of all the repetitions in Japanese – in particular, the repetition of the English 'it', being more customary, does not have the same effect as the repetition of the Japanese '*sore wa*':

> They crawled <u>busily</u> around the entrance to their hive but they gave no sign whatever that they had any relation to the dead bee. These <u>busily</u> working bees <u>all the more</u> gave me the feeling that they were living things. And, again, whenever I saw the dead one beside them, morning, noon or night, lying face down always in exactly the same place, it <u>all the more</u> gave me the feeling that it was a dead thing. <u>It</u> lay there for more than three days. When I looked at <u>it</u>, it <u>all the more</u> gave me a feeling of quietness. And of <u>loneliness</u>. It was <u>lonely</u> to see the one dead bee left on the cold roof-tile when the others had all gone into their hive after nightfall. But also <u>it</u> was <u>all the more</u> tranquil.

To quote Yoshida again:

> In this brief passage alone, there is one sentence in which there are four repetitions of the same word or phrase, two sentences in which there are three and two in which there are two. That there should be so many repetitions even after the writer has omitted and deleted as much as possible is probably a fault from the point of view of rhetoric. But it is all a necessary and unavoidable part of Shiga's mode of expression. The repetitions are a part of his poetic sense of rhythm, and give forceful expression to those impressions which have made the deepest impact on his mind.[42]

Indeed, the repetitions may serve a thematic as well as a stylistic purpose. Yoshida illustrates this with the following passage, also from *At Kinosaki*:

> *Ima <u>jibun</u> ni ano nezumi no yō na koto ga okottara <u>jibun</u> wa dō suru darō. <u>Jibun</u> wa yahari nezumi to onaji yō na doryoku o shiwa shimai ka. <u>Jibun</u> wa <u>jibun</u> no kega no baai, sore ni chikai <u>jibun</u> ni natta koto o omowanai de wa irarenakatta. <u>Jibun</u> wa dekiru dake no koto o shiyō to shita. <u>Jibun</u> wa jishin de byōin o kimeta.*[43]

> (What would <u>I</u> do now if <u>I</u> were placed in the same situation as the rat? Wouldn't <u>I</u> too, after all, put up

the same kind of fight? I couldn't help thinking that
something similar had happened to me when I was
hit by the train. I had tried to do everything I could
to survive at that moment. I had decided by myself
which hospital I should be taken to.[44])

Again, of course, all these repetitions of *'jibun'* in Japanese
create a stronger impression than the repetitions of 'I' in
English – since in English this is more usual. Thus Yoshida is
moved to ask:

> What about these eight repetitions of the word *jibun*?
> If we were to isolate this passage and examine it as an
> example of bad style, it would probably be possible
> to delete many of the repetitions. But if we look at it
> as embedded in its original context, and try to
> discern how this *jibun* works, then this mode of
> expression which emphasizes the self assumes a
> necessary role as part of the honest self-absorption of
> the passage.[45]

Shiga's use of repetition as a powerful way of communicating
his basic theme is also evident, throughout his Kinosaki story,
in his repeated use of the word *sabishii* (lonely) – but more on
this presently. For the moment, we may note that Yoshida's
analysis seems to support Shiga's contention that there is more
to good style than mere skill or technique, whether this involves
following textbook rules of rhetoric or any other 'artificial'
standards. Shiga himself, as we have seen, used the word
'rhythm' to try to define the quintessence of what he regarded
as good style. But, as we may see from the above example, this
involves more than just patterns of sound – it is also, we might
say, the very pattern of a writer's feelings and thoughts.

Although he did not see eye-to-eye with Shiga's apologists on
the innate superiority of the *shi-shōsetsu* genre *per se*, Tanizaki
Jun'ichirō, who was certainly no mean stylist himself, was as
unreserved as anyone else in his praise of Shiga's style.[46] Of the
Kinosaki story in particular, he said that it had the finest style
he had ever encountered.[47] He quotes from it extensively to
illustrate the virtues of Shiga's style in his *Stylistic Reader*
(*Bunshō Tokuhon*). What he seems to admire above all is the
economy or 'practicality' (*jitsuyō*) of Shiga's writing. As an
example, he quotes the partial sentence: '*Ta no hachi ga mina su
ni haitte shimatta higure tsumetai kawara no ue ni hitotsu nokotta
shigai o miru koto wa ....*'[48] ('...to look at this one dead bee left
alone on the cold roof tile when, after sunset, all the other bees

had entered the hive.') Any ordinary writer, says Tanizaki, would have written this in a far more roundabout way: '*Hi ga kureru to ta no hachi wa mina su ni haitte shimatte sono shigai dake ga tsumetai kawara no ue ni hitotsu nokotte ita ga, sore o miru to ....*' ('After it had grown dark and the other bees had all gone into the hive, only the dead body would be left behind, all alone, on the cold tile; when I saw it ....') Tanizaki describes Shiga's sentence as having been 'tightened up' (*hikishimeta*) and says that 'this very "tightening up" enables the sentence to convey its impressions with all the more clarity.'[49] As a further illustration of this point he quotes Shiga's graphic description of the activity of the bees:

> *Hachi wa hame no awai kara surinukete deru to hitomazu genkan no yane ni orita. Soko de hane ya shokkaku o maeashi ya ushiroashi de teinei ni totonoeru to sukoshi arukimawaru yatsu mo aru ga sugu hosonagai hane o ryōhō e shikkari to hatte buuun to tobitatsu. Tobitatsu to kyū ni hayaku natte tonde yuku.*[50]

> (When the bees slipped out through the gaps between the boards, they would land for a while on the entrance-hall roof. There they would carefully arrange their wings and antennae with their fore- or rear-legs – and some would walk around a little – then they would suddenly stretch both their long thin wings out tight and fly up with a buzz. Once aloft, they would suddenly gain speed and fly quickly off.[51])

Tanizaki comments on this passage:

> Here the bees' movements are described precisely as one would see them through close observation. The reader feels that he is actually seeing each motion because all waste has been eliminated in the description; any word that is not absolutely necessary has been left out.[52]

Responding to Tanizaki's analysis, Tanikawa Tetsuzō, perhaps more in consonance with Shiga's own way of thinking, emphasizes that the power of Shiga's writing derives not merely from his talent for 'close observation' but also from his deep sensitivity towards the natural world and even from his personal strength of character:

> I feel a special interest in the passage which describes the rat's death. What is shown here is Shiga's power

as a realist – I mean not merely his powers of description but the power of his heart to gaze unflinchingly and without regret at any scene whatsoever. Furthermore, Shiga has the sort of temperament that is more than usually responsive to such scenes. In this case also he says finally: 'I felt lonely and unhappy.' But having said this, he does not turn his eyes away from the scene. One can find this kind of example everywhere in Shiga. He is the same in regard to the human heart. He sees what he must see, he feels what he must feel; he does not, like the faint-hearted, turn his eyes away or try to cover things up.[53]

From the comments of these major Japanese writers and critics, then, we may take it that *At Kinosaki* is regarded, on grounds of style alone, as a masterpiece of the *shi-shōsetsu* genre, and thus may fairly stand to represent this genre in any comparative study of it with, say, the modern Western short story. It is fortunate, then, that there happens to be a highly 'representative' Western story built around largely the same idea as Shiga's, but written very much in the European manner: Tolstoy's *Three Deaths* (and who could represent the Western fictional tradition better than Tolstoy?) It will tell us much, I think, about the distinctive nature and special merits of the *shi-shōsetsu* genre to compare the way in which these two very different writers handle a basically similar story concept.

The question of influence may be quickly disposed of. Although Shiga was a great admirer of Tolstoy, it is unlikely that this is a case of 'direct influence'.[54] As Japanese biographical critics never tire of telling us, Shiga based the story on events he had actually experienced. It is one of the obvious virtues of 'autobiographical' writers in general that they are fairly immune to any kind of direct influence. Whether Shiga was 'indirectly' influenced to make a story out of the events he witnessed because he had read the Tolstoy story is a rather esoteric question, and one that is anyway more of biographical than of critical interest.

Tolstoy's story, as its title implies, is structured, like *At Kinosaki*, around three separate deaths: in this case, the deaths of a wealthy lady, of an old peasant and of a young tree. The story is divided into four numbered parts. In the first part, we are introduced to the lady, travelling from Russia to Italy by stagecoach with her husband, her doctor and her maidservant. The group has stopped at a post-station and here the doctor advises the husband not to continue with the journey, as his wife will surely die along the way. The husband tries to prevail upon his wife to turn back, but she, acting like a rather petulant, spoiled child, insists that, if only she can reach the warm climate of the south, her tuberculosis will vanish.

In the second part we are taken inside the drivers' room at the post-station and here introduced to Uncle Theodore, an old driver who is also, like the lady, dying of tuberculosis. In sharp contrast to the lady, however, he accepts his coming death with calm stoicism, even apologizing to the woman of the house for the inconvenience his illness has caused her. When a young driver asks for his boots, since he will no longer be needing them, the old man accedes without complaint, asking only that the youth buy a gravestone for him when he is dead.

In the third part it is about half a year later and the scene is the wealthy lady's house in Russia. She did not go on to Italy after all and now we witness the solemn scene of her grieving family gathered around her deathbed. The solemnity of the occasion, though, is somewhat marred by the lady's continuing insistence that, if only her husband had allowed her to proceed to Italy, she would be fully recovered by now. Up to her last moment she refuses to accept the inevitable; she rejects the very idea of death with an instinctive ferocity which recalls the futile struggle of Shiga's rat. Only when death finally comes does she achieve a dignified calm. Now we are reminded of the quietude of Shiga's dead bee: 'The dead woman's face looked stern and majestic. Neither in the clear cold brow nor in the firmly closed lips was there any movement.'[55]

In the story's fourth and final part we are taken back to the post-station. Uncle Theodore has been dead now many months but he still has no gravestone. The young driver who promised him one is prodded by the woman of the house until finally he agrees to go out and cut down a tree, so that the old man might have at least a wooden cross over him. In the final scene of the story Tolstoy 'draws back' and describes the tree's death not through the young driver's eyes but as if from the point of view of Nature itself – the way the axe-blows, for instance, disturb the silence of the forest. And when the young ash has fallen, the other trees around it are described as having 'flaunted the beauty of their motionless branches still more joyously in the newly cleared space.'[56]

As this last quote immediately suggests, the two stories have more in common than merely their overall conception. In this case, it is the use of the device of contrast in a quite specific way: to give a profound sense of the difference between life and death. We have already seen how Shiga's contrast of the motionless dead bee with the busily active ones succeeded in giving this sense. The final sentence of Tolstoy's story achieves the same effect in much the same way: 'the sappy leaves whispered gladly and peacefully on the treetops, and the branches of those that were living began to rustle slowly and majestically over the dead and prostrate tree.'[57] Tolstoy, in fact, uses this device more extensively than Shiga. For example, he contrasts the feeble, irritable dying lady with her energetic, cheerful maidservant who possesses a 'full bosom' and 'quick black eyes', and likewise he contrasts the gentle old Theodore with the young driver, insolent but full of life, who demands his boots.[58]

Both authors also, of course, contrast the three deaths described in their respective stories, but now to quite different effect. In Tolstoy the contrast serves largely a moral and satiric purpose: as his English translator remarks, he contrasts 'the querulous invalid lady with the dying peasant and the useful tree which made no demands on anyone.'[59] In other words, even in this early Tolstoy story we find his perennial theme of the decadence of the upper classes, especially as opposed to the peasantry and to the natural world in general (to which, in Tolstoy's view, the peasantry also belong) – a world represented here by the tree. As we would expect, Shiga is far less ideological or even cerebral. What he contrasts mainly are his different emotional responses to the three deaths, ranging, as we have seen, from the positive to the negative.

A similar difference may be remarked in the role that nature plays in the two stories. In the context of Shiga's total *opus*, *At Kinosaki* is important in that it records the 'Shiga hero's' first really significant contact with the world of nature.[60] *One Morning*, as we have seen, was concerned exclusively with the narrow world of human relations within a family setting that seemed 'claustrophobic' for a young man yearning to express his individuality. *At Kinosaki* provides the first indication of how the Shiga hero will seek escape from these oppressive confines: by turning more and more towards the wider world of nature. We can discern the growth of this tendency throughout Shiga's later works until, as we shall see, it reaches a kind of climax in his *magnum opus*, *A Dark Night's Passing*. In his final years Shiga turned away from the human world even more,

49

saying that 'the troublesome complications of human affairs have gradually come to be most distasteful to me.'[61] His very last stories are concerned almost entirely with plants and animals. As Francis Mathy says: 'Now that Shiga had established an almost perfect rapport with nature he no longer felt the urge to write about the complications of human affairs, but was content to live immersed in nature, quietly enjoying the beauty that surrounded him.'[62] In *At Kinosaki*, then, there is already some hint of what we might call Shiga's growing 'distaste' for human nature. The only human beings to appear in the story, besides the narrator himself, are the onlookers who cruelly torment the dying rat. And even the narrator himself is not presented in an entirely favourable light: through careless-ness, albeit unintentionally, he is the agent of the unfortunate lizard's death.

In Tolstoy's story too there is a strong sense of the purity of the natural world as opposed, at least, to the world of the Russian aristocracy; but still the story is centred far more on human life. For one thing, the stoical peasants are seen as every bit a part of nature as the trees in the forests. And Tolstoy is, after all, a nineteenth-century Western writer – what he is interested in above all is the portrayal of human character. Even in this story of only about fifteen pages (almost three times the length of Shiga's story but very short indeed for Tolstoy!), a whole gallery of characters is presented, and even the minor ones seem to spring to life with just a few strokes of the master's pen. In Shiga's story there are no 'characters' in this sense, only the 'disembodied' consciousness of the narrator. But I shall consider the significance of this point in more depth presently.

Because Tolstoy employs 'nature', including the peasantry, largely for the moral purpose of satirizing the aristocracy, his view of nature, as we might expect, tends to be idealistic, even sentimental. He is well known for having persistently idealized the Russian peasant, but in the present story we can see how he also tends to idealize inanimate nature, by a kind of anthro-pomorphism that is rather unconvincing to the modern mind. We see this, for instance, in the sentence already quoted: 'The trees flaunted the beauty of their motionless branches still more joyously in the newly cleared space.'[63] Tolstoy's picture of the tree's death, in fact, seems an altogether too pretty one if we compare it with Shiga's uncompromisingly realistic portrayal of the rat's desperate struggle for survival and the lizard's absurd death by mischance. Although Shiga, like Tolstoy, turns to nature as a welcome alternative to the human world, he describes what he sees there with a clear, unflinching eye, perhaps because he has no 'vested interest' in making a moral point. There is, as I have mentioned, some hint here of his growing 'distaste' (I use the word advisedly, to connote more an emotional than a moral response) for human beings – but this is by no means the main point of the story.

In setting himself up as the judge instead of as merely, like Shiga's narrator, the experiencer of the world, Tolstoy naturally assumes the God-like, 'omniscient' point of view. A judge, after all, must appear to be 'objective', and this pretence to objectivity would be far less convincing if a first-person narrative viewpoint were used. Here lies, it seems to me, the very crux of the difference between Shiga's story and Tolstoy's – and indeed between the *shi-shōsetsu* and the mainstream tradition of Western fiction in general. It is not merely a technical difference but a difference in the way the writer handles his material and even, one might say, in his way of apprehending the world. On these specific grounds, Shiga and the *shi-shōsetsu* seem to offer certain distinct advantages, especially to the modern reader who is wary of a writer who makes absolute judgements.

The feeling that the third-person 'omniscient' narrative viewpoint is in some way 'artificial' is certainly not confined to Japanese critics. In his seminal study, *The Rhetoric of Fiction*, Wayne Booth remarks:

> One of the most obviously artificial devices of the storyteller is the trick of going beneath the surface of the action to obtain a reliable view of a character's mind and heart. Whatever our ideas may be about the natural way to tell a story, artifice is unmistakably present whenever the author tells us what no one in so-called real life could possibly know. In life we never know anyone but ourselves by thoroughly reliable internal signs ....[64]

Unintentionally, I am sure, this distinguished American critic has here written a convincing defense of the *shi-shōsetsu* aesthetic.

I have already used Makoto Ueda's term, the 'natural plot', to describe an 'associative' rather than a causal narrative line, but now we can see that this 'naturalness' is also related to the narrative viewpoint. As Booth points out, there is something undeniably artificial about an author telling us the inner thoughts and feelings of a variety of characters – and this artificiality becomes particularly apparent in Tolstoy's case, as we have seen, when he goes so far as to tell us the 'inner feelings' of natural objects such as trees. But I would go further than Booth and say that this artificiality extends even to the narrative structure of a story written from an 'omniscient' point of view. The 'three deaths' of Tolstoy's story, for instance, are not integrated into a natural, seamless whole as successfully as those of *At Kinosaki*. This is made immediately apparent by the fact that Tolstoy is obliged to divide his story into four distinct numbered parts, whereas Shiga's story is all 'of a piece'. In 'Three Deaths', the relation of the lady's death to that of the old peasant is, on the surface level of the action, purely coincidental: it just so happens that the lady's carriage has stopped at the post-house where the peasant lies dying. On a deeper, thematic level, the reader is aware that the author has brought these two deaths together to contrast them and so to make a moral point. The tree's death is causally related to the peasant's death in the usual 'syllogistic' manner of Western narrative: because A, therefore B. But again, it is related to the lady's death thematically only to make a moral point; indeed, if the reader were unaware of these thematic relationships which have been 'artificially' imposed upon the three deaths by the author's moral will, then the story would seem pointless.

What enables *At Kinosaki* to have such a 'natural' structure is its complete and undisguised subjectivity. In the first paragraph of the story the narrator informs us of his near escape from death just before his trip to Kinosaki. It therefore seems perfectly natural, in the first place, that he is especially observant of death in the world about him, even in small forms that a 'normal' person might fail to notice, and, in the second place, that he should respond to even these 'small' deaths with exceptionally deep feeling. In other words, the first paragraph defines the nature of the consciousness through which all the events of the story will be filtered; there is no pretense at all, as in Tolstoy's story, that we are to be presented with an 'objective', God's-eye view of reality. As a result, the reader is prepared to accept the events described as a natural, indeed inevitable, expression of the narrator's state of mind (thus it is a *shinkyō shōsetsu* in the fullest sense of the term).

At Kinosaki, then, is an excellent example of the total subjectivity of the *shi-shōsetsu* genre. This is not merely a matter of the story being written in the first-person singular or being faithfully autobiographical. If, for instance, we examine *At Kinosaki* more closely, we find that the narrator's 'state of mind' permeates the whole story even in the smallest details. The entire story is pervaded by the psychological atmosphere of a traumatized mind, the mind of a man still in a mild state of shock after having suffered a serious accident. The narrator tells us himself in the second paragraph of the story: 'My head still was not quite clear somehow.'[65] And indeed he seems to wander about Kinosaki, itself a rather 'unreal' resort town, as in a waking dream. There is a dream-like quality, for instance, to the intensity and minute detail of his observation of the bees. But the final scene of the story in particular verges on the surrealistic. The narrator is out for a walk one evening on a mountain road above the town. He feels strongly compelled to go on and on as in a dream: 'I was continually on the point of turning back, but kept urging myself on to the next corner visible in the distance, and then the next one.'[66] And the nature surrounding him takes on a mysterious, dream-like ambience:

> Everything looked pale in the evening light, the touch of the night air chilled my skin, and the deep silence made me feel somehow, perversely, rather restless. Large mulberry trees grew beside the road. On a mulberry tree branch which extended over the road up ahead, a single leaf fluttered in a continual rhythmic movement all by itself. There was no wind and, apart from the stream, only that leaf disturbed the deep stillness, busily fluttering on and on. It gave me an eerie feeling. And it frightened me a bit. But it also aroused my curiosity. I went down to the foot of the tree and stood looking up at it for a while. Then I felt a breeze. And the single fluttering leaf stopped fluttering.[67]

This seemingly irrational behaviour of the single leaf creates the proper air of mystery for what is about to happen. The narrator spots a water lizard sitting on a rock beside a stream. It just so happens that lizards have a kind of personal symbolic significance for him:

> Ten years before in Ashinoko, when I would see the lizards that often used to gather at the water flowing out of the drain of my inn, I had often felt that, if I were one of them, I wouldn't be able to bear it. I often wondered what I would do if I were reincarnated as a lizard. Every time I saw a lizard in those days such thoughts would enter my mind, so I hated to see them.[68]

It is therefore as if this present lizard has sprung from some deep 'obsessive' region of his own unconscious mind, again as in a dream. Thus when he casually throws a stone and 'accidentally' kills the lizard, one need not call on the good doctor of Vienna to see the obvious symbolic meaning that this 'dream-like' action has.

With this last example, though, we are moving from the formal to the thematic level, and indeed it is an indication of how well-integrated these two levels are in Shiga that it is difficult to talk of them separately. Not only is the narrator's consciousness the 'filter' of all external events but this consciousness itself is also the actual subject of the story. This too is characteristic of the *shi-shōsetsu*: the central interest of the story lies in the series of changes which the narrator's consciousness undergoes as it witnesses or experiences the events the story describes. The genre thus may claim a unique reciprocal interaction between form and content: the subject of the narration is the changes in the narrator's consciousness, which are in turn reflected in the narrative style and structure – and so on, one might say, *ad infinitum*.

Lest this all begin to sound overly abstract, what it means in more concrete terms is an extraordinary depth of insight into the human psyche. As we have seen, Shiga's story cannot begin to compare with Tolstoy's in terms of breadth – that is, in the range of 'characters' it presents. In fact, one might well say that Shiga offers us no full-blooded, 'rounded' characters of the type E.M. Forster has delineated in his celebrated study of the novel.[69] Even the narrator in Shiga's story is little more than a 'disembodied' consciousness. Shiga employs none of the tricks of which Tolstoy was such a master, those little details of physical appearance, personal mannerism or idiosyncratic behaviour which can make even a minor character spring to life. We know nothing 'personal' about Shiga's narrator except that he is a writer; he is, in fact, hardly identifiable as an individual. This is perhaps the central paradox that emerges from a comparison of the two stories: the *shi-shōsetsu* is deeply subjective but, at the same time, almost completely impersonal; the Western story, on the other hand, despite its pose of objectivity, is far more 'personal' in the sense that it presents individual human personalities and, as we have seen, even tends to 'personify' natural objects such as trees. Of course, we would expect an 'objective' writer such as Tolstoy to present a wider range of characters, but then we would also expect that

Shiga's narrator, at least, since the whole story is focused on him, would be more highly 'individuated' than any of Tolstoy's characters. But this is certainly not the case. If, however, we examine more closely the nature of human personality – at least as it usually appears in fiction – what seemed to be a paradox may no longer seem so. What gives Tolstoy's characters personality is his use of such largely surface details as the character's appearance, mannerisms, opinions and so on. Shiga's narrator, on the other hand, is presented at such a deep level of his psychic being that he appears to be almost a non-individuated 'everyman'. It seems that the deeper a writer goes into the human psyche the less distinguishing features he finds there – at the deepest level, perhaps it is quite literally true that 'all men are one'. And this sense of universality is added to by the fact that the problem that the narrator confronts in this story is, after all, the most universal problem of all: death itself.

This aspect of 'impersonality' also explains why the reader is not offended by the self-absorption of the *shi-shōsetsu* genre, at least as practiced by Shiga. Edward Fowler has noted that Shiga often uses the rather impersonal word for oneself, *jibun*, rather than the more personal *watakushi*, in order 'to distance himself from his experience, and at the same time draw the reader into it . . . .'[70] But Shiga's works are also 'impersonal' in a sense that goes far beyond mere self-detachment. I quoted earlier Flaubert's condemnation of the 'egotism' of any work 'in which the author's face is reflected.'[71] But in Shiga's work, one might counter, it is not the author's 'face' that is reflected but his 'soul', and, one might add, the impersonality of the human psyche at its deepest level is attested to by Western psychology (e.g., Jung's 'collective unconscious') as much as by Eastern philosophy (e.g., Zen Buddhism). In this sense, too, the *shi-shōsetsu* differs significantly from the Western autobiographical or confessional novel, which usually aims at the 'self-portrait' of a highly individuated personality.[72] Indeed, Karatani Kōjin, in his extensive and fascinating study of the creation of the 'subject' in modern Japanese literature, goes so far as to claim that, although that literature 'may be said to have come into existence together with the confessional literary form,' this form 'should not be confused with an act of confession, for in this case it is the form itself that produces the "inner life" that is confessed' – in other words, the work writes the author rather than the other way round.[73] Although, of course, such ideas have become very fashionable in the West since Roland Barthes announced the 'death of the author,' and although I would not wish to follow Karatani to quite that extreme of 'pure formalism,' nevertheless the impersonality of the *shi-shōsetsu*, at least as practiced by Shiga, undeniably makes his claim more plausible than such claims usually are in a Western context.

At any rate, in the particular case of East/West comparison I am concerned with here, the point emerges more clearly if we contrast the way in which Shiga and Tolstoy approach death, which may be regarded as the central theme of both stories. There is a difference in their approaches here much like that we already encountered in the ways they dealt with nature. Tolstoy is mainly interested in using his 'three deaths' to make a moral and satiric point, namely by showing the way in which different human types die. Shiga, on the other hand, attempts to confront the very nature of death itself, with its sense of peace but also with its cruelty and arbitrariness. He is thus working on a far more universal level: a basic human consciousness, stripped of almost all 'personality', confronting a fundamental human problem. Thus there is no question of the author's 'egotism' preventing the reader's identification with the narrator – because the only part of himself that he 'exhibits' to us is the deepest part, the part that we share with him. In this sense the 'I' of a Shiga story is the same as the 'I' behind, say, a Bashō *haiku* or a Western lyrical poem – it is human consciousness at its most basic and universal level. I think we are justified, then, in saying that what Shiga – and the *shi-shōsetsu* at its best – sacrifices in 'breadth' is compensated for by a commensurate gain in 'depth'.

I have already remarked on the 'reciprocity' of form and content in Shiga's story, but the ultimate example of it is this: not only is the narrative voice largely impersonal, but impersonality itself is the narrator's final 'goal' – that is, the series of changes which the narrator's consciousness undergoes, and which are the story's true focal point, are all in the direction of impersonality.

The critic Yoshida Sei-ichi, as we have seen, demonstrated how Shiga often makes use of the repetition of a word or phrase to establish the 'psychological atmosphere' of his stories.[74] In *At Kinosaki* the most important of these words is *sabishii*, usually translated as 'lonely'. In its adjectival or nominal form, the word is used to describe the narrator's emotional response to each of the three deaths he witnesses. Seeing the dead bee: 'I was overcome by a feeling of profound quietness. And of loneliness. It made me feel lonely to look at this one dead bee left alone on the cold roof tile when, after sunset, all the other bees had entered the hive.'[75] Watching the doomed rat: 'gave me a lonely and unpleasant feeling.'[76] And, having killed the lizard:

> I felt that now there was only myself and the lizard, I became one with him and felt how he felt. I pitied him, but at the same time shared with him a feeling of the loneliness of all living creatures. By chance I had not died. By chance the lizard had died. I began to feel lonely and finally headed back towards the hotspring inn.[77]

Obviously if a writer such as Shiga, famous for not wasting words, repeats one word so often, we might expect that word to carry more than its normal weight of meaning. Unfortunately, the English word 'lonely' is not able to bear that weight – it has, of course, none of the rich cultural associations of the Japanese word *sabishii*. As William Sibley points out, *sabishii* in the context of Shiga's story describes a 'quite positive, if largely passive, esthetic-emotional experience ....'[78]

The word *sabi*, derived from *sabishii*, is a key term of Zen aesthetics, and has particular resonance, for instance, in the poetics of Bashō's school of *haiku*. Bashō himself, as Makoto Ueda points out, often used the word *sabishii*. But he conceived of loneliness, says Ueda, 'as an impersonal atmosphere, in contrast with grief or sorrow, which is a personal emotion. The contrast cannot be over-emphasized, because loneliness thus conceived lay at the bottom of Bashō's view of life, pointing toward a way in which his plea "return to nature" can be fulfilled.'[79] Sorrow, in other words, belongs to the human world, whereas 'loneliness' belongs to the world of nature. Thus, if it were possible for men to escape from sorrow, 'it would be only through a denial of humanity, through men's dehumanizing themselves. They can escape from sorrow only when they transform it into an impersonal atmosphere, loneliness.'[80] This transformation is brought about by a deep communion with nature, as in the following haiku of Bashō:

> My sorrowful soul –
> Make it feel lonesome,
> You, a cuckoo.[81]

The poet, says Ueda:

> .... as he set out to compose the poem, was still in
> the world of humanity, with a personal feeling like
> sorrow. The cuckoo, on the other hand, seemed to
> have already transcended sorrow, as it was closer to
> the heart of nature. Thereupon the poet wished that
> the bird's cry might enlighten his soul and eventually
> lead him into the realm of impersonal loneliness,
> where he would no longer feel sorrow .... Such a
> dissolution of personal emotion into an impersonal
> atmosphere constitutes the core of Bashō's attitude
> toward life.[82]

If we review the way in which Shiga uses the word *sabishii*, we
find that more and more throughout the story it comes to take
on Bashō's sense of an 'impersonal atmosphere' pervading
nature. And the effect which the absorption of this 'atmosphere'
has on the narrator's consciousness is to produce a greater and
greater sense of detachment. His contemplation of the dead bee
gives him a sense of 'loneliness' but 'at the same time it was
tranquil, soothing.'[83] Already, then, in Bashō's terms this is not a
'personal sorrow' but a liberating, impersonal feeling derived
directly from nature. His response to the sight of the doomed rat
struggling for survival at first seems more 'sorrowful' and
therefore 'personal' – in fact, it reminds him of his own struggle
to survive after his accident. But further contemplation leads
him on to the kind of 'transformation' Bashō demands from the
cuckoo in his *haiku*: by identifying with the rat, he comes to see
that to struggle to survive is a universal instinct, present in the rat
as much as in himself, and that therefore it would be absurd for
him to take it 'personally', i.e., for him to feel ashamed because
he had acted 'like an animal' after his accident, because he too
had been driven by an irresistible force. This realization gives
him the necessary sense of detachment:

> Undoubtedly I would have behaved in much the
> same way as the rat. And when I tried to imagine
> how I would act if the same thing happened again -
> would I struggle hard or would I give in to my
> longing for peace? – since I hadn't changed much
> and since one's behaviour is not really influenced so
> easily by such moods as the longing for the quiet of
> death, I concluded that I'd probably still struggle to
> survive. But both possibilities seemed real, and I felt
> that either way would be alright. Whatever happened
> would happen inevitably.[84]

The narrator's profound sense of detachment is even further intensified by his accidental killing of the lizard. He is filled with 'a feeling of the loneliness of all living creatures. By chance I had not died. By chance the lizard had died. I began to feel lonely . . . .'[85] In other words, by identifying with the lizard as he had with the rat, he receives a further insight: that death strikes arbitrarily. He feels that he himself might just as easily be dead now – if he had been as unlucky as the lizard at the time of his accident. The thought is enough to make him lose his attachment to life:

> And now I, who had not died, was walking along like this. Such were my thoughts. I felt that I should be grateful. But in reality no feeling of joy arose within me. Living and dying were not polar opposites. I felt there was not so much difference between them.[86]

Thus, it seems, the narrator has reached an ultimate level of 'impersonality' and detachment since, though he knows he will instinctively struggle for survival if the need arises, he no longer really cares, intellectually at least, whether he lives or dies.

But what is the purpose, the reader may well ask, of achieving such an 'unhuman' detachment? What is its wider significance? We have already seen that Bashō advocated the development of an impersonal state of consciousness as a way of 'returning to nature'.[87] According to Francis Mathy, it is exactly this sense of closeness to nature that Shiga is expressing in *At Kinosaki*: after his encounter with death, he 'found himself entering a new world of union and harmony with nature.'[88] William Sibley emphasizes the 'Shiga hero's' mature acceptance of death that has been brought about by his deep communion with nature. And Sibley relates this to the 'more fully delineated experience of Kensaku', the hero of *A Dark Night's Passing*.[89] In the penultimate chapter of this long work, Kensaku retreats like a traditional hermit to Mount Daisen and there undergoes a 'mystical' experience of self-dissolution and union with nature. Shortly before he has this experience, we are told that 'he was irresistibly attracted to the realm the Buddhists call "*nirvana*" or "*jakumetsu iraku*" (the bliss of annihilation).'[90]

Undoubtedly there is some relation between Kensaku's experience of 'self-annihilation' and union with nature and the experience of detachment and 'impersonality' of the narrator of *At Kinosaki*, but I doubt that it is as straightforward as Mathy and Sibley would have us believe. If we look again at the final part of the story, we find that the narrator's experience has by no means left him in an unalloyed state of bliss. He feels none of the euphoria that Kensaku experiences on Mount Daisen. In fact, he feels rather miserable and confused. The final scene of the story makes it quite clear that his 'dark night' has not yet passed:

> Only the distant lights were dimly visible. Unable to see where I was stepping, I walked forward uncertainly. My mind alone worked on as it pleased. And this led me all the more into those kinds of thoughts and feelings.[91]

These last two sentences in particular, it seems to me, tell us why the narrator has not yet achieved the psychic breakthrough – the '*satori*' – he is after: he continues to intellectualize, to fantasize, and therefore to stand apart from nature. He has not yet surrendered his whole mind and soul to nature as Kensaku does on Mount Daisen. There is, in fact, something suspiciously 'intellectual' even about his sense of detachment. When he says: 'To be alive and to be dead were not two opposite extremes', he is stating an idea rather than describing an experience – and it is doubtful whether any Zen master (or, for that matter, any reader) would accept this as real proof of spiritual transformation.

When Kensaku experiences complete union with nature on Mount Daisen, he remembers that he has had similar experiences before, but that he had 'always tried instinctively to resist it, and on finding such resistance difficult, he had felt a distinct uneasiness. But this time, he had not the slightest will to resist; and contentedly, without a trace of the old uneasiness, he accepted nature's embrace.'[92] If, like Kobayashi Hideo and William Sibley among others, we see the 'Shiga hero' as one consistent character throughout, at least, Shiga's 'autobiographical' works, then we might say that *At Kinosaki* describes one of those earlier experiences when he 'tried instinctively' to resist 'nature's embrace'.[93] Without dwelling on the problematical relation of *nirvana* to death in orthodox Buddhist philosophy, we might certainly claim that the *At Kinosaki* narrator's early attraction to the quietude of death may be related to Kensaku's attraction to the 'bliss of annihilation'. What seems to be yearned for in both cases is the death of the troublesome individual human self so that it may be replaced by an 'impersonal' state of consciousness that is totally at one with the natural world. This would explain why the narrator is troubled by his own 'instinct to survive' after he is reminded of it by the struggling rat – this instinct to resist death is, after all, an expression of that same instinct that Kensaku speaks of, to resist complete mergence with nature. The narrator of *At Kinosaki* is obviously not yet ready for such a complete surrender of self, though he is moving hesitantly in that direction. Before he is capable of so unreservedly 'letting go', the grip of his ego must be loosened by a whole series of traumatic shocks. But we shall see this more clearly when we come to *A Dark Night's Passing*.

CHAPTER THREE

A FIRE IN THE HEART

*B*onfire (*Takibi*, 1920) shares a place with *At Kinosaki* as one of Shiga's two or three most celebrated short-story-length *shi-shōsetsu*. Just as *At Kinosaki* was offered as a paragon of the Shiga style by Tanizaki Junichirō, *Bonfire* was selected by another great contemporary, Akutagawa Ryūnosuke, to serve as a model of what he considered to be the finest qualities of Shiga's art of fiction, which was a 'kind of fiction approaching poetry'.[1] What was quintessential to this art, according to Akutagawa, was its traditional Japanese lyricism, its intensely 'sincere', exalted mood that transformed the rather ordinary, everyday events the story described into pure poetry. Although he saw Shiga as 'a realist who does not depend on fancy or fantasy'[2] (i.e., as an 'autobiographical' writer), he was also convinced that 'what makes Shiga's realism unique is his poetic spirit which is deeply entrenched in Oriental tradition'[3]; this, 'coupled with his technical mastery, endows his most prosaic work with a singular beauty'.[4] Thus it was possible for a 'pure story' (*jun shōsetsu*) such as *Bonfire* to be a 'plotless story' (*hanashi no nai shōsetsu*[5]) because the pervasive lyrical mood, and not a highly structured plot-line, was the unifying principle of the work.

As I shall make clear later, it seems to me that Akutagawa, perhaps a little too eager to make a point, presented here an over-simplified analysis of Shiga's art, since he tried to reduce it to merely one of its major ingredients. Nevertheless, if we compare *Bonfire* with *At Kinosaki* for a moment, we may see why it was a highly appropriate choice to illustrate Shiga's 'lyricism'. The world of nature plays a dominant role in both stories but in *At Kinosaki*, as we have seen, the narrator's response to this world is an ambiguous one. He is at first attracted to the absolute stillness at its core – whether this be called 'death' or '*nirvana*' – but then he recoils back into the shell of his own ego when he sees the violence and suffering that necessarily precedes that stillness. *Bonfire*, written about three years later, is the product of a far different frame of mind; without troubling himself about 'life versus death' as an intellectual problem, the Shiga hero is now able to immerse himself without restraint in the natural world and, as a somewhat paradoxical result, he is also able to commune more comfortably with his fellow humans. In contrast to the rather dark, somber mood of *At Kinosaki*, then, the overall mood of *Bonfire* is one of profound tranquillity and joy. The 'narrative progression' of the story may be seen as a steady deepening of this mood – rather than, as in conventional fiction, the building up of causally-related events towards a 'climax'. At first, the mood is anything but lyrical, as the opening paragraph of the story makes clear:

> It rained that day from morning on. All through the afternoon I played cards in my room upstairs with my wife, the painter S., and K., the innkeeper. The smoke-filled room made everyone feel drowsy. By three o'clock we were sick of card-playing and had over-stuffed ourselves with cakes.[6]

Significantly, then, the narrator and his friends are first presented to us indoors, and they are in a bored and restless mood. In other words, they are confined within the same narrow, claustrophobic world as the narrator of *One Morning*, and the stuffy, smoke-filled room seems to aptly represent this world. But relief is soon at hand:

> One of us stood up and slid open the paper-screen window. At some point the rain had stopped. Chill mountain air charged with the scent of fresh green streamed into the room, driving the tobacco smoke into swirls. We all exchanged glances, as if suddenly coming to life.[7]

In the second paragraph of the story, then, there is already a turn away from the human world and towards nature. The windows are literally thrown open to let in some of nature's fresh air, which clears out the tobacco smoke and makes the people inside feel as if they have been brought back to life.

At this point, it might be appropriate to make a few remarks on Shiga's use of imagery. In the hands of a more cerebral writer than he, the use of imagery such as the above could well seem like a form of simplistic, over-obvious 'symbolism'. But this is another important advantage of the casual, diary-like style of the *shi-shōsetsu*: even if the author does insert some imaginary details to suit his thematic purpose, the reader still has the sense that he is simply describing things 'as they happened', and is not straining to create meaningful but artificial 'symbols'. As Shiga himself said of another story: 'In a relaxed frame of mind I wrote down the day's happenings as they actually occurred.'[8] The important point is that he maintains this 'relaxed' style even in his more 'fictional' and more 'symbolic' works, as we shall see when we come to *A Dark Night's Passing*. Thus the reader would usually fail even to notice that there is any form of symbolism present – although, of course, it might all the while be having its cumulative effect on his mind, subtly and unnoticed. In this as in other areas, we may see the success of Shiga's aesthetic 'program' to abolish all traces of artificiality.

In fact, one hesitates even to apply the term 'symbolism', which usually carries such a weight of metaphysical connotation in the West, to Shiga's simple – indeed, almost primitive – use of imagery. An object in Shiga rarely stands for something other than it is in itself: the stream of fresh mountain air does not really 'symbolize' nature – it is nature; likewise, the stuffy, smoke-filled room does not merely 'represent' the claustrophobic human world – it is that world. In other words, Shiga's 'symbolism' does not usually amount to anything more than the most elementary form of synecdoche, perhaps the oldest and most natural of all symbolic uses of language, since it is embodied in such everyday expressions as 'thirty head of cattle'. In *Bonfire* there is one important exception to this which we shall note later, an exception which stands out conspicuously because it is a more complex kind of symbol. For the most part, though, Shiga's imagery is concrete and 'this-worldly'.

To return to our story, the net effect of the in-rushing stream of 'chill mountain air' is to entice the group of bored, restless humans out into the world of nature, where they know their spirits will be further refreshed. Eventually they all climb to a place some way up the mountain where together they are building a small hut for the narrator and his wife to live in. This working together outdoors gives them a very real sense of satisfaction:

> Twilight on the mountain always puts one in a
> mellow mood, especially after a rainfall. And when,
> as now, we had been working and paused to observe

our day's work while having a smoke, a fleeting kind
of joy arose between us.[9]

Already we see here an important difference between *Bonfire*
and *At Kinosaki*: now there is none of the sense of 'loneliness'
which was the dominant mood of the earlier story. The narrator
no longer confronts nature alone. On the contrary, there is now
a strong sense of 'communal spirit' that is manifested not only
in the group's working together but also, throughout the story,
in their sharing the joys of communing with nature. This sense
of 'joyful sharing' is further intensified in the following
paragraph when the narrator recalls the good time they had
had together on the previous day:

> On the day before it had also cleared up in the
> afternoon and the twilight had been beautiful. It was
> made all the more beautiful by a great rainbow that
> extended all the way from Torii Pass to Black
> Cypress Mountain. We had lingered near the hut
> for a long time. It was placed among a grove of oaks
> and we couldn't resist climbing them. Even my wife
> had wanted to climb up to have a good look at the
> rainbow, so K. and I helped her climb to a height of
> more than six meters.
> 'It's as comfortable as an armchair', K. had shouted
> down to us. He lay face up in a fork of high branches
> that were conveniently wide-spread and, puffing on a
> cigarette, he set the branches swaying like great
> waves.[10]

This happy memory leads the narrator to suggest that they
should all go boating on the lake that night. Thus begins, in this
highly casual manner, the story's main event: the group's
expedition on a mountain lake one quiet evening in spring.

Significantly, on their way to the lake the group passes
through 'the dark precincts of a *Shintō* shrine that was hidden
among tall fir trees.'[11] As we shall see, the group's coming
encounter with the natural world will give them a 'primitive',
animistic sense of the awesome, mysterious power of nature –
the story, in fact, takes on an ever-deepening atmosphere of
'nature-worship' that is strongly reminiscent of Shintō. Thus
the shrine forms a highly appropriate 'gateway' for the group's
entrance into the natural world.

At first, though, the group's high spirits set them apart from the
nature that surrounds them. They act like excited children out for
a night's adventure. When they see a bracken-gatherer's bonfire

burning on the opposite shore of the lake, they row over out of curiosity to take a look. There is a subtle contrast set up between the group's light-hearted chatter and the quiet, solemn mood of the natural world as darkness descends. Vivid images of nature are interposed with snatches of conversation. On the one hand:

> It was a tranquil evening. Some faint after-glow of the sunset still remained in the western sky. But the mountains on all sides were black, and I thought they resembled the backs of crouching water lizards.[12]

And:

> From Bird Island to the mainland the water was especially calm. Looking over the sides of the boat, we could see below us a perfect mirror-image of the star-filled sky.[13]

On the other hand:

> 'It seems a little cold', I said, dipping my hand into the water. 'But when I spent a few days viewing the autumn leaves around Ashino Lake a while ago, I went swimming there early one morning and it wasn't as cold as I thought it would be. I have even gone swimming around there in early April.'
> 'My, you were really something in the old days', said my wife teasingly, knowing full well how I am usually so sensitive to cold.[14]

But gradually this playful, light-hearted mood of the four people diminishes as they are drawn deeper and deeper into the quieter, more solemn mood of nature itself. What seems to make for a 'turning point' in this regard is the lighting of the bonfire which, as indicated by the title, stands as the central image of the story. Now they are no longer merely passive observers of the natural scene; by the 'ritualistic' act of lighting a fire, they themselves become active 'celebrants' of nature's mysterious beauty and power. In fact, before they can even attempt to light the fire, they must begin to relate to their environment in a more intimate way that naturally heightens their awareness of it:

> To collect materials for the bonfire, we all entered the dark forest. There was everywhere a luxuriant growth of ferns, wild plants, yellow-flowered shrubs and so on. We all went our separate ways but, whenever K. or S. puffed on a cigarette, we could see where they were by the small red glow. Where the

old bark of the white birches was already peeling, its rough edges turned out, it was easy to tear off. Every now and then, the sound of K. snapping off a branch broke the deep silence of the forest. When we had gathered as much as we could handle, we carried it back to the beach.[15]

And when finally they light the fire, it is as if the whole world around them is transformed by this act:

The area around us suddenly grew bright. The firelight was reflected across the water and even onto the trees opposite us on Bird Island.[16]

As we shall see, Shiga uses the image of fire to great effect again in *A Dark Night's Passing*, but now connected more explicitly with a Shintō ritual, the 'fire festival' of Kurama.[17] Fire plays an important role in Shintō purification rites – along, of course, with water – which, significantly, is the other dominant image of *Bonfire*.[18] When we remember that the group has first crossed over a body of water (according to Norman Friedman, a 'universally understood' symbol of 'some sort of spiritual transition'[19]) and then lit a bonfire, it becomes evident that Shiga is using these elemental images to suggest the deeper nature of the group's experience. But why do these people stand in need of 'purification' and what manner of 'spiritual transition' do they undergo? If we recall the first scene of the story – the tired, bored, restless group of people who have overstuffed themselves on cakes – I think the answer becomes clear. Lighting the bonfire completes the process of psychic 'purification', of spiritual as well as physical refreshment, that the inrush of fresh mountain air first began; and by crossing over the lake the group has literally removed itself far from the stuffy, smoke-filled room – the human world – and so is now able to become immersed ever deeper into the world of nature. As the four people experience this immersion, their mood or state of mind changes perceptibly.

What gives expression to this change of mood primarily are the stories told as the group sits around the bonfire by K., the innkeeper. K. is the only long-time resident of the mountain in the group and his closeness to this particular spot on earth is emphasized by the stories he tells. Thus he is the appropriate person to lead the others to a greater sense of harmony with the surrounding nature – his voice, in fact, comes to seem, if not the voice of nature itself, at least of the *genius loci*.

K.'s first story 'deepens' the group's mood by reminding them, in a way reminiscent of *At Kinosaki*, that not beauty alone but also terror and death are present in nature:

'Were there any wild dogs about in the old days?' asked S.

'As a boy I often heard them,' answered K. 'Sometimes in the middle of the night I heard them howling in the distance and I remember it gave me a terrible feeling of loneliness.'

He then told us a story about his father, now dead, who had liked to go night-fishing. One night the wild dogs had surrounded him and, to escape them, he had had to make his way home through the water along the shoreline. And the year when they had first put their horses out to graze on the mountain, he had seen one of them that had been attacked and half-devoured by the dogs.[20]

K.'s second story is a kind of ironic prelude to his final and most important one:

The story was that K., as a child, was coming home from Maebashi one night when he saw this thing in a large pine grove about eight kilometers past Kogure. An area about three hundred meters in front of him glowed with a vague light and a black figure over two meters high moved within it. But when he walked further on he came across a man with a large pack on his back resting by the roadside, and he realized that it had been this man, occasionally striking a match to light a cigarette as he walked along, whom he had taken for the giant within the halo of light.[21]

This experience of K.'s with the pseudo-giant leads the group to a discussion of 'mysteries' in general:

'Mysteries usually turn out that way, don't they?' said S.

'But I think there are some real mysteries,' said my wife. 'I don't know about giants and such but I believe, for instance, that things are sometimes revealed to us in dreams.'

'Well, that's something else again now, isn't it?' said S. And then, as if suddenly remembering something: 'Say, K.-san, that story about when you were trapped in the snow last year, that's pretty mysterious, isn't it?' And, turning around to me: 'Have you heard about that yet?'

'No, I haven't.'

'Yes, that was really quite strange,' said K. And he proceeded to tell the story.[22]

Thus the second story of a 'false mystery' leads to K.'s extended account of a genuine mystery he has experienced, and this last story-within-a-story really forms a kind of 'climax' (or high-point, at least) to the whole development of *Bonfire* as we have been tracing it.

The incident had occurred during the previous winter. Returning to the mountain from a trip to Tokyo, K. had arrived at the nearby town of Mizunuma at about three o'clock in the afternoon. Since it was still early and home was so near, he did not feel like waiting until the next day to ascend the mountain.

> Thinking that he would go as far as the foot of the mountain anyway and then decide whether to climb or not, he left Mizunuma.
> Dusk had just settled as he approached the second of the series of Shintō archways at the foot of the mountain. There was ample moonlight and he felt no tiredness in either body or mind. He decided to climb.[23]

One notes again that K. must pass through a *torii* (a Shintō 'archway') before he enters more deeply into the world of nature as the group itself had done earlier in the story before they crossed the lake.

K. soon finds himself, in fact, in danger of being 'immersed' in nature not just spiritually but in a literal, physical sense. The snow grows deeper the higher he climbs, so that even he, who has grown up on the mountain, loses the trail. All he can do is head upwards, higher and higher:

> He continued climbing, urging himself on step by step. He didn't feel especially afraid or uneasy. But he felt a certain vagueness encroaching upon his mind. 'Thinking about it now, I know I was in real danger', said K. 'People who die in the snow usually get that way and then they fall asleep. They end up dying in their sleep.' Strangely enough, even though he had known all this, K. had not felt the slightest uneasiness at the time.[24]

Thus the theme of the attraction of death, of the 'bliss of annihilation', appears at this point in *Bonfire* too, and just as in *At Kinosaki* and *A Dark Night's Passing*, it is associated with Shiga's major theme of the achievement of total union with nature.

But K. manages to resist the 'siren-song' of death and finally reaches the top of the mountain pass. As he begins his descent, he notices two lanterns coming towards him in the distance. He is surprised that anyone should be out at this late hour. He is even more surprised, though, when he meets up with the lantern bearers and finds that it is his brother-in-law with three guests of their inn. Even though no-one could have known that he was coming back at this time, they tell him that his mother had got them up and sent them out to meet him. She had assured them that K. had just called out to her. She had spoke so clearly and firmly that they had not thought to question what she said.

> 'When I asked about it later,' says K., 'it turned out that this was exactly the time when I was most weak and had that slight feeling of vagueness. On the mountain we go to bed early, at seven or eight, so it was just around that time when everyone had fallen into the deepest sleep. Even so, my mother woke up four men and sent them out into the night – so I think she must have heard that call very clearly.'
> 'And did you in fact call out to her?' asked my wife.
> 'No, I certainly didn't. Because no matter how hard I had called from the other side of the pass, no-one would have heard me.'
> 'Of course,' said my wife. Obviously she had been very moved by the story. There were tears in her eyes.[25]

K.'s tale of real-life mystery reduces the group to an awe-struck silence that is in telling contrast to their earlier light-hearted chatter. Whereas up to this point in the evening they have enjoyed communing with nature and with each other on a rather superficial level, K.'s story reminds them of the much deeper level of communion possible between human beings – in this case, the love between mother and son. The narrator gives further emphasis to the point with some comments of his own:

> If one knew about the relationship between K. and his mother, one was even more deeply moved by this story. I didn't know him very well but K.'s dead father, who was nicknamed 'Ibsen' because of his resemblance to the playwright, didn't seem a particularly bad man but, to say the least, he didn't amount to much as a husband. They say that he lived most of the time around Maebashi with his

> young mistress and, come summer, he would bring
> her with him to the mountain, pick up his earnings
> from the inn and then leave. K. was deeply upset by
> his father's behaviour and often clashed with him.
> And this made K. all the more deeply attached to his
> mother and his mother all the more deeply attached
> to him.[26]

But it is important to note that this moving insight into the
depths of a human relationship does not distract the group
from the world of nature which surrounds them. On the
contrary, what they come to feel is that this mother's love,
which is able even to transcend the bounds of time and space, is
as awesome, mysterious and elemental a power of nature as the
fire they have lit on the beach this evening. In other words, at
this deepest level man and nature are one, since both are an
expression of that same elemental, ineffable force that Shiga
has elsewhere called 'rhythm'. Earlier we saw that it was the
sharing of this elemental force that made possible a deep
communion between writer and reader; now, on a much wider
scale, we can see that it is likewise this all-pervasive 'rhythm'
which enables man to achieve union both with his fellow man
and with nature.

Thus, in the closing passages of the story, when the group
turn their eyes back to the world around them, it is with a vastly
deepened sense of oneness. This is brilliantly symbolized by
their final 'communal' (in more senses than one) action:

> K. picked a well-charred branch out of the fire and
> hurled it with all his might far out over the lake. Red
> sparks scattered from the branch as it went flying
> through the air. In simultaneous reflection, a branch
> scattering red sparks went flying through the water.
> The upper and lower branches described the same
> arc, one through air, the other through water, until,
> the instant they came together at the water's surface,
> they sizzled out and the surrounding area fell back
> into darkness. The effect was fascinating. The rest of
> us also began to pick up smoldering branches and
> hurl them out over the lake.[27]

There is a sense of exhilaration, almost of ecstasy, in the self-
abandonment of these four people as they fling fiery branches
out over the lake. There is also a sense of ritual-like participa-
tion in the creation of an awesome and beautiful natural
phenomenon, as there was when they first lit the bonfire – but

now with this sense of joyful abandon. We may also note how Shiga, in this final brilliant scene, brings together the three elemental images he has used so effectively throughout the story: air, water and fire. And now we can see clearly the full symbolic meaning of 'fire', the story's central image. It is both the agent and the symbol of that 'mystical union' which is the main theme of *Bonfire* and indeed, one might say, of Shiga's entire *opus*. Just as the ritual of lighting the bonfire precipitated the group's feeling of oneness with nature, so now it is fire, in the form of burning branches, that brings together the mountain air (which streamed into the smoke-filled room in the story's first scene) and the water (the lake the group has earlier crossed) in a symbol of perfect union and, it is even suggested, of final death or *nirvana*:

> The upper and lower branches described the same arc, one through air, the other through water, until, the instant they came together at the water's surface, they sizzled out and the surrounding area <u>fell back into darkness</u>.[28] (My emphasis.)

As the story closes the group is silent, thoroughly immersed in the peace and beauty of the world around them. In fact, they are as much an integral part of the landscape themselves as the tiny figures in a traditional Far Eastern *sansui* (landscape) ink-painting – an art which Shiga greatly admired and even tried to emulate in his writing.[29] As in *At Kinosaki* we are left with the 'impersonal' atmosphere of the natural world. But whereas in the earlier story the sense was of 'man alone with nature', now it is just simply of 'nature alone with nature':

> We boarded the boat. The bracken-gatherer's bon-fire across the lake had now also died out. Our boat rounded Bird Island and glided quietly towards the woods around the Shintō shrine.
> The calls of the owl grew more and more distant.[30]

The narrative line of *Bonfire* thus may perhaps better be seen as 'oscillating' rather than as straight: that is, it swings like a pendulum back and forth between the human and the natural worlds until finally these two worlds are brought together and the pendulum stops. Or, to use a 'sonic' figure that is perhaps more appropriate, it is as if a bell were struck in the wilderness and we listen to its gently dying reverberations: the narrative movement between the two worlds may be seen to form the 'wave-length' of this sound, the peaks of which gradually

diminish until finally they come together and there is silence –
or, in other words, the end of the story. At any rate, it is the
movement between the two worlds that forms the essential
dynamic of the story, its basic narrative 'rhythm', rather than
the movement from conflict to resolution of conventional
fiction.

In *Bonfire*, then, we have another form of Shiga's 'natural
plot'. Whereas in *At Kinosaki* the incidents arose by virtue of
the associative working of the narrator's death-obsessed consciousness, in the present story they arise from the yearning of a
group of people, confined too long in a stuffy room, to refresh
their spirits by communion with nature. (And perhaps, in the
end, they get more 'communion' than they bargained for.)
Both stories arise naturally from the state of mind of the
narrator (and, in the latter case, of his friends). In this sense
they are ultimately 'subjective'. And, though the dynamic
principle of their narrative structures is somewhat different, in
both case the 'plot' is structured in an unconventional way that
may even make the stories seem 'plotless', as Akutagawa
claimed. It is doubtful, though, whether there can exist any
such *rara avis* as a 'plotless story' – one might as well speak of
'soundless music' or 'invisible painting'. A truly plotless story
would have no discernible narrative structure whatsoever – and
then, of course, it would no longer be a story. Certainly Shiga's
stories, as I hope to have shown, have an integral structure, an
almost rigorous internal logic of their own, and even a definable
movement towards a kind of climax and denouement (albeit
very different in nature to those of conventional fiction), so that
to call them 'plotless' is, in the end, an absurd misrepresenta-
tion. One suspects either that Akutagawa and like-minded
critics had failed to look closely enough at the works themselves
or, what is more likely, were over-influenced by nineteenth-
century Western paradigms of the short story. Plot, after all, as
the Oxford English Dictionary reminds us, has to do with the
way events in a story are connected to each other.[31] Whereas, in
traditional Western fiction this connection is usually causal, in
Shiga it usually takes other forms – but still a connecting
principle is very much there if a critic takes the trouble to look
for it.

Shiga's real problem in regard to narrative structure, it seems
to me, is quite an opposite one. Given the elemental, almost
epic-like nature of the underlying action of his stories, as shown
by his use of certain universal, archetypal symbols – crossing

the lake and lighting the fire in *Bonfire*, the 'journey through dark night' and the final ascent of the mountain in *A Dark Night's Passing* – there is actually a danger that his stories might become too schematic, too formalized in structure for modern taste. It is here that the diary-like informality of the *shi-shōsetsu* genre has come to his rescue, disguising the epic-like or parable-like formality of the Shiga story's thematic conception so successfully that, as we have seen, some near-sighted critics have accused it of 'formlessness'. But I shall pursue this point at greater length when I come to deal with *A Dark Night's Passing*.

In the previous chapter we found some fundamental differences between the Shiga *shi-shōsetsu* as represented by *At Kinosaki* and the traditional Western short story as represented by Tolstoy' *Three Deaths*. If we look among more contemporary Western writers, however, it is possible to find, if not exact parallels, at least much closer analogies to Shiga's 'naturally plotted' stories. I am thinking, in particular, of the early short stories of a writer who made his debut just over a decade after Shiga, Ernest Hemingway.

I have already mentioned the remarkable similarity between Shiga's style and Hemingway's – that is, of course, after we have taken into account the gulf that separates their two respective languages.[32] There is in both writers a desire to eschew all forms of 'artificiality', including the kind of 'big words' and abstract rhetoric that characterize 'intellectual discourse' in any language. Their preference is for a simple, down-to-earth mode of expression. As a result, they both tend to write short declarative sentences free of subordinate clauses and this gives their prose a strong, almost staccato rhythm. They also both use a simple, colloquial diction which includes only a few of the most commonplace of those adjectives which express emotional or intellectual judgements (i.e., words such as 'good' or 'nice'). A wider use of such adjectives, they both seem to feel, would make their writing overly intellectual and abstract. Concomitantly, they fill their writing with simple, concrete nouns that name actual physical objects. This 'anti-intellectualism' is also expressed by the preference of both writers for the 'non-logical' use of language – most notably, the way in which both will repeat a key word or phrase constantly rather than resort to explicit argument to make their point.[33] Above all, the styles of both writers are characterized by such a disciplined economy – packing the greatest possible meaning into the fewest possible words – and by such a vivid immediacy – capturing the exact feeling of the experience – that critics of both have often claimed that their prose approaches the quality of poetry. At the same time, however, these critics insist on its extreme 'naturalness', and they often use images taken from the natural world to illustrate this point. I have already quoted the beautiful series of metaphors that Kobayashi Hideo used to describe the 'immediacy' of Shiga's style, saying that it was like 'the wings of the ptarmigan turning white with the advent of winter' and so on.[34] The following passage that Ford Madox Ford wrote on Hemingway's style is much in the same vein:

> Hemingway's words strike you, each one, as if they were pebbles fetched fresh from a brook. They live and shine, each in its place. So one of his pages has the effect of a brook-bottom into which you look down through the flowing water.[35]

But since 'le style est l'homme même',[36] it is hardly surprising that, on closer observation, there are some deeper affinities between these two writers whose styles have so much in common. Their ultimate affinity, it seems to me, is that both belong to that seemingly paradoxical category of man, the modern 'primitivist'. As M.H. Abrams has pointed out, there is a strong tradition of 'cultural primitivism' in the West which may be traced back to Rousseau and the Romantics – in other words, to about the time the Industrial Revolution was beginning to make its impact felt:

> Cultural primitivism is the preference of 'nature' over 'art' in any field of human culture and values. For example, in ethics a primitivist lauds the 'natural', or innate, instincts and passions over the dictates of reason and prudential forethought; in social philosophy, the ideal is the simple and 'natural' forms of social and political order in place of the anxieties and frustrations engendered by a complex and highly developed social organization; in milieu, a primitivist prefers outdoor 'nature', unmodified by human intervention, to cities or artful gardens; and in literature and the other arts, he puts his reliance on spontaneity, the free expression of emotion, and the intuitive products of 'natural genius', as against the reasoned adaptation of artistic means to foreseen ends and the reliance on 'artificial' forms, rules, and conventions.[37]

To this obviously apposite summation, I might add something that also seems quite germane to our present discussion: namely, that the literary 'primitivist', because of the great value he places on 'spontaneity, the free expression of emotion, and the intuitive products of "natural genius"' – in other words, on immediacy – has usually tended to take himself as his first and foremost subject, because, as Hemingway once asked: 'Does a writer know anyone better?'[38] Rousseau himself, of course, began this tradition with his great *Confessions*, and the figure of the self-absorbed, Byronic 'egotist' became a familiar one in Romantic literature.

The career of Ernest Hemingway is an interesting case in point. Generally speaking, it seems that the further he drew away from his own immediate experience, the more his writing lost its original power. Critics are generally agreed that his early stories and his first two novels are his most successful works and these are also his most closely autobiographical.[39] The change is reflected in the noticeable deterioration of the famous 'Hemingway style' in his later works. As Scott Donaldson points out, his style changed 'from an early economy of language and objectivity of presentation to a much longer, more discursive, and, for almost all observers, less successful later style. It was the first style that became famous and imitated.'[40]

It is also pertinent to our discussion of Shiga's *shi-shōsetsu* to note that such later, non-autobiographical Hemingway novels as *For Whom the Bell Tolls* (1940) are more conventionally structured than his earlier works. The closely autobiographical 'Nick Adams stories', on the other hand, may well be regarded as being 'naturally plotted' in a way similar to Shiga's *shi-shōsetsu*. To early readers, in fact, they appeared not as 'well-made' stories but as formless 'slices of life'. Reminiscing about the difficulties of his early career, when publishers refused to accept his radically new versions of the short-story form, Hemingway once wrote of 'all of the stories back in the mail . . . with notes of rejection that would never call them stories, but always anecdotes, sketches, contes, etc.'[41] As we have already seen, Shiga still has the same problem with certain Western critics – perhaps because they have not yet caught up with the remarkable developments in the Western short story between Tolstoy and Hemingway.

Although, of course, there can be no question of any direct influence either way between Shiga and Hemingway (since the latter read no Japanese and the former had written the bulk of his work before Hemingway was published), there is, nevertheless, an interesting and important 'Japanese connection' in Hemingway's case which may account, to some extent, for the affinities between them. During the years of his 'apprenticeship' in the early 1920s in Paris, Hemingway came under the direct influence of the so-called 'Imagists', and especially of the mentor of them all, Ezra Pound. Pound, in fact, exercised his 'blue pencil' on Hemingway's early stories in the same way as he did on the early poetry of T.S. Eliot. The Japanese influence on Pound and the other Imagists has been well documented, and this influence, in turn, may be seen to have reached Hemingway mainly through Pound.[42] What it amounts to in Hemingway's case, above all, is a very precise and concrete use of imagery to create an emotion or a psychological atmosphere. It is the technique made famous under Eliot's term of the 'objective correlative', although, as Jackson Benson has pointed out, James Joyce's 'epiphany' expresses a very similar concept.[43] In fact, this central doctrine of Imagism may be seen to lie at the core of the aesthetic theory of the whole 'Pound-Lewis-Ford-Joyce-Stein-Eliot "group"', so that, if we add, as we must, the name of W.B. Yeats to this list, it is hardly an exaggeration to say that the Japanese influence on early twentieth-century literature in English was a crucial one.[44]

Characteristically, Hemingway himself expressed his imagist credo in rather more concrete terms than 'epiphany' or 'objective correlative'. What he tried to capture in his work, he once wrote was 'the real thing, the sequence of motion and fact which made the emotion.'[45] Hemingway's concept here of the 'real thing' seems remarkably close to Shiga's 'real feeling' (*jikkan*) which, as already noted, was central to his aesthetic program. Both writers, then, might be called 'lyrical realists', and it is this combination of the precise image with the true emotion in their work that links it to the Japanese poetic tradition. As Jackson Benson points out in regard to some of Hemingway's 'haiku-like' sentences:

> ... there is a sense of timelessness: the vision of an instant and all its internal stresses, isolated and captured, yet speaking for itself. The matter-of-factness is journalistic, but it is also poetic. These sentences are very much like Pound's *In a Station of the Metro* which he called a 'hokku-like sentence'.[46]

What Benson says here of Hemingway's style is very similar to what Akutagawa says of Shiga's style in the passage I have already quoted.[47] Needless to say, one need not look for a Pound in Shiga's background – he comes by this tradition quite 'naturally'.

In Hemingway's case, as in Shiga's, the emphasis on emotional veracity leads the writer perforce to a heavy reliance on the data of his own life – for, as Hemingway pointed out, he knows his own feelings best. Carlos Baker has described the way in which the young Hemingway arrived at this 'autobiographical' preference:

> 'All you have to do is write one true sentence', he told himself. 'Write the truest sentence that you know.' It must be above all a 'true simple declarative sentence' without scrollwork or ornamental language of any sort. It must deal with something he knew from personal experience. Stories like *The Passing of Pickles McCarty* or *Wolves and Doughnuts* had been largely invented. They grazed his own experience in Italy and Illinois without keeping the central facts in focus. Now he wanted to place his faith in the direct transcription of what he saw. That and no more. Somehow the emotion that he wanted to convey would filter through the reported facts.[48]

It was inevitable that, with his primary emphasis on personal emotion, Hemingway, like Shiga, would write a new kind of fiction. Being so self-centred, he would obviously not write the traditional English 'social novel', nor, with his distrust of abstract ideas, would he write the more French-style 'thesis-novel'. Especially in his earlier (and best) works, Hemingway, like Shiga, was a practitioner of that fictional form that has risen to prominence only in this century, which Ralph Freedman has called the 'lyrical novel'[49] As a result, the 'Hemingway hero', like the 'Shiga hero' is a fairly consistent character who appears as the protagonist of all Hemingway's major works, from the 'Nick Adams' of his first stories to the 'Thomas Hudson' of his final, posthumous novel, *Islands in the Stream* (1970), and this character is an identifiable *persona* of the author himself.

It is interesting also to note that, because of his primary reliance on the 'facts' of his own experience, Hemingway, like Shiga, did not make the rigid distinctions between 'fiction' and 'non-fiction' that have been customary in the West. As

Sheridan Baker points out, Hemingway 'consistently shows a kind of wilfulness in reporting fact with journalistic accuracy and then insisting that it is all fiction, that "there are no real people in this volume".'[50] Indeed, some of the works included in his short story collections were first written and published as newspaper reports, just as a Shiga story such as *One Morning* was first written as a diary entry. *Green Hills of Africa* (1935) is a very literal account of one of Hemingway's African safaris, but it is presented in the form of a novel, complete with extensive dialogue. As Hemingway says in the foreword: 'The writer has attempted to write an absolutely true book to see whether the shape of a country and the pattern of a month's action can, if truly presented, compete with the imagination.'[51] Similarly, his Paris memoir, *A Movable Feast* (1964), is presented in a novelistic form and Hemingway writes in the preface: 'If the reader prefers, this book may be regarded as fiction.'[52] In his *Memoir as Fiction*, Fraser Sutherland defends this practice of Hemingway's by arguing that 'since the writer's mind is always at work, everything he writes is fiction. And whether the writer pretends to write "pure" fiction or pure non-fiction, he produces a new image.'[53]

Jackson Benson, however, tells us that there is really nothing new about this mixing of 'journalistic' fact with fiction – the very word 'novel', after all, is related to 'news'. Hemingway's use of journalistic style and content:

> ... was really a new application of an old approach that goes back to the 'true accounts' of Defoe and the early novelists. Fiction, the history of fiction tells us, must never be fiction, never 'made up', but always presented as something that really happened – either history, a discovered 'document', or biography, a discovered 'diary'. But the modern temper demands more immediacy, more authenticity, more impersonality.[54]

Another way of putting this, as we have seen in Shiga's case, is that the story must seem 'natural' (i.e., taken directly from nature) as opposed to 'artificial'. In this sense Hemingway, like Shiga, wanted to write an 'anti-literary literature'.[55] As Robert Weeks has testified, Hemingway's 'consummate art' is an 'art so unobtrusive as to elicit the charge of not being art at all' – in other words, the best art of all to Hemingway, as to Shiga, is one that appears to be 'artless'.[56]

At this point a sceptical reader might well ask: exactly

wherein, then, does the seemingly invisible art of such writers lie? The answer, of course, is: first and foremost, in the very process of selection. This was summed up by Ezra Pound in his famous bilingual motto, obtained by chance from a German-Italian dictionary: 'Dichten=condensare'.[57] According to Jackson Benson, it was Hemingway's 'reportorial skills' that enabled him to put this motto into practice and, by doing so:

> ... writing prose in the manner of modern poetry.
> His effort involved looking carefully, getting at the
> essential facts of the situation he observed, putting
> these facts down in a straight-forward, economical
> fashion and then letting this 'condensed essence'
> speak the emotion for itself.[58]

But the famous 'economy' of Hemingway's style, as of Shiga's, is not merely a matter of packing the greatest possible meaning into the fewest possible words; the writer is also 'economical' in his selection of his material, so that what is left out is often as important as what is included.[59] 'I always try to write', Hemingway once remarked, 'on the principle of the iceberg. There is seven eighths of it under water for every part that shows. Anything you know you can eliminate and it only strengthens your iceberg.'[60]

This 'iceberg principle' is brilliantly illustrated by the major story of Hemingway's first collection, *In Our Time* (1925). The story, *Big Two-Hearted River*, is, as it happens, admirably suited for comparison and contrast with *Bonfire*. As in Shiga's story, very little seems to happen on the surface: we are shown Nick Adams, the protagonist of a whole series of early Hemingway stories, returning alone to fish a river in northern Michigan where he often fished when younger. He hikes a few miles, sets up camp, cooks himself a meal, beds down for the night, gets up the next morning and catches a few trout – this is the extent of the story's action and it is all described with almost microscopic realism. Nevertheless, there are hints throughout the story that this is no ordinary 'fishing trip' – that it is, in fact, a rather desperate attempt on the part of the protagonist to administer therapy to his own deeply wounded psyche. And the source of this wound? 'The story,' Hemingway himself said years after he wrote it, 'was about coming back from the war but there was no mention of the war in it.'[61] Once we have realized this fact, the story's imagery and action become comprehensible on a much deeper level.

The 'burned over' country which is the opening image of the story, for instance (and which is so reminiscent of T.S. Eliot's *Waste Land*, written just a couple of years before) now seems to symbolize both the physical ruin of the war Nick has just returned from, and the psychic scars it has caused in him. Hemingway's 'burned-over' country, in fact, performs much the same function in the structure of this story as Shiga's 'stuffy, smoke-filled room' does in *Bonfire*: it serves as a very concrete imagistic embodiment of all that the protagonist is about to escape from – which, in both cases, may be described as the 'ills of civilization'. Shiga's group take a boat out over the lake, Hemingway's protagonist hikes up to the 'good country' not yet devastated by man; the principal action of both stories, in other words – as we would only expect from two 'primitivist' writers – is an escape from civilization into the world of nature.

But the similarity between these two stories does not end there. Just as the Shiga group engaged in certain 'primitive' rituals to bring themselves into deeper harmony with nature – lighting the bonfire, throwing the fiery branches out over the lake – to an even greater extent the Hemingway protagonist is shown engaged continuously in ritualistic actions: making camp, cooking meals, preparing his fishing equipment, fishing itself – indeed, these activities occupy almost the entire story, and they are described in such minute, almost monotonous detail that the reader can have no doubt about their 'ritualistic' nature.

In the Hemingway story, these rituals seem to have a double purpose: as in the Shiga story, they help to bring the protagonist into closer touch with nature, but they also have a more urgent function – they help him to exercise control over his own disordered, traumatized mind. The war-scarred Nick, as Elizabeth Wells point out, 'does not want to think. He wants to act. He is, in fact, consciously putting himself through a ritual that will keep him from thinking.'[62]

Nevertheless, there is a strain of Shigaesque 'nature mysticism' in Hemingway too, and Nick's rituals do bring him at least a momentary 'unitive' experience with nature. This comes through the story's central ritual (and, as Jackson Benson points out, the central ritual of all the Nick Adams stories[63]): fishing. When he catches his first trout, Nick achieves a momentary oneness with the fish which releases him briefly from the oppressive confines of his own troubled self. As Philip Young points out, this momentary release is reflected even in the language of the story:

> When there is the extreme excitement of a big strike
> from a trout the style changes abruptly. The pressure
> is off the man, he is nowhere but right there playing
> the fish, and then the sentences lengthen greatly and
> become appropriately graceful.[64]

Hemingway describes an identical kind of experience more explicitly in an earlier story of *In Our Time* called *Cross-Country Snow*, but this time Nick is skiing: 'The rush and the sudden swoop as he dropped down a steep undulation in the mountainside plucked Nick's mind out and left him only the wonderful flying, dropping sensation in his body.' [65] As Sheridan Baker says: 'The peace for which Nick is searching, in our time, is not unlike – in a tough, earthbound sort of way – that which passes all understanding.'[66]

In some ways, *Big Two-Hearted River* may seem to remind us more of *At Kinosaki* than of *Bonfire*. In the earlier Shiga story, as we may recall, the protagonist also retired alone to nature to try to recover from the recent trauma of a near-fatal accident. Like Nick too he had trouble exercising control over his traumatized mind. In the final scene of the story he is fairly overwhelmed by thoughts of death: 'My mind alone worked on as it pleased. And this led me all the more into those kinds of thoughts and feelings.'[67]

While the mood of *Big Two-Hearted River* is not as light or as tranquil as that of *Bonfire*, however, neither is it as dark or as tortured as that of *At Kinosaki*. Through the studied practice of his 'rituals', Nick does manage to keep his thoughts in check: 'His mind was starting to work. He knew he could choke it because he was tired enough.[68] And, as we have seen, he does achieve a few moments of self-oblivion and union with nature. Now he knows, at least, the direction his recovery must take. There is hope here for the future. The story, in fact, ends on this emphatically optimistic note: 'There were plenty of days coming when he could fish the swamp.'[69]

On the other hand, the mood of *Bonfire* is not as unreservedly 'light-hearted' as might first appear. Here too there are shadows in the background and, again, they are not made very explicit because Shiga, like Hemingway, believes in the power of 'the thing left out'. (And, unfortunately, this minimalist aesthetic does not seem to be fully understood or appreciated by those critics who point to all the undisclosed facts about his life as evidence of his 'insincerity'.) On closer view of the story, in fact, we find that, just as Nick's war experience is an 'unspoken presence' in *Big Two-Hearted River*, so too the Shiga narrator's near-fatal accident still looms in the background of *Bonfire*. Francis Mathy perceptively notices this when, in speaking of Shiga's life on Mount Akagi, the site of *Bonfire*, he remarks:

> The quiet melancholy that Shiga had begun to experience after his brush with death was further deepened here on this mountain. It is this feeling of quiet melancholy that informs the story *Bonfire* . . . .[70]

In the same way as Hemingway refers symbolically to the war with his image of the 'burnt-over' country at the opening of his story, early in *Bonfire* Shiga makes use of a striking image that immediately puts us in mind of *At Kinosaki* and the near-fatal accident: 'But the mountains on all sides were black, and I thought they resembled the backs of <u>crouching water lizards</u>.'[71] (My emphasis.) When we recall the final episode of *At Kinosaki* in which the narrator kills a water lizard, as well as the deep symbolic significance which he tells us these creatures have for him, then it is difficult to believe that this is just a casually dropped simile – and, of course, it is also made conspicuous by the fact that Shiga rarely uses such similes.

As the story progresses, too, this darker note emerges more explicitly when K. tells his story of the wild dogs who had once killed a horse on the mountain and who had even, one night, threatened to kill his father; and the narrator himself then tells of the skull of 'a small wild animal' he had found in 'Hell Valley' just a few days before. Death being perhaps <u>the</u> major theme of Shiga's work, as it is of Hemingway's, it is hardly surprising that it is not entirely absent even from *Bonfire*, one of Shiga's most 'light-hearted' stories.[72] Nevertheless, amidst the beauty of the mountain and the lake on a tranquil evening in spring, death seems but a distant shadow – albeit a necessary 'foil' to set off the joyful sense of life that occupies the foreground. Thoughts of death no longer overwhelm the Shiga narrator, as in *At Kinosaki*, disturbing the quietness of mind necessary for him to achieve harmony both with nature and with his fellow man. As the final scene of *Bonfire* shows, he is, in fact, well on the way to the 'enlightenment' that is, as we shall see, the culminating experience of *A Dark Night's Passing* and, indeed, of Shiga's entire *opus*.

CHAPTER FOUR

AN ARTLESS ART, A SELFLESS SELF

With writers more prolific than Shiga Naoya, there may be some dispute as to which of their works should be regarded as the most important or the most representative. In Shiga's case, however, there is only one work which can be singled out unreservedly as his *magnum opus*: *A Dark Night's Passing* (*An'ya Kōro*, 1937). It is his only really substantial, novel-length work (about four hundred pages in its English translation, for instance) – all his other fictional writings are either of short story or novella length. Furthermore, *A Dark Night's Passing* contains the clearest, most forceful expression of Shiga's major themes and the finest passages of his celebrated prose style. Indeed, he seemed to have put all that he had into this one novel-length *shi-shōsetsu*, as evidenced, firstly, by the fact that it took him about twenty-five years of intermittent effort to write it (from 1912 to 1937) and, secondly, by the fact that, after it was finally done with, he wrote very little else, though he lived on for another thirty-four years. Regarding this work Agawa Hiroyuki has written: 'Here is to be found everything Shiga possesses, everything that he aspired to in his life and work.'[1] And, as Francis Mathy points out: 'Some Japanese critics go so far as to call it the highest peak of modern Japanese literature.'[2]

Nevertheless, *A Dark Night's Passing* is not so 'pure' an example of the quintessential Shiga Naoya *shi-shōsetsu* as the shorter pieces we have examined up to this point. It is that seemingly adulterated form, the 'fictional autobiography', in two distinct senses. On the one hand, if we regard it as the author's autobiography, we discover that, though the protagonist, Tokitō Kensaku, is obviously a *persona* of Shiga himself, many of the events the work describes are fictitious. As Shiga once wrote: 'Kensaku's actions and feelings represent what I myself would do if placed in similar circumstances, or what I would want to do, or what I have actually done.'[3] On the other hand, the work is also a 'fictional autobiography' in the sense that it is presented as the actual autobiography of the fictional character, Tokitō Kensaku. On this level, *A Dark Night's Passing*, as we shall see, may be regarded as a *shi-shōsetsu* about a man trying to write *A Dark Night's Passing* – in other words, it is as 'self-reflective' as some other major 'autobiographical' novels which were being written at about the same time in the West, by writers such as Proust, Joyce, Lawrence and Thomas Wolfe. In my discussion of the work, I shall be more interested in it as an autobiography in this second sense – that is, as the autobiography of the fictional character, Tokitō Kensaku, rather than of the actual author, Shiga Naoya. Previous critics of the work have failed to emphasize this distinction, though it seems to me crucial to a full understanding of its aesthetic achievement and thematic significance.

With their largely 'biographical' approach, Japanese critics seem to content themselves with ferreting out those correspondences which do exist between the author's life and this particular work. One rather hostile critic, Nakamura Mitsuo, even goes so far as to say that readers contemporary with Shiga accepted *A Dark Night's Passing* as a great novel, even though the main character is 'never more than a kind of abstract existence', only because they 'saw behind the abstract hero the figure of the writer himself. It was because the readers accepted the novel unconditionally as an autobiographical novel presenting the idealized self of the author.'[4] A Western critic such as Francis Mathy, on the other hand, seems to regard it as a kind of 'admission of defeat' on Shiga's part that he would write a fictional autobiography rather than a pure *shi-shōsetsu*. The way Mathy sees it, Shiga did not have enough material in his own life to fill a novel-length *shi-shōsetsu*, and so had to resort to some of the very 'fabrications' he had always frowned upon.[5] He also wished to avoid the pain of introspection:

> To salvage the parts he had already written and go on to complete the novel, he had recourse to fiction: he designed the structure of the two 'sins', the 'sin' of the hero's mother and that of his wife, and into this structure were fitted the individual parts. Since it was never more than a convenient technical device, it is no wonder that it has so little organic function in the novel. Shiga's inability to continue the work without recourse to fictional elements is eloquent testimony of the degree to which the desire to 'mine what is in me' had begun to yield to the desire for harmony and peace.[6]

In making these various points, however, Mathy, like the Japanese critics, is still regarding *A Dark Night's Passing* as a fictional autobiography only in the first and, it seems to me, lesser sense – as the autobiography of Shiga the man. I hope to show that, once we regard the work in its proper light – as a fictional autobiography in both senses – we discover that the complex mixture of fiction and reality it contains, far from being 'inorganic', is an integral part of the work's form and theme from the very beginning. With this work, in fact, Shiga consciously confronts the nature of the *shi-shōsetsu* and the problems, both personal and aesthetic, that the writing of it involves. Furthermore, the tension between the 'real' and the 'fictional' is a part of that larger tension which Shiga, as a 'primitivist', inevitably felt, and which forms the basic dynamic of *A Dark Night's Passing*: the tension between man/art/ civilization on the one hand and nature on the other. This is the tension that is ultimately resolved in the union of man and nature in the climactic scene on Mount Daisen, and I intend to show that, once we regard *A Dark Night's Passing* as the autobiography of Tokitō Kensaku, we find that it is because of this ultimate resolution that Kensaku is able to go on to write this very work. Not to regard the work as Kensaku's autobiography is, then, to miss a good part of its meaning.

A Dark Night's Passing opens with a short prologue entitled, *The Hero's Reminiscences*, in which Kensaku recalls five major episodes from his childhood. All five deal with his difficult, involved relations with his family. In the first it is his 'grandfather': the boy Kensaku's impressions of the old man are unfavorable from the beginning – he is 'seedy' and disreputable-looking – so that when Kensaku is sent to live with him he is baffled and resentful that of all his family he has been singled out for this special treatment, although 'since my infancy I had come to expect injustice.'[7]

The second episode concerns Kensaku's relations with his mother. Once, when he was four or five years old, his mother found him perched dangerously high on a roof. She held him there by the riveting force of her eyes until he could be rescued by two menservants. Kensaku still cherishes this memory as a proof that he was loved by at least one member of his family:

> For years after, my eyes would fill with tears whenever I remembered it. And I have thought to myself: whatever else, my mother at least loved me very much.[8]

The third episode also concerns Kensaku's relations with his mother. When she refuses to give him some cake that his father has bought, he persistently and aggressively continues to demand some. As the narrator remarks in retrospect, he did not really want the cake, he only wanted 'to cry my heart out, or to be shouted at, or to be beaten – it didn't matter which, so long as something was done to soothe my nerves, to get rid of the terrible feeling of oppression.'[9] Thus he paints a picture of himself as a rather gloomy, high-strung boy who feels sorely neglected – characteristics which, as we presently discover, stay with him into adulthood.

The fourth episode concerns the young Kensaku's life at his grandfather's house where 'everything was slovenly'.[10] The house was a gathering-place for all sorts of disreputable characters, who dropped in at night to play cards. Kensaku's only consolation was his grandfather's young mistress, Oei, who acted as a kind of substitute mother for him (since his own mother was dead by then). When she had had a few drinks and was in a good mood, 'she would pick me up and put me on her knees and hold me tight in her strong, thick arms. I would feel such ecstasy then, I hardly cared that I could not breathe.'[11]

In the fifth and final episode Kensaku is shown relating with his father. On this particular day his father is in a good mood, so he invites the boy to wrestle with him. What starts as a harmless play-fight between the two suddenly becomes a fight in earnest when they both allow their true feelings towards each other to surface. Kensaku is roughly pushed away by his father and, when he still persists, he is finally bound hand and foot. As he lies helpless on the floor, he is filled with rage and hatred towards his father.

The first question that must arise, it seems to me, in any critical analysis of *A Dark Night's Passing*, is: why does Shiga use this unusual device of opening a long third-person narrative with a short prologue written by the hero in the first person? Of course, we might begin to answer by saying that it forms a splendid introduction to the work's themes and motifs, since in Kensaku's case particularly 'the child is father of the man'. There is even an element of suspenseful mystery in the way the prologue poses questions for which the work proper provides the answer. Why is Kensaku's grandfather presented as such an unsavory character? Why is Kensaku himself continually singled out for 'unjust' treatment by his family, including being shipped off to live with his grandfather? And why is there a certain tension in his relations with his mother and outright animosity in his relations with his father? To all of these questions the answer comes in *Part Two*, when we discover, along with Kensaku, that his mother was seduced by his supposed 'grandfather' when his 'father' was away from home and that he himself is the product of this 'sinful' union. Thus Kensaku's 'dark night' begins at the very moment of his birth and, as the prologue shows, continues through his childhood.

One may see, then, how skillfully Shiga introduces his major theme – Kensaku's struggle to overcome his 'dark fate' – in the few pages of the prologue, without, at the same time, giving too much away. (We are reminded here again of Hemingway's 'principle of the iceberg' and the strategic 'thing left out'.) Nevertheless, it seems to me that the prologue serves another function that is at least as important: it establishes Kensaku as a writer of *shi-shōsetsu* and so, at least potentially, as the author of *A Dark Night's Passing* itself. The prologue, after all, might have been written, like the rest of the work, in the third person and in this form might have presented its 'introductory' material just as well. By casting it as a *shi-shōsetsu* written by Kensaku, Shiga actually accomplishes three things: he introduces, as I have said, Kensaku as the author of *shi-shōsetsu*; he introduces the concept of a fictional character being the author of a work that we know, of course, was actually written by Shiga himself (thus preparing us to accept the idea that the work as a whole is also meant to have been written by this character); and, finally, he introduces the *shi-shōsetsu* genre itself, and the complex problem of 'fiction versus reality' that it involves, since the prologue is a 'pure' example of the *shi-shōsetsu* only as authored by Kensaku. (If we regard Shiga as the author then it contains several fictitious elements, most notably the character of the grandfather, who is purposely made to be diametrically opposite to Shiga's own greatly revered paternal grandfather – a *samurai* of the old school.)

The question then arises: why did not Shiga go on to write the rest of the work in the first person, presenting it outright, like the prologue, as the *shi-shōsetsu* of Tokitō Kensaku? Generally, one might answer that to have done so would have been to have upset the delicate balance of fiction and reality which forms the work's underlying aesthetic tension. But since the work operates in two different senses as a 'fictional autobiography', the question must be answered on two different levels. Firstly, although there is a 'spiritual' identity between the author and his protagonist, there are also large elements of fiction in the work, so that it was necessary for Shiga to establish some distance between himself and Kensaku. In a lengthy *shi-shōsetsu* such as *Reconciliation* (*Wakai*, 1917), for instance, Shiga does write in the first person while calling himself by a fictitious name, but this work is a more or less direct transcription of events from his own life. By writing *A Dark Night's Passing* in the third person, he serves notice that it is not as straightforwardly autobiographical as his earlier works. Furthermore, in this work, as I intend to show, he wished to write not merely a *shi-shōsetsu* ('fictional' or otherwise) but an extended if informal commentary on the *shi-shōsetsu* genre, and for this purpose also he needed some distance from the form itself.

Secondly, the fact that most of *A Dark Night's Passing* is written in the third person does not prevent us from regarding it as Kensaku's *shi-shōsetsu*. On the contrary, it seems to point more in this direction. Although, as we have seen, Shiga usually wrote his own 'pure' *shi-shōsetsu* in the first person, this practice was by no means universal among other writers of the genre – including the 'founder', Tayama Katai – despite its general designation as literally an 'I-novel'.[12] After all, it is easy enough for a writer to change 'I' to 'he' if he wants to maintain some semblance of fictionality. (And also, as Edward Fowler has so persuasively argued, there is much less distance between 'I' and 'he' in Japanese than in English anyway – a word such as *jibun*, much favoured by Shiga, may refer to either.[13]) But the important point, in the case of *A Dark Night's Passing*, is that the whole work, with one brief but important exception that I shall discuss later, is told from Kensaku's point of view. Just as, in the prologue, we do not know the root cause of the boy Kensaku's 'dark fate' because he himself does not know it, so, throughout the rest of the work, we perceive the world almost entirely through his eyes.

But there is, it seems to me, a deeper reason, related to the work's central theme, why Kensaku should be made to write his spiritual autobiography in the third person, a reason which I shall briefly outline here but return to in more detail later. Throughout the work we are presented again and again with Kensaku as a frustrated writer unable to bring any of his *shi-shōsetsu* to a successful conclusion. By the work's end we know why: he has been insufficiently detached from the complications of his life and, above all, from his own tyrannically egotistical self; without this detachment, quite naturally, it has been impossible for him to write, as an author of *shi-shōsetsu* must do, about either his life or himself. Only when he has achieved the supreme detachment that comes with his final union with nature on Mount Daisen is he free to write – and, I would argue, what he goes on to write is this very work called *A Dark Night's Passing*. That he has written it in the third person, then, signifies his new-found detachment from his formerly oppressive self.

Shiga continues the *shi-shōsetsu* motif in the first chapter of the work proper, but now in a lighter, even satirical vein. The chapter opens with a scene reminiscent of *One Morning*: the protagonist, unable to sleep, reads in bed until the early hours of the morning. What Kensaku is reading here, though, is also significant: it is a *shi-shōsetsu* written by an acquaintance, Sakaguchi. And it does not please Kensaku; in fact, it leaves 'a nasty taste in his mouth' and confirms the 'mounting dislike for Sakaguchi' that he has felt for some time.[14] He throws the story aside and, interestingly enough, seeks refuge in a 'harmless little book', a 'historical romance' called *Tsukahara Bokuden* (the adventures of a master swordsman of the Muromachi period).[15] Thus the fiction/reality dialectic is introduced in a rather humorous fashion from the very beginning.

But there is more. When Kensaku awakes the following afternoon, he finds that Sakaguchi himself has come to call on him, together with another acquaintance, Tatsuoka. Kensaku at first refuses to see Sakaguchi, but quickly relents. We are then told:

> The story by Sakaguchi that Kensaku had found so unpleasant was about a man who has an affair with his fifteen-year-old housemaid; the housemaid becomes pregnant and is sent to an abortionist. Kensaku thought it most likely that it was based on the author's own experience. The facts described were in themselves unpleasant enough; but what he really disliked was the obvious flippancy of the author. He could have forgiven the facts if he had been allowed to feel some sympathy for the protagonist; but the flippancy, the superciliousness of the protagonist (and of Sakaguchi) left no room for such sympathy.
> He was angered, too, by the way the protagonist's friend, who he was certain had been modeled on himself, was described.[16]

Because Sakaguchi portrays him in the story as 'an unknowing observer, harboring what amounted to a secret longing for the girl', the irate Kensaku is surprised that Sakaguchi would have the nerve to come call on him.[17]

> Had he expected to get an angry letter from Kensaku, and when it didn't come, become uneasy and begun to feel threatened by the uncanny silence? Or had he come to play the stage villain, gloating over his own nastiness? He had better be careful, Kensaku thought, or I'll give him a piece of my mind. Thus his fancies about Sakaguchi became less and less restrained; and by the time he had finished washing his face, he was in a state of considerable agitation.[18]

When Kensaku joins his guests, however, he finds that Tatsuoka is equally convinced that he is the model for Sakaguchi's unintelligent character. "'He says most of the story is imagined'", he tells Kensaku, "'but I doubt it. He's just the sort of fellow who'll write about his friends behind their backs.'"[19] Sakaguchi himself maintains a haughty silence in the face of these accusations:

> One thing at least was clear – he was enjoying himself. Why else would he have that smirk on his face? In his characteristic fashion, he was flaunting his superiority.[20]

When he finally tries to silence Tatsuoka, though, the two men come close to blows. But Sakaguchi must beat a hasty retreat, because he is 'no match for Tatsuoka physically, who was not only twice as large but a third-grade black belt in judo.'[21] Kensaku finds himself thrust into the unexpected role of mediator between the two. But he is still not convinced that the friend in the story is Tatsuoka. To protest about it, though, would be to admit that he sees some similarity between this unadmirable character and himself, so that Sakaguchi, who is such a 'slippery customer', might easily ask: "'Do you really have such a low opinion of your own character that you should see yourself in him?'"[22] Kensaku even suspects that Tatsuoka is only pretending to think that he is the model for the character, hoping that, by doing so, he will prevent Kensaku, the real model, from breaking off his friendship with Sakaguchi.

At any rate, one thing these rather convoluted agonies of suspicion seem to illustrate, with more than a touch of humour, is the occupational hazards of a writer of *shi-shōsetsu*, the perils of mixing fiction with reality. Although the scene approaches farce when the engineer and the writer almost come to blows, there is, nevertheless, an undercurrent of serious comment here. To begin with, Sakaguchi's story, as an account of the author's affair with his young maid, is highly reminiscent of Tayama Katai's *The Quilt* (*Futon*, 1908), generally regarded as the 'naturalist' progenitor of the *shi-shōsetsu*, and the work which, more than any other, led to the popularization of the genre in early twentieth-century Japan. Shiga, then, seems to be serving notice here that his *shi-shōsetsu* is to be in some important way different to those of Tayama and his fellow 'naturalists'.

How he perceives this difference becomes clear if we look again at Kensaku's criticism of Sakaguchi's story. It is not the 'unpleasant' facts that disturb him (and the 'naturalists' were well known for wallowing in the mud), it is the unsympathetic attitude of the author and of the protagonist, his *alter ego*. 'He could have forgiven the facts if he had been allowed to feel some sympathy for the protagonist; but the flippancy, the superciliousness of the protagonist (and of Sakaguchi) left no room for such sympathy.'[23] The cynical protagonist is shown cruelly mistreating the young maid for his own amusement, although the real girl was, as Kensaku knows, 'innocent and good-hearted'.[24] In other words, Sakaguchi lacks the one quality that, in Shiga's view, is absolutely essential in a writer of *shi-shōsetsu*: sincerity. If the author lacks this quality then so, inevitably, will his fictional *persona*, and his work, no matter how brilliant intellectually, will fall flat because, as Kensaku tells us, it will fail to arouse our sympathy – i.e., it will not bring about that all-important communion of spirit between reader and writer which Shiga called 'rhythm'.

By establishing this close relation between personal character and aesthetic value in the writing of *shi-shōsetsu* – a relation which has always been emphasized in traditional East Asian aesthetics, with both Buddhist and Confucian encouragement – Shiga also prepares us for the theme that I have already suggested is central to the work: Kensaku must solve his fundamental 'problem of the self' before he can succeed as a writer – and go on to write this very *shi-shōsetsu* called *A Dark Night's Passing*. Already in the first scene, despite its almost comic tone, we are given some hints of the depths of the problem: his anger and mental agitation, which seem out of all proportion to their rather trivial cause; his suspicion, amounting almost to paranoia, not only of Sakaguchi but even of the harmless Tatsuoka; and, finally, his self-doubts revealed, as he himself admits, by the very fact that he identifies with the disagreeable character portrayed by Sakaguchi, not on the basis of any external evidence but entirely because of what he perceives as a 'similarity of character'.[25]

On the other hand, this opening scene also gives us just as clear indications that there is much to be hoped for from Kensaku. In telling contrast to the smug, self-satisfied Sakaguchi, Kensaku is at least aware – painfully aware – that something within him is seriously awry. He admits to himself that he is being 'far too suspicious of Sakaguchi' and that, 'ever since his experience with Aiko', he has found it 'increasingly difficult to trust people'.[26] (As is consistent with this being Kensaku's *shi-shōsetsu*, his own 'stream of consciousness', we do not understand this reference to 'Aiko' until later.) He also admits that he does not 'like this tendency in himself, but there was not much he could do about it.'[27] Nevertheless, by this very act of painful self-awareness, he has taken the first step on the road that will lead him ultimately out of his 'dark night'. What this first scene shows us, in Shiga's admirably economical fashion, is that Kensaku, unlike his fellow-writer, Sakaguchi, possesses at least the sincerity necessary to make progress as a human being – and so as a writer of *shi-shōsetsu*.

Throughout the remainder of Part One, however, Kensaku's development seems more in the nature of a 'rake's progress'. He begins to frequent the teahouses and, eventually, the brothels of Yoshiwara, conducting liaisons with several different *geisha*, but without being really satisfied with any of them. Ultimately he must admit to himself his inability to control his sexual desires, as he admitted earlier that he could not control his suspicions; and this too is a symptom of some deeper malaise:

> The truth was that he was drawn to almost every woman he saw .... And before he could stop himself, he was asking himself the unwelcome question: 'What is it that I want?' He knew the answer; but it was so unpleasant, he wanted to hide from it.[28]

Finally, Kensaku's sexual desire becomes fixed on Oei, his 'grandfather's' ex-mistress who is now living with him as a kind of housekeeper. He recognizes instinctively, though, that his increasing 'self-indulgence' might lead him now to violate some deep taboo, which could prove disastrous:

> With every passing day, his self-indulgence became more intense. As his life grew more anarchic, so did his mind, and his lewd fantasies about Oei became more and more uncontrolled. He wondered fearfully what would happen to them if his present condition were to persist. This woman, who had been his grandfather's mistress, was almost twenty years older than he. He imagined their future together. What he saw – and he shrank before the prospect – was his own destruction.[29]

As Part One ends, Kensaku decides that he must get away from Tokyo for six months or a year, to try to come to grips with himself on his own, away from Oei and from the distractions of his perpetually carousing friends. As he tells Oei, he also hopes that in solitude he will 'get a lot of work done'.[30] This is the first important statement in the work of the link between Kensaku's spiritual well-being and his capacity to write. Also, by going away to face himself alone, he acknowledges, at least unconsciously, that his fundamental problem does not lie in his external circumstances but in his inner condition – which he alone can change. This is the beginning of a process of progressive 'internalization' in Kensaku's perception of his own problem which, as we shall see, culminates in the final part of the work when he openly confronts his own 'tyrannical' egotism. His going into hermetical retreat to seek peace of mind in the traditional East Asian fashion at the end of Part One also foreshadows his final 'retreat' to Mount Daisen at the end of Part Four.

As Part Two opens, Kensaku is on his way by ship to Onomichi, a small provincial town beautifully situated on the Inland Sea, which he has chosen as the site of his retreat. Standing alone on the ship's deck, he has an experience that is an important prelude to the experience he will have on Mount Daisen several years later:

> Above and below, to his right and left, the darkness stretched without limit. And here he was, standing in the very middle of this enormous thing . . . . He alone stood face to face with nature, as mankind's chosen representative. But together with this exaggerated sense of self-importance came the hopeless feeling that he was about to be swallowed up by the great

darkness around him. It was not altogether unpleasant. He fought against it nevertheless. As if to prove to himself his own presence, he tightened the muscles in his lower abdomen and breathed deeply. As soon as he stopped doing so, however, he again felt in danger of being swallowed up.[31]

It is obvious from this that Kensaku is not yet ready to 'let go' and completely lose himself in nature, even though he already recognizes that the experience is 'not altogether unpleasant'. And it is also obvious what is stopping him: his 'exaggerated sense of self-importance' – i.e., his ego – the other side of which is fear, the fear of losing himself, of being 'swallowed up'. To counteract this fear of what in Zen is called 'nothingness' (*mu*), Kensaku tightens his abdominal muscles and breathes deeply, 'as if to prove to himself his own presence'. The Zen way, of course, and the way Kensaku himself will come to eventually, is to embrace this nothingness; but, for the moment, his excessive egotism prevents the kind of self-surrender that this requires.

At first Kensaku responds well to his peaceful life on the mountainside above Onomichi. 'At last he felt relaxed enough to start on a long-range project he had been planning. This was to be a work based on his life from childhood to the present.'[32] In other words, he has begun to write *A Dark Night's Passing* – specifically, we may speculate, the part that later becomes the prologue, the 'hero's reminiscences' of his childhood. This also would account for the prologue's being written in the first person: it was written before Kensaku had attained the 'post-Daisen' detachment I spoke of earlier.

The fact that he lacks such detachment is shown by his inability to continue writing at Onomichi. A writer of *shishōsetsu*, as Shiga once said, must 'mine' what is in him, but this often involves painful introspection and self-analysis.[33] Kensaku, for instance, is troubled by a memory of having touched his mother's genitals while sleeping with her as a four-year-old and having been reprimanded by her for doing so:

> He felt shame still as he remembered the incident. He was also puzzled by the memory. What had made him do such a thing? Was it curiosity or was it some kind of urge? .... Perhaps, he thought wretchedly, he had inherited such an inclination; perhaps even with such things, one may be cursed by the sins of one's forefathers.

> It was with childhood reminiscences like these, then,
> that he began his writing.[34]

But, after about a month of reawakening such painful memories, the pressure of the past becomes too much for Kensaku: 'For about a month his work progressed at a steady pace, and both his daily life and his health seemed satisfactory. Then gradually everything began to deteriorate.'[35] And: 'As his work faltered he began to suffer from the monotony of his life. Every day was the same.'[36] Here we have, then, a somewhat more serious example of the hazards of writing *shi-shōsetsu* than was presented in the work's opening scene, and one that demands from the writer a good deal of self-detachment, since the 'self' is his principal subject.

Finding, then, that the internal pressure that builds up during solitude is, as yet, too much for him to bear, Kensaku turns to an external source for relief: he writes to his brother Nobuyuki, asking him to convey his proposal of marriage to Oei. Nobuyuki's answer brings a double shock; not only does Oei adamantly refuse his proposal, but Nobuyuki reveals the reason why she must: the 'shoddy, common, worthless old man' to whom she was mistress is Kensaku's real father. This unwelcome piece of information is the deepest blow yet to Kensaku's sense of self; it shakes him to the very core:

> It was all like a dream to him. The being that was
> himself, the person he had known until now as
> himself, seemed to be going farther and farther into
> the distance like a thinning mist.[37]

Again, then, Kensaku feels threatened by a sense of 'nothingness'. Significantly, what saves him at this point is the sudden surge of sympathy he feels for his dead mother:

> His mother and that shoddy, common, worthless old
> man – the mere thought of the association was ugly
> and unclean. He was then suddenly filled with
> overwhelming pity for his mother, his mother who
> had been defiled by that man. 'Mama!' he cried out,
> like a boy about to throw himself into his mother's
> arms.[38]

By this spontaneous cry from the depths of his soul Kensaku turns all his attention away from himself and towards another, thus freeing himself, at least momentarily, from his own personal pain. Although this is an entirely instinctive action here, it is, nevertheless, an important indication of the way which, ultimately, Kensaku must consciously embrace: the way of self-transcendence, of 'freeing the self from the self'.

In the letter that he sends back to his brother, Kensaku makes it clear that he is determined to make positive use of his new 'self-knowledge', however painful, both as a man and as a writer of *shi-shōsetsu*:

> Through my new knowledge about myself I shall be able to do my work with greater determination than before. And in that new determination I shall seek my salvation. There is no other way for me. By that means, I shall be able to accomplish two things at once: do the work I want to do and find myself.[39]

Here, then, we have the most explicit statement yet of the intimate relation between Kensaku's 'finding himself' and his capacity to write.

There is also some ironic, almost comic comment here on a subject familiar by now: the perils of writing *shi-shōsetsu*. Nobuyuki has expressed his concern that the 'family scandal' will make its way into Kensaku's writings, so that Kensaku must try to reassure him:

> I can sympathize with your fear lest the affairs of our family should appear in my writings. I cannot promise that they will not appear in some form or other. But I shall try to be careful not to cause discomfort.[40]

Left alone with his thoughts at Onomichi, Kensaku naturally is tempted to brood at times about being born a 'child of sin'. But, already, long before his experience on Mount Daisen, he knows intuitively that relief can be found only if he is able to 'dissolve' his troubled self in the vast world of nature that surrounds him:

> He made himself think of the vastness of the world around him ....in the midst of this vastness there was this minute particle that was himself, busily weaving a web of misery in the little world of his mind. Such was his customary way of combatting his own fits of depression ....[41]

Nevertheless, Kensaku does not yet feel strong enough to heal his own wounded spirit all by himself. He decides to return to Tokyo, although with misgivings that he might relapse again into his old life of dissipation:

The thought of living once more the way he had done those last three months in Tokyo was almost enough to detain him. There was his work too, nowhere near completion. How could he live like that again, he wondered, rushing about frantically yet always with that oppressive feeling of guilt?[42]

Back in Tokyo, Kensaku finds that his brother has decided to resign from his company and take up the study of Zen. The startled Kensaku 'could hardly share Nobuyuki's confidence in the efficacy of Zen. Zen was becoming awfully fashionable, and Kensaku naturally felt animosity toward it.'[43] He also disapproves of the Zen master Nobuyuki has chosen to study with:

He was the sort that spoke to large audiences at such places as the Mitsui Assembly Hall. For men like him, who went about scattering seed indiscriminately on barren ground, Kensaku had no respect.[44]

This is the first significant mention of Zen Buddhism in *A Dark Night's Passing*. There is an interesting dialectical relation between this work and the 'meditation' sect that has exercised such an overwhelming influence on Japanese culture. As some of my comments have already suggested, Kensaku's 'journey through dark night' – his struggle to free himself from his own egotism and his eventual achievement of this by total union with nature – fall perfectly within the Zen view of life and of the basic human predicament. Later in the work, in fact, Kensaku is shown to be reading and admiring the Zen classics: the 'enlightenment stories', in particular, 'appealed deeply to his susceptible mind. And each time he heard the words, "Thus in an instant there was enlightenment", he would feel like crying.'[45] And, just before his Daisen experience, we are told: 'Though he knew nothing about Buddhism, such realms believed in by Buddhists as "nirvana" and "the realm of bliss" seemed irresistibly attractive to him.'[46] While living on Mount Daisen, in fact, he even comes close to attending a Zen *sesshin*, an extended period of meditation and lectures by a Zen master.

Nevertheless, *A Dark Night's Passing* is not a religious tract but a work of fiction, so that Shiga, whatever his personal views on the matter, is wise to balance Kensaku's positive feelings about Zen in its 'pure' form with some rather negative feelings about Zen as a modern organized religion (an example of which we saw in his contemptuous opinion of the 'indiscriminate' Zen master quoted above). The important point, though, is that Kensaku, although undoubtedly somewhat under the sway of Zen ideas, does not, in contrast to his brother, take up the actual practice of Zen. If his Mount Daisen experience is a genuine Zen *satori*, it has been achieved 'naturally' and not by *zazen* (seated meditation) or *kōan* (meditation problem) practice. Kensaku is definitely the type of man who must go his own way – if only because of the enormity of his ego! As we are told: '. . .it distressed him to imagine himself sitting humbly at the feet of some smug Zen priest'.[47]

On one level, then, *A Dark Night's Passing* may be regarded as part of that series of major modern Japanese works of fiction which try to come to terms with this fundamental aspect of Japanese culture, the ineffable wisdom of Zen. The list includes Mori Ōgai's *Kanzan Jittoku* (1916), Natsume Sōseki's *The Gate*, (*Mon*, 1910), a number of works by Kawabata Yasunari, and Mishima Yukio's *The Temple of the Golden Pavilion* (*Kinkakuji*, 1956).[48] Of all these works, though, it seems to me that Shiga's, despite its apparent rejection of 'orthodox' Zen, comes closest to presenting the authentic Zen experience of a great spiritual liberation achieved after years of painful effort. Perhaps this accounts for the work's very palpable spiritual power, which gave it something of a 'cult following' among several generations of Japanese readers.

To return to the story itself, though: as Part Two draws to a close, Kensaku, despite all his good resolutions, does return to his former life-style of frequenting the teahouses and brothels of Yoshiwara. He 'once more began to decline, both in spirit and in body . . . . His way of life again became disorderly'.[49]

At the same time, however, he dreams of escaping entirely from the world of men, much like a traditional hermit:

> He would find a world where the very air he breathed was different. He would live at the foot of some great mountain, among peasants who knew nothing. And if he could live apart even from them, all the better . . . . How good it would be to live and eventually die in that condition – forgotten, unknown, untouched by the outer world![50]

Walking through the Ginza one night, he tries to evoke within himself the spirit of a Zen man of old like Hanshan:

> He must look straight ahead with the eyes of a calm and controlled man and not look about him nervously as he was wont to do. He wanted to be

like a man striding alone through the wilderness in
the twilight, unmindful of the crying pines and the
whispering grass. (Had Nobuyuki said the image was
to be found in a poem by Hanshan?) He wanted to
capture the spirit of such a man – even here on
Ginza. And he did not altogether fail to do so. In his
present frame of mind he needed desperately to cling
to some such ideal.[51]

As we would expect from his present mental condition,
Kensaku also fails to make any progress in his writing: 'There
was the long piece that he had worked on in Onomichi and was
still unfinished, but he did not want to touch that for the time
being.'[52] Kensaku is referring here, of course, to *A Dark Night's
Passing* itself. Since he is in no mood to engage in the kind of
painful introspection that the writing of his lengthy *shi-shōsetsu*
would require, he feels that he might try writing a work of
conventional fiction, drawing on his experiences in the 'gay
quarter'. While visiting a teahouse one night he had heard from
two geisha the story of Eihana, 'the most wicked *geisha* in
town', whom Kensaku had seen perform when she was a girl.[53]
She had trained when young to become a ballad-singer but had
run away before her training was finished to live with the son of
a local bookseller. But the boy was soon taken back by his
parents and she was disowned by hers. She was pregnant by
then and rumour had it that she had destroyed her own child
and taken up with the first man who happened along, who
turned out to be a pimp. She had disappeared from Tokyo for a
few years but now she was back and working as a *geisha* in
Yanagibashi, one of the pleasure quarters frequented by
Kensaku.

This tale of Eihana is the first of a series of 'stories within the
story' that appear in *A Dark Night's Passing* (other examples are
the *samurai* tale told by Naoko's uncle, Oei's misadventures in
China, the story of the Korean nobleman mistreated by
Japanese colonial authorities and the gossip that Kensaku
hears on Mount Daisen about the melodramatic goings-on that
surround the 'sluttish' wife of the woodcutter, Take). As we saw
in *Bonfire*, this is a favourite device of Shiga's. Just as the
'supernatural' material in *Bonfire* is made more acceptable by
being presented in this kind of framework (since the author
seems 'detached' from the material – he is merely 'reporting'
something he has heard), so is the rather melodramatic
material here made more palatable by being presented merely

as gossip Kensaku has heard. Nevertheless, these 'conventional-style' stories do have an important function in the work as a whole. Quite apart from their intrinsic interest as stories *per se*, they serve to represent traditional, conventional fiction within the *shi-shōsetsu* proper (the story of Eihana, for instance, sounds like something out of the popular *gesaku* literature of the Tokugawa period, with its highly coloured tales of the 'floating world'); and thus they function, within the fiction/reality dialectic, as the opposite end of the pole to the *shi-shōsetsu*. In other words, Shiga makes good use of the principle, here as elsewhere, that the best way to define something is by contrast with its opposite. When, for instance, Kensaku's friend Ishimoto suggests that 'all that background stuff about Eihana' would make a good short story, Kensaku's reaction is telling:

> 'Quite so,' said Kensaku with an obvious lack of enthusiasm. 'At least, it's good conversation material.' This last remark was ungracious, but he had to make it; for he resented Ishimoto's assumption that the stuff of gossip could immediately be translated into writing.[54]

In other words, the mere fact that something has actually happened does not qualify it as material for a writer of *shi-shōsetsu*. Life itself is often as full of melodrama as the most vulgar soap opera, but the writer, as an artist, must select as his material only what seems most appropriate and 'natural' to him.[55]

Nevertheless, Kensaku has a momentary change of heart about the Eihana story as material for his writing, and this tells us much about what motivates him as a writer. When he and his brother return home from the teahouse:

> Nobuyuki recounted for Oei's benefit the story of Eihana. It was a tale told with little pity and in a spirit of censure about a woman steeped in evil .... Kensaku was filled with anger. He thought of that little pale-faced girl on the stage, so helpless yet proud, and wanted to tell them, 'It's not Eihana that's bad!' But they had never seen the girl, and they would not know what he meant; and as he sat there trying to contain his anger, it suddenly occurred to him that here was something he could write about.[56]

It is clear, then, that, as an essentially 'lyrical' writer in the mainstream Japanese tradition, Kensaku must have strong personal feelings about something before he is able to write about it. In the case of Eihana, there is, in fact, an even deeper personal reason than the one indicated in the above quote: as a 'fallen woman', she reminds him of his mother.[57] Still, there is one crucial stumbling-block: as an author of *shi-shōsetsu*, how is he to write about someone other than himself?

> He tried writing about Eihana from his own point of view; quickly it became evident that the story would be too bare told that way, and he decided to tell it from her point of view, <u>giving his imagination free rein</u>. He toyed with the idea of having her meet Omasa the Viper .... He liked his story less and less as it developed. It seemed to him to become particularly <u>contrived</u> after the heroine's journey to Hokkaidō. Besides, he found telling a story from a woman's point of view, which he had never attempted before, far more difficult than he had imagined.[58] (my emphasis)

Here we have one of the most explicit statements of Kensaku's 'credo' as a writer of *shi-shōsetsu*: that, at least for himself, to try to tell a story from any point of view other than his own would be to risk the kind of artificial, 'contrived' writing he associates with conventional fiction. As for Shiga, the actual author, one may note that, even if we look at his more 'fictional' stories, we find that, in almost every case, the protagonists are more or less identifiable (although, of course, never completely identical) projections of himself: the 'Han' of *Han's Crime* (*Han no hanzai*), the 'Kakita' of *Akanishi Kakita*, the 'Claudius' of *The Diary of Claudius* (*Kurâdiasu no nikki*) and so on.[59]

As Part Three opens, Kensaku's spirits have revived somewhat from the doldrums we last saw him in. He has moved to Kyoto, the old capital of Japan and still the main repository of its traditional culture, where 'ancient temples and works of art' have 'led him gently back to ancient times, inviting a response from him that he had not thought possible.'[60] He spends most of his time just walking around the old city, admiring its temples, gardens and art works and soaking in its peaceful atmosphere. On one such outing he happens to catch sight of a young woman in a nearby house, who presents an inviting picture of domesticity to the lonely Kensaku as she goes about her household chores. 'She was a pleasing and wholesome sight, and he was immediately drawn to her.'[61] So drawn is he, in fact, that the impulsive Kensaku resolves to marry her, more or less on the spot. In doing so, he identifies himself, interestingly enough, with perhaps the most famous of all fictional characters, Don Quixote, and hopes that his new-found love might raise him above himself as did the 'blind' love of Quixote for Dulcinea. These hopes seem to be realized, at first, when the girl and her family accept his proposal and Kensaku settles down with his new bride, Naoko, to a life of comfortable domestic bliss in the beautiful suburbs of northern Kyoto. But there is some suggestion that, for a writer of *shi-shōsetsu*, his life is now a little too comfortable: 'He would often sit at his desk and simply stare at the view, not writing a word.'[62]

But marriage soon brings its own great trials. About a month after the newly wed couple's first child is born, it dies a slow, agonizing death from erysipelas. Kensaku, who had felt great delight at becoming a father, is plunged back into the depths of despair. He feels great bitterness towards what he perceives to be his evil fate, which has destroyed his new-found happiness just at its inception: 'why must he be betrayed now, when after years of journeying down the dark road, he had thought that the waiting and seeking had not been in vain, that the dawn had at last come? . . . .he could not in the end escape the conviction that he was the victim of some evil force bent on hurting him.'[63] Significantly, then, Kensaku is still inclined to place the blame for his misery on some power exterior to himself. He turns to his writing for therapy, but that too fails him: 'Kensaku sought to immerse himself in his work, which had lain discarded too long. But he felt so weighed down by a sense of fatigue – it was like a heavy chain wrapped around him – that he was incapable of such immersion.'[64] Part Three ends at this point, with Kensaku at the nadir of his despair.

One final great trial still awaits him, and this is recounted in the opening chapters of Part Four. He is obliged to make a ten-day trip to Korea to rescue Oei, who has been stranded there after having failed to set up a '*geisha*' business. When he returns to Kyoto, the intuitive Kensaku immediately senses, from his wife's behavior, that something is seriously wrong. He presses Naoko to reveal what is troubling her and finally she breaks down and tells him. During his absence she was visited by her cousin, Kaname. When they were children, he and Naoko had once played a game together that had distinctly erotic over-tones, so that she still felt uncomfortable in his presence. Nevertheless, she had allowed him to stay with her and, one night after they had played cards until late, she had offered to massage his back. Taking advantage of the situation, Kaname had forced himself upon her. Naoko resisted for some time, but eventually she 'felt herself drained of all power to resist. Indeed, she soon lost even the capacity to think.'[65] The incident is thus ambiguous, half seduction and half rape, but this does nothing to lessen Kensaku's shock.

He struggles bravely, however, to overcome his emotional turmoil and do the best thing for both his wife and himself:

> 'I do not want to condemn her', he said to himself, repeating what he had said to Naoko the night before. 'I want to forgive, not because it's virtuous to forgive, but because I know that if I can't forget what she did, the unhappy incident can only cause more unhappiness. I have no choice but to learn to forgive her.'[66]

But, with his large ego so badly bruised, this is easier said than done: 'A moment later, however, he could not avoid adding, "And so I shall be the only fool in the entire affair, the only loser."'[67]

An important hint as to the only way out of this emotional labyrinth is provided by Kensaku's friend, Suematsu. Though still unaware of the real cause of Kensaku's present 'touchiness', Suematsu berates him for the quick, 'irrational' way in which he judges people:

> In matters involving your feelings, you really are a tyrant. You're a terrible egoist, you know. True, you're not a calculating person, and I suppose that's a good thing. But you can be very thoughtless .... Let me put it another way. Perhaps you yourself aren't tyrannical; rather, it's as though a little tyrant is living inside you somewhere. I suppose it's possible that the real victim is therefore you.'[68]

Because of his friend's basic 'sincerity', Kensaku is forced to admit to himself the truth of his words:

> Kensaku had always allowed his emotions to tyrannize over him; but he had not before thought to describe his own condition quite in these words. Now, as he remembered the various incidents in his life, he had again to grant that more often than not he had been wrestling with himself, that his enemy had been a creature residing within him.[69]

This is the culmination of the process of 'interiorization' I mentioned before. Kensaku now no longer perceives his fundamental problem as caused by some exterior 'evil fate' – he knows now that the problem lies within. With this realization he has taken a major step towards his spiritual freedom. Although there are a few more struggles to come, he is sure now, at least, of the direction he must travel to emerge from his 'dark night'. And a prophetic promise of what lies at the end is also given by Suematsu. When Kensaku asks: '"If I am going to spend the rest of my life fighting with this thing that's inside me, what was the point of my having been born?"', Suematsu tells him, with a 'consoling look': '"Perhaps it isn't so bad, if at the end of it all there's peace of mind waiting."'[70]

Suematsu's point about the 'tyrant' ego is further driven home to Kensaku by an incident that occurs a few months later. By this time Kensaku has been blessed with another child, and one would expect to find him in a better frame of mind. On the surface all does seem to be calm but the fact that Kensaku is still subject to unpredictable rages shows that he has by no means resolved his inner tensions.

One day he takes Naoko with some others on an outing to a nearby resort. At the train station she goes to use the toilet and Kensaku is infuriated by her slowness. The train has already begun to pull out when Naoko tries to board it. Kensaku orders her to return home. When she persists in trying to get aboard, Kensaku, 'as in a reflex action', pushes her off.[71] She falls onto the station platform, injuring herself slightly. Thinking that he must have had 'some sort of fit',[72] Kensaku is naturally very shocked by his own behaviour: 'He could still see the strange look in Naoko's eyes as she fell off the train. It was unbearable. Oh God, he thought, I've done something irreparable.'[73] And 'he dared not contemplate what his action had done to their future relationship.'[74] It is indeed as if some uncontrollable 'tyrant' within him had acted, rather than his true self.

Naoko's reaction is one of deep but knowing sadness. She accuses Kensaku of having not really forgiven her in his heart of hearts:

> 'I was terribly pleased when you said you weren't going to hate me, you weren't going to brood about it, since hating and brooding did no one any good. But you can't expect me to go on believing what you said when you do something like what you did the

other day. I can't help thinking that deep inside, you
do resent me.'[75]

Although Kensaku is angered by her suggestion that even his
forgiveness is tinged with egotism, still he must admit that: '"As
you say, my feelings aren't as magnanimous as my ideas."'[76] He
sees this, though, as a problem which he must solve alone. '"A
doctor may say I'm suffering from a nervous breakdown. But
even if I am, I don't want to go to a doctor for help."'[77] As a
result: '"I want merely to go away to some mountain for half a
year, and live quietly by myself."'[78]

As his place of retreat this time Kensaku chooses Mount
Daisen, 'a holy place of the Tendai sect', where he can stay in a
Buddhist temple.[79] Before leaving he tells Naoko jokingly that
he will '"concentrate on attaining Buddhahood"' and '"shall
return as Buddha"'.[80] But there is a serious undertone to this
jesting: 'He was indeed leaving in a frame of mind akin to that
of a man about to take holy orders, but he could hardly tell
Naoko so.'[81] When Oei objects that the similar retreat he had
made to Onomichi a few years before did him little good, he
explains to her that his motives now are quite different:

> 'I went to Onomichi to force myself to get some work
> done; I found that it was too difficult, and I failed.
> But this time, work is not my primary concern. I'm
> going in order to find spiritual well-being, you might
> say, and to recover my physical strength.'[82]

This difference makes clear how serious – and how desperate –
Kensaku has become about his spiritual quest, now that he has
seen the terrible depths of his own egotism. And, although his
'spiritual well-being' and not his writing is now his 'primary
concern', because he is an author of *shi-shōsetsu* the two are
really inseparable. A spiritual break-through will also enable
him to break through the writer's block he has suffered from
the work's beginning.

As soon as Kensaku arrives in the vicinity of Mount Daisen,
his spirits begin to revive. He is immediately struck by the great
contrast between people who live in the city and those who live
close to nature. 'As though for the first time, he was made aware
that such a world as this existed. There are people, he thought,
that live like wild cats in a cave, forever snarling at each other;
and then there is this life.'[83] When he ascends the mountain
itself, he comes across a 'serene old man' at a teashop who seems
an ideal example of a man who lives close to nature:

> He must have gazed at the same scene countless times before; yet here he was, still gazing at it without apparent boredom .... he was like an ancient tree in the mountains, he was like a moss-covered rock that had been placed there in front of the view. If he was thinking at all, he was thinking as an old tree or a rock would think. He seemed so tranquil, Kensaku envied him.[84]

Here, then, is a perfect image of what it means to be 'dissolved' in nature, 'mindless' in the Zen sense, untroubled by any of the petty concerns of the human world – free even of one's own memories, one's own 'identity'. Here is an image, in fact, of everything that Kensaku hopes to become.

There is another 'natural' man whom Kensaku meets later on the mountain: Take, the Christ-like carpenter who fixes the temple buildings without pay. His wife is a notorious 'slut' with several lovers but Take, in telling contrast to Kensaku, 'could not bring himself to hate her'.[85] Kensaku marvels at Take's forbearance which, he speculates, probably comes from 'his total understanding of what his wife was .... Of course Take must have suffered, he must be suffering now. Yet he had somehow managed to rise above his misfortune.'[86] This simple carpenter, then, has attained the state of egolessness that Kensaku aspires to.

In his new conciliatory mood, Kensaku writes a letter home to Naoko. He explains to her the changes that have already occurred in his state of mind:

> 'Since coming to this mountain I've spent a lot of time looking at the little birds, the insects, the trees, the water, the rocks. As I observe closely all these things by myself, I find that they give rise to all kinds of feelings and thoughts that I never had before. That a world which had never existed for me before has opened itself up to me has given me a sense of joy.'[87]

Significantly, with his psychic condition improved he has also begun to write again, and he encloses a sample of his work in his letter to Naoko – as we would expect, a 'nature sketch'.

We now approach what may be regarded as the climactic scene not only of *A Dark Night's Passing* but of Shiga's entire *opus*. Kensaku decides to hike up to the top of Mount Daisen one night, so as to watch the sunrise from there the following morning. He is accompanied by a group of company employees from Osaka, whose boisterous holiday spirits contrast sharply with Kensaku's own quiet, subdued mood. Indeed, they share little of his growing sensitivity to nature. When he tells them he has already been on the mountain a fortnight, they ask: "'How can you stand it? We'd go mad after two days here.'"[88] We are thus given a distinct sense of irony when they all break into a traditional pilgrim's chant as they begin to ascend the 'holy mountain': 'Begone all the senses, let the spirits guide us to the clear sky above.'[89] Regarded from Kensaku's present state of mind, however, these words have an entirely appropriate tenor, and may even be regarded as prophetic of his coming experience.

That there are still, for the moment, some traces of worldly egotism left in him, however, is made clear by the 'competitive' feeling he has, as the only Tokyo man in the group, towards the other young men, who are all from the rival city of Osaka. This makes him push on up the mountain at the same pace as theirs, in spite of the fact that he is still suffering the aftereffects of a 'severe attack of diarrhea' he had earlier that day.[90] When the group pauses to rest after about an hour's hike, Kensaku feels that he has no more strength to continue. He tells the others that he will rest there until dawn, and then return home by himself. Reluctantly, the group continues on up the mountain without him.

Left alone on the mountain in the quiet of the night, Kensaku is now able to commune with nature as never before. He sits down on the grass and begins 'breathing deeply through his nose, his eyes closed'[91] (interestingly, the traditional way a Zen adept quiets his mind before meditation). Then comes perhaps the most celebrated passage in all of Shiga:

> He felt his exhaustion turn into a strange state of rapture. He could feel his mind and his body both gradually merging into this great nature that surrounded him. It was not nature that was visible to the eyes; rather, it was like a limitless body of air that wrapped itself around him, this tiny creature no larger than a poppy seed. To be gently drawn into it, and there be restored, was a pleasure beyond the power of words to describe .... He had experienced this feeling of being absorbed by nature before; but this was the first time that it was accompanied by such rapture. In previous instances, the feeling perhaps had been more that of being sucked in by nature than that of merging into it; and though there

had been some pleasure attached to it, he had at the
same time always tried instinctively to resist it, and
on finding such resistance difficult, he had felt a
distinct uneasiness. But this time, he had not the
slightest will to resist; and contentedly, without a
trace of the old uneasiness, he accepted nature's
embrace.[92]

It is important, first, to note Kensaku's condition immediately preceding this experience: he is thoroughly worn out by
his illness and by the effort of competing with the boisterous
Osaka men. Beyond this, of course, we must recall all the great
trials he has undergone throughout the course of the work,
which have taxed his spirit close to breaking-point. As the
familiar Christian phrase has it: 'Man's extremity is God's
opportunity.' And this truth has also been made an integral part
of Zen training, as we know from the innumerable 'enlightenment stories' recounted in the works of D.T. Suzuki in which
the adept frequently attains *satori* only when pushed to the very
end of his tether.[93] It is claimed that the vise-like grip of
egotism on human consciousness can be loosened only in this
exacting way, and certainly in Kensaku's case this seems to be
borne out. As he himself recalls in the above passage, when he
had experienced a similar feeling of being 'dissolved' in nature
before (as I have noted earlier, on the boat to Onomichi), he
had 'instinctively' resisted it, fearing loss of his identity (as he
says, of being 'sucked in'). The great difference now is that his
sense of individual self has since received a good many shocks,
which have greatly reduced its hold on him and, more
importantly, Kensaku himself, as we have seen, has admitted
his own egotism to be his fundamental problem and has
consciously taken measures to overcome it – for one thing,
coming to this mountain. And so, 'this time, he had not the
slightest will to resist; and contentedly, without a trace of the
old uneasiness, he accepted nature's embrace.'[94]

Here, then, is the culmination of that process of increasing
union with nature which I have traced through four of Shiga's
major works. In his earliest story, *One Morning*, the bare outline
of the problem was presented: how was a hypersensitive young
man to cope with the frictions that inevitably resulted from his
relations with others, especially within the narrow, rather
oppressive confines of the traditional Japanese family? By *At
Kinosaki* he has received a more severe shock to his delicate
sense of self – a near-fatal accident – but he also is given some

inkling of a way out: by turning away from the human world and towards nature. Nevertheless, he is not yet ready for the degree of self-surrender that a total mergence with nature would require, as is evidenced by his intellectual doubts towards the story's end, which arise from his equating such a state of union with death. Significantly, these doubts are answered by Kensaku in the paragraph following the passage quoted above:

> He felt as if he had just taken a step on the road to eternity. Death held no threat for him. If this means dying, he thought, I can die without regret. But to him then, this journey to eternity did not seem the same as death.[95]

In *Bonfire* the Shiga protagonist has already attained some degree of union with nature but, shared as it is among a group of convivial friends, this seems more like a passing mood – like the momentary calm of the lake's surface in the story – rather than the profound experience of self-surrender that the solitary Kensaku undergoes, an experience that one feels will have lasting and radical effects on the man's whole being and character. *A Dark Night's Passing*, in fact, contains all the stages we have observed in the previous stories, but in much larger dimensions: that is, the wounds that Kensaku receives to his sense of self are far more critical and prolonged than those of the earlier protagonists, just as his ultimate experience of liberation is far more profound.

But the cycle is not quite yet complete: since it began in the human world, not in the world of nature, it must also end there. As we have seen, the Shiga protagonist's first perception that something was basically awry – both in *One Morning* and in *A Dark Night's Passing* – arose from his difficulties in relating with other people. Now that, supposedly, he has eliminated the root cause – his own egotism – it is only natural that he be shown descending from his mountain retreat and relating with others in a new and freer way. This would correspond to the traditional final stage of the 'enlightened' man's life known as 're-entering the marketplace' and invariably illustrated in the last of the Zen ox-herding pictures one finds in monasteries all over East Asia.

Such, in fact, is the import of *A Dark Night's Passing*'s final scene. Perhaps so as not to be overly obvious about it, Shiga keeps the scene short and, rather than employ the symbolism of

Kensaku actually descending from the mountain, he has the human world below – in the form of Naoko – come to Kensaku instead. But the true significance of the scene is nevertheless quite apparent. When Naoko arrives, Kensaku is lying prostrate in bed, thoroughly exhausted, and his worn appearance initially shocks her. But when she draws near to him, she soon forgets her anxiety and falls under the spell of his new presence:

> His gaze was like a caress. She thought she had never seen such gentleness, such love, in anyone's eyes before. She was about to say, 'Everything is all right now,' but she refrained, for in the presence of such contentment and quiet, the words seemed hollow.[96]

That one word describing the quality of Kensaku's gaze – 'caress' (*nademawasu*) – tells us volumes about his new-found capacity for communion with others. As was revealed in *Bonfire*, an increased capacity for union with nature brings an equally increased capacity for union with one's fellow human beings since, at the deepest level, man and nature are one. As we recall, Shiga used the term 'rhythm' to express that fundamental power which is shared by all natural phenomena, including man, and it is this 'rhythm', more a spiritual than a physical quality, that the narrator seems to be referring to by the word 'nature' in the passage quoted above: 'It was not nature that was visible to the eyes . . . .'[97] Thus, when Kensaku becomes identified with this universal 'rhythm', he also becomes identified with the innermost nature of man. On the level of human relations the word for this 'unitive' capacity is, of course, 'love', and so Naoko 'thought she had never seen such gentleness, such love, in anyone's eyes before.'[98]

The final few paragraphs of the work contain an unusual device: the narrative viewpoint, having been that of Kensaku throughout the entire work, suddenly changes to that of Naoko. This has disturbed some critics who might have got the *idée fixe* from the Jamesian critic Percy Lubbock and his many disciples that any work of narrative fiction must have a rigidly consistent point of view.[99] Regarded with the above explication in mind, however, it seems a perfectly appropriate 'objective correlative' on a formal level for what is, on a thematic level, the profound depth of union achieved between Naoko and Kensaku. Despite her initial wifely anxiety, Naoko has been so drawn into Kensaku's 'tranquility' that she is now prepared to accept even the idea that he might die:

> She had never seen him look so tranquil. Perhaps, she thought, he is not going to live through this. But the thought somehow did not sadden her very much. As she sat there looking at him, she felt herself becoming an inseparable part of him; and she kept on thinking, 'Whether he lives or not, I shall never leave him, I shall go wherever he goes.'[100]

But there is another significance to this change of viewpoint which has been missed by a critic such as Francis Mathy, who fails to take Kensaku as the 'fictional' author of the work.[101] Naoko does not only achieve union with Kensaku; above all, Kensaku achieves union with Naoko – it is he, after all, who has just been 'enlightened' on the mountain. With his new-found capacity for union with others, Kensaku, the erstwhile writer of *shi-shōsetsu*, who had been so totally absorbed in himself that, as we saw when he tried to write the story of Eihana, he could never write from any viewpoint other than his own, is now able to commune with others to such an extent that he can even write down their innermost thoughts. The fact that the work ends with a thought of Naoko's rather than of Kensaku's signifies the depth of selflessness that he has attained, and the new and 'novelistic' dimensions that have opened for him both as a man and as a writer.

One of the questions often raised by readers of *A Dark Night's Passing* concerns Kensaku's presumed fate after the work's end: does he succumb to his illness or does he recover?[102] It is not the sort of question literary scholars generally take very seriously but, nevertheless, it does have some relevance to my reading of the work. It seems to me that, if Shiga had meant Kensaku to be presumed dead, the work would lose much of its meaning as an analysis of the *shi-shōsetsu* and the problems involved in its creation: principally, the fact that, because of the intimate link between an 'autobiographical' writer's life and work, Kensaku's 'writer's block' can be overcome only by a breakthrough on the personal, psychic level, a breakthrough that will enable him to go on to write *A Dark Night's Passing* itself. Though on the level of everyday factual reality we know, of course, that Shiga Naoya is the author of *A Dark Night's Passing*, on the level of 'fictional reality' it seems to me imperative that we believe that Tokitō Kensaku survived and went on to write this very work. Thus the implications of Shiga's fiction/reality dialectic resonate on even beyond the work's ending.

And it is important to recognize that both sides of the dialectic play a necessary role in Shiga's 'artless art'. Elements which seem conventionally fictional – which in Shiga's view, as we have seen, confer a sense of 'artificial' form – must be balanced by more 'natural-seeming', informal, diary-like elements – a process of 'deformation' or 'making irregular' which is very much in tune with the tradition of Zen aesthetics.[103] It may be tempting for the Western critic, reacting against the overwhelming tendency of Japanese critics to regard the work purely as Shiga's autobiography, to go to the other extreme and insist exclusively on its status as a work of fiction. But this would be an equally one-sided approach and would fail to account for the rich ambiguities and the full interplay of tensions which forms the inner dynamic of Shiga's art.

To be more specific: even though there is much invented material – for instance, the 'illicit' birth of the hero and his wife's 'semi-rape' – we also know that many details of Shiga's own life went into the work.[104] Most important of these is undoubtedly his own experience of deep union with nature while on Mount Daisen in the summer of 1914.[105] How significant the experience was for him may be judged by the fact that he used it, almost a quarter of a century later, as the basis for the 'climax' of his *magnum opus*. To deny *A Dark Night's Passing* its autobiographical side would be to deprive it of an important dimension of its significance. This is certainly true in the Japanese cultural context, where such a high value is placed on 'sincere' autobiographical literature, but for a work of this nature, which might be valued even more as a spiritual document than as a work of fiction, its essentially 'autobiographical' character is likely to carry some weight among Western readers too. And certainly there are major precedents for this in our own literature. If, for instance, some clever scholar of English literature were ever to prove that Wordsworth's nature mysticism were all a sham, a mere 'rhetoric of mysticism', and that the great poet himself had never had any such experience, then certainly two centuries of devoted Wordsworthians would feel profoundly disappointed, and an important part of English spiritual heritage, if not of English literature, would seem sadly vitiated. Or, to take an example closer to Shiga's own generation and genre, a similar disappointment would overwhelm those who regard *A la Recherche du temps perdu* as almost a sacred text if it could ever be proven that the real Marcel had never been sent into time-transcending raptures by the taste of 'une petite madeleine'. But, happily, the fact of the matter is that no evidence or argument is ever likely to convince Wordsworthians, Proustians – or Shigaites – that their author was 'insincere', that he was not being fundamentally true to to his own experience (fundamentally, because one must make certain allowances, of course, for poetic or fictional license).

But, of course, the Mount Daisen experience did not occupy quite the same position in Shiga's life as in Kensaku's: it did not mark the climactic high-point of his growth as man and artist, nor did it enable him to live the rest of his days as an all-compassionate, enlightened Buddha. In other words, through the process of *fictionalization* the Daisen experience and the character of Shiga himself have been made 'larger than life' – they have assumed, in fact, almost mythic proportions. This may be seen as an inevitable process, regardless of how much an author draws his material from his own 'everyday' life. Just as an *objet trouvé* – say, an old shoe – takes on a formal, symbolic aspect if placed on a pedestal in a museum, so too an author's own experience, regardless how 'trivial' or private, takes on a symbolic, universal aspect when placed within the framework of a work of fiction. All the more so is this true, then, when the 'experience' in question is such a fundamental one as a man's 'journey through dark night' towards spiritual liberation. And this mythic, archetypal aspect of *A Dark Night's Passing* accounts, of course, for much of its underlying power. It is not simply the story of one man's spiritual struggle but a kind of 'pilgrim's progress' of a modern Everyman (and, in keeping with this, Kensaku is a rather 'impersonal' character in the sense I noted in Chapter Two).[106] Indeed, Karatani Kōjin claims that '*Anya Kōro* has a configuration resembling the *monogatari* more than the *shishōsetsu* and contains a mythological-ritualistic space.'[107] Nevertheless, on the other side of the equation, this strong tendency towards formality and abstraction on the thematic level is balanced by the very informal structure and particular everyday content of the *shi-shōsetsu* genre itself, which is, in this respect, a worthy descendant of the medieval *nikki* (diary) and *zuihitsu* (random essay). Thus the fiction/reality dialectic which Shiga establishes in *A Dark Night's Passing* is one of a delicate and masterful balance, both terms of which may be seen as absolutely essential to the total aesthetic effect.

It is, however, this very mixing of 'fiction' and 'non-fiction', and the supposed 'formlessness' that results from it, which has disturbed some Western critics of the work. In an article on the *shi-shōsetsu*, Edward Seidensticker, in fact, expands this complaint into a criticism of Far Eastern literature in general:

> In the Orient, the notion of genre has been at once too elaborate and not elaborate enough, if these fundamental Western distinctions between fiction and non-fiction, lyric and drama, are accepted .... Some Japanese categories, such as *shōsetsu* and *monogatari*, seem so broad as to be meaningless. They include virtually everything, and cut across what in the Western tradition seem like the most fundamental distinctions. Others, like *sharebon* and *kibyōshi*, seem so narrow as to be meaningless. They cover tiny realms, and within their tiny realms seem capable, in a most perverse fashion, of mixing fiction and non-fiction, quite as in the *monogatari* empire.[108]

As a matter of fact, though, even the 'fundamental Western distinctions' – if they ever really existed – are not what they used to be. This becomes obvious if we look at, say, American fiction over the latter half of this century. The rambling autobiographical journals of Jack Kerouac, for instance, works such as *On the Road* (1957) and *The Dharma Bums* (1958), were among the most celebrated 'novels' of the 'fifties 'Beat generation'. Writing in a more 'documentary' vein, Truman Capote claimed to have invented a new genre, the 'non-fiction novel', with his *In Cold Blood* (1965), a 'novelized' account of an actual incident of mass murder. Norman Mailer also followed this trend with his 'reportorial novels' such as *The Armies of the Night* (1968), subtitled 'History as a Novel, the Novel as History', and *The Executioner's Song* (1979), subtitled 'A True Life Novel'. *Time* magazine even invented an ugly neologism for such works: 'faction', though serious literary scholars generally prefer the now-fashionable term, 'postmodern novel'. During the 1980s and 1990s such novels have proliferated throughout the English-speaking world.

Whatever we may think of the literary value of this form of fiction, it is likely that, because of their widespread acceptance, the younger generation of English-speaking readers will be less disturbed than their elders by the 'blurred lines' between fiction and non-fiction in the works of Shiga Naoya and other Japanese writers. Perhaps, then, it is no coincidence that *A*

Dark Night's Passing finally appeared in English translation in 1976, about forty years after its first publication in Japan, even though it had long been recognized in its own country as a modern classic. Shiga, in fact, seems at the same time both peculiarly modern and very much within the Japanese tradition. This seeming paradox is by no means unprecedented: traditional Japanese architecture, for instance, with its simple lines and uncluttered decor, seems more 'modern' to the Western eye today than the ornate architectural styles of our own recent ancestors – nor is this entirely fortuitous, in view of its seminal influence on such 'modernist' Western architects as Frank Lloyd Wright. In the same way, as we saw in Chapter Three, the *haiku* has a way of seeming ultramodern because of its affinity with and influence on Imagism and the many offshoots of that early modernist movement. Whether the recent breakdown in the Western novel of the formerly strict divisions between fiction and non-fiction is due in part to Japanese influence is more difficult to determine. Certainly there was a strong Japanese (especially a 'Zen') influence on the 'Beat' writers which led them to emphasize 'spontaneity', an emphasis that resulted, for instance, in the 'automatic' diary-like writing of a Jack Kerouac. But there seems, anyway, something in the modern temper – shaped so much by newspapers and television – that demands at least a greater illusion of 'reality'. (As any book publisher knows, non-fiction generally sells better than fiction.)

At any rate, Shiga's works too may be seen, on one level, to appeal to the reader's appetite for 'the facts'. Just as early English novelists such as Defoe and Richardson used the letter and the diary form to impart a sense of 'reality' to their fictional works, in *A Dark Night's Passing* Shiga uses the *shi-shōsetsu* for the same purpose. Aesthetically, this results in an impression of 'artlessness' (since the writer seems merely to be 'transcribing' reality) which enables Shiga to avoid what he considered to be the 'artificiality' of conventional fiction. But there is another side to the 'artless art' equation: the writer's art itself. This lies not merely in his invention of certain fictional details but in the essential vision which orders the selection of all his material – 'fiction' and 'non-fiction' alike – and which unifies the entire work. In Shiga's case, as we have seen, this central vision is redolent of the mainstream spiritual culture of the Orient, especially of Zen Buddhism. In its conception of the human predicament and of the way to wisdom and liberation, it is a restatement of an ancient tradition in modern terms. It is primarily as such, I would suggest, that the works of Shiga Naoya will find their way into the hearts of Western readers.

PART TWO

SELECTED TRANSLATIONS

AT KINOSAKI

To recover from injuries I suffered on being hit and sent flying by a train of the Yamanote line, I travelled by myself to the Kinosaki hot spring in Tajima. If the wound to my back turned into spinal tuberculosis it could prove fatal, but the doctor assured me this wouldn't happen. He told me that, if tuberculosis didn't appear within two or three years, there would be nothing more to worry about – but anyway the main thing was to be careful. And so I came to the hot spring to recuperate. I came with the idea that I would stay about three weeks – or five weeks if I could stand it.

My head still was not quite clear somehow. I had become terribly forgetful. But emotionally I was calmer than I had been in years – it was a good feeling, quite serene. It was just about the time they had begun to harvest the rice crop, so the weather also was pleasant.

I was all by myself so I had no one to talk to. I could either read or write, or just sit absent-mindedly in the chair in front of my room, gazing at the mountains or at the traffic in the street – or, if not doing any of these, I could spend my time going for walks. There was a good place for walking, a road which led gradually uphill out of town, following alongside a small stream. Where it circled around the foot of a mountain the stream turned into a small pool which was full of trout. And when you looked closer you could spot some big river crabs with hair on their legs, sitting there as motionless as rocks. I often went walking on this road in the evening, just before supper. The kind of thoughts I had while following the small, clear stream through the lonely, autumnal mountain gorge, pierced through by the evening chill, were often, as one might expect, rather dark thoughts. Lonely thoughts. Nevertheless, a quiet and pleasant feeling arose from these thoughts. I often dwelt upon the way I'd been injured. I thought to myself, for instance, that, if the accident had been just a little bit worse, I'd be lying now asleep forever, face-up in the earth of Aoyama

Cemetery. My face would be blue, cold and stiff, the wounds on my face and back would never heal. The corpses of my mother and my grandfather would lie beside me. But there would be no communication between us.... These are the kind of thoughts that floated up into my mind. They made me feel lonely but they did not frighten me much. After all, it happens to everyone at some time. The only question was when that 'some time' would come. Until now when I thought about it that 'some time' seemed to lie in some unknowably distant future. But now I had come to feel that I really could not know when it would be. I had been saved from a likely death, something had failed to kill me, there was some work which I had to accomplish – in a book about Lord Clive I had read in middle school, it said that he had taken courage from such thoughts. In reality I also felt about my near-fatal accident in the same way. Such was my sense of it too. But my heart had become strangely serene. An unfathomable intimacy with death had awakened in my heart.

My room was on the second floor, without neighbors, and thus relatively quiet. When I was tired of reading or writing, I would often sit out on the veranda. The roof of the entrance-hall was below me, and there was some clapboard placed over the gap where it joined the main house. There seemed to be a beehive underneath the boards and every day, if the weather was fine, big fat tiger-striped bees worked busily thereabouts from morning until close to dusk. When the bees slipped out through the gaps between the boards, they would land for a while on the entrance-hall roof. There they would carefully arrange their wings and antennae with their fore- or rear-legs – and some would walk around a little – then they would suddenly stretch both their long thin wings out tight and fly up with a buzz. Once aloft, they would suddenly gain speed and fly quickly off. Some hedge flowers had just begun to bloom and the bees crowded around those. When bored I would often lean over the railing and watch their comings and goings.

One morning I noticed a dead bee on the entrance-hall roof. His legs were stuck tight to his underbelly, his antennae were drooping down sloppily over his face. The other bees passed him by with absolute indifference. Busy as they were going in and out of the hive, they did not hesitate at all to crawl over anything in their way. These bees going so busily about their work gave one the sense of something intensely alive. And the one bee lying beside them – which, whenever one looked at it, morning, noon or night, was still curled up face-down and motionless in exactly the same spot – this gave one just as intensely the sense of something dead. It lay there like that for about three days. Whenever I looked at it I was overcome by a feeling of profound quietness. And of loneliness. It made me feel lonely to look at this one dead bee left alone on the cold roof tile when, after sunset, all the other bees had entered the hive. But it was also very quiet.

During the night it rained very heavily. In the morning it cleared and the leaves, the ground and the roof all looked as if they'd been washed beautifully clean. The dead bee was no longer there. The other bees were all still energetically at work, but the dead bee had probably been washed down to the ground through the drain-pipe. Perhaps he was lying motionless somewhere, covered in mud, his legs pulled in, his antennae stuck against his face. No doubt he would have to stay there until some force in the external world moved him again. Or would some ants carry him off? Even so, it all seemed a very quiet process. It seemed so quiet because the bee who had spent his whole life working so busily now could not move at all. I felt close to that quietness. I had written a short story called *Han's Crime* a little while before. The story told about a Chinese named Han who had murdered his wife because he was jealous of the affair she had conducted with his friend before marriage, and also because his mental state was further aggravated by certain physiological pressures he was under. I had written the story from Han's point of view, but now I wanted to rewrite it from his wife's point of view – in short, to write out of the feeling of quietness of his murdered wife lying in her grave.

I planned to call it: *The Murdered Wife of Han*. Although I didn't write it in the end, I did feel the need to write it. And this depressed me, because it meant I had begun to think and feel in a way very different to the hero of *A Dark Night's Journey*, a novel I had been writing for some time.

Without my even seeing it go, the dead bee had been swept away. One morning I left the inn, planning to walk to Higashiyama Park, from whence could be seen the Maruyama River and the Japan Sea, into which the river flowed. In front of 'Ichinoyu' a small stream gently crossed the road and flowed into the Maruyama River. When I walked a little further on, some people were standing about on a bridge and on the riverbank making a lot of fuss about something in the river. It was a large rat which had been thrown into the water. The rat was swimming with all his might, desperate to escape. A seven-inch-long fish skewer had been run through his neck. It protruded about three inches above his head and three inches below his throat. He was trying to scramble up a stone wall. Two or three children and a ricksha man of about forty were throwing stones at him. For a long time the stones failed to hit their mark. They struck sharply against the stone wall and bounced off. The spectators laughed loudly. The rat finally managed to hold onto a gap in the stone wall with his forepaws. But when he tried to squeeze through the fish skewer immediately got caught. And again he fell into the water. The rat tried with all his will to save himself. His facial expressions may not have been comprehensible to a human being, but one understood how determined he was from his actions. As if thinking he would be saved if only he could escape somewhere else, he swam back out into mid-river, his neck still pierced through by the long skewer. The children and ricksha man threw stones at him all the more eagerly. Two or three ducks searching for food at the washing place on the river-bank were startled every time the stones came flying and stretched their necks out to look all around. The stones made a big splash as they fell into the water. With their necks still outstretched and with alarm on their faces, the ducks cried out and paddled busily upstream. I didn't feel like watching the rat's last moments. The image of the rat who could not be killed but who, while enduring his fate, used every last ounce of his energy running around, trying all means of escape – this image lingered strangely in my mind. It gave me a lonely and unpleasant feeling. I thought to myself that this was reality. It was terrible that, before I could enjoy the quietness I longed for, I would have to endure that kind of suffering. Though I felt close to the peace which followed death, I feared the struggle which must precede it. Animals do not know how to commit suicide and so must struggle on like that until death comes at last. What would I do now if I were placed in the same situation as the rat? Wouldn't I too, after all, put up the same kind of fight? I couldn't help thinking that something similar had happened to me when I was hit by the train. I had tried to do everything I could to survive at that moment. I had decided by myself which hospital I should be taken to. I had even specified which mode of transportation should be used. Concerned that, if the doctor was out, any necessary operation could not be performed the moment I arrived, I asked someone to phone ahead to warn the hospital I was coming. When I thought about it later, it seemed strange to me that, even in its half-conscious state, my mind dealt efficiently with those matters it considered of utmost importance. It also seemed strange to me that, even though I had wondered whether my wounds would prove fatal, I had wondered this in a strangely detached way, without being overcome by any fear of dying. I had asked some friends who were with me what was the doctor's prognosis. They assured me that he'd said the wounds wouldn't be fatal. When I heard this, I suddenly felt invigorated. I grew cheerful with the excitement. How would I have reacted if they'd told me I was going to die? I couldn't imagine. I probably would have grown weak. But it seems to me that I wouldn't have been so overcome with the fear of death as one usually expects. But, though I say that, I think that I would have struggled hard to save myself somehow. Undoubtedly I would have behaved in much the same way as the rat. And when I tried to imagine how I would act if the same thing happened again – would I struggle hard or would I give in to my longing for peace? – since I hadn't changed much and since one's behavior is not really influenced so easily by such moods as the longing for the quiet of death, I concluded that I'd probably still struggle to survive. But both possibilities seemed real, and I felt that either way would be alright. Whatever happened would happen inevitably.

One evening shortly after this I went by myself for a walk out of town again, following the small stream gradually upwards. Once I had crossed the tracks in front of a tunnel on the Sanin line, the road grew narrow and steep and the stream alongside it began to flow more quickly. There were no more houses anywhere in sight. I was continually on the point of turning back, but kept urging myself on to the next corner visible in the distance, and then the next one. Everything looked pale in the evening light, the touch of the night air chilled my skin, and the deep silence made me feel somehow, perversely, rather restless. Large mulberry trees grew beside the road. On a mulberry tree branch which extended over the road up ahead, a single leaf fluttered in a continual rhythmic movement all by itself. There was no wind and, apart from the stream, only that leaf disturbed the deep stillness, busily fluttering on and on. It gave me an eerie feeling. And it frightened me a bit. But it also aroused my curiosity. I went down to the foot of the tree and stood looking up at it for a while. Then I felt a breeze. And the single fluttering leaf stopped fluttering. The cause was obvious. It occurred to me that somehow I had known about such phenomena before.

Gradually it became darker. No matter how far I went, there was always one more corner up ahead. I kept thinking that I would turn back hereabouts. For no particular reason I looked over at the stream beside me. Something small and black sat on a rock about the size of half a *tatami* mat which jutted out of the water onto the opposite bank. It was a lizard. It was still wet and this made its colour seem more attractive. It sat very still, hanging its head down the slope towards the stream. A stream of black water dripped from his body and flowed for about an inch over the dry rock. Unconsciously I crouched down to watch. I no longer disliked water lizards as much as I used to. Land lizards I rather liked. Among creeping and crawling things I disliked gecko the most. I neither liked nor disliked lizards. Ten years before in Ashinoko, when I would see the lizards that often used to gather at the water flowing out of the drain of my inn, I had often felt that, if I were one of them, I wouldn't be able to bear it. I often wondered what I would do if I were reincarnated as a lizard. Every time I saw a lizard in those days such thoughts would enter my mind, so I hated to see them. But I no longer had such thoughts. I only wanted to scare the lizard into the water. He seemed to begin to move, waddling his body awkwardly from side to side. Still crouching, I picked up a stone the size of a small ball and threw it. I wasn't particularly aiming at the lizard. In fact, it didn't even occur to me that I might hit him – even if I had tried, it would have been a very difficult shot, especially for someone like me, who was so poor at throwing things. The stone struck something with a sharp sound and then fell into the stream. At the same time as I heard the stone striking, the lizard seemed to fly about four inches sideways. He curled his tail and lifted it up high. I wondered what had happened. At first I didn't think the stone had hit him. His curled-up tail quietly and naturally uncurled again. He seemed to brace himself so as not to slide down the slope. But then he retracted the claws on both his forelegs and fell helplessly forward. His tail lay completely flat against the rock. He no longer moved. He was dead. I felt sorry for what I'd done. Though I had often killed creatures of that sort, what gave me a strange and unpleasant feeling was that I had killed it without intending at all to do so. Although it had happened because of something I'd done, this made it seem all the more a matter of chance. For the lizard it had been a totally unexpected death. I continued squatting there for a while. I felt that now there was only myself and the lizard, I became one with him and felt how he felt. I pitied him, but at the same time shared with him a feeling of the loneliness of all living creatures. By chance I had not died. By chance the lizard had died. I began to feel lonely and finally headed back towards the hotspring inn. It was still light enough for walking on the road. The lights on the outskirts of town became visible in the distance. What had happened to the dead bee? Probably he had been washed underground by the rain that swept him away. And how about the rat? He'd probably been swept out to sea and by now his bloated body might have been washed ashore with some garbage. And now I, who had not died, was walking along like this. Such were my thoughts. I felt that I should be grateful. But in reality no feeling of joy arose within me. Living and dying were not polar opposites. I felt there was not so much difference between them. By now it had grown rather dark. Only the distant lights were dimly visible. Unable to see where I was stepping, I walked forward uncertainly. My mind alone worked on as it pleased. And this led me all the more into those kinds of thoughts and feelings.

I spent three weeks in Kinosaki. More than three years have passed since then. I have been spared at least from getting spinal tuberculosis.

BONFIRE

It rained that day from morning on. All through the afternoon I played cards in my room upstairs with my wife, the painter S., and K. the hotel manager. The smoke-filled room made everyone feel drowsy. By three o'clock we were sick of card-playing and had over-stuffed ourselves with cakes.

One of us stood up and slid open the paper-screen window. At some point the rain had stopped. Chill mountain air charged with the scent of fresh green streamed into the room, driving the tobacco smoke into swirls. We all exchanged glances, as if suddenly coming to life.

'I think I'll go do a little work on the hut', said K., half standing and fidgeting about restlessly with both hands thrust deep into his trouser pockets.

'Maybe I'll go do some painting', said S.

The two of then left together.

Seated on the ledge of the box window, I watched as the white clouds gradually thinned out and a delicate celadon blue spread over the sky. S., with a paint-box slung over his shoulder, and K., with a waist-length overcoat draped over him like a caps, were talking something over as they climbed up towards the hut. They stood and talked for a while longer in front of the hut and then S. went off alone into the woods.

I lay down to read a book.

I had begun to tire of this too when my wife, who was sewing beside me, asked if I wasn't going up to the hut.

The 'hut' was just a small rough shack which young Mr. K. and the old charcoal-maker, Haru, were building for my wife and I to live in.

I climbed up to where they were working and found that they had just finished the outhouse.

'It's turned out a fine piece of work', said K.

I had helped to build it. Even my wife had sometimes lent a hand.

More than half an hour later, S. emerged from the woods, trampling over soggy piles of last year's leaves.

'It's looking good', he said, eyeing the workmanship of the outhouse. 'With the roof extended like that over the sides, it looks just like a regular house'.

'Yes, I thought it would be just a chore to make, but it's turned into something really fine', answered K. with a broad smile.

I had left K. entirely in charge of building our hut. He was interested in the art of building. Not only in its practical aspects - he took great pains over such things as the overall design of a building and the use of materials. So he tried to make our hut as pleasant a place to live in as possible.

A nighthawk cried out with a sharp sound like clappers of hard wood struck together. It was growing dark, so we stopped work.

'We'll have to hurry and make a fence in case the horses and cows climb up here', said Haru, emptying some tobacco embers onto his palm and using them to light a new pipe-full.

'That's right. It would be a nuisance if they chewed all this up before we had finished building it', K. answered.

I laughed at the idea of a house being eaten. On this mountain there wasn't any mud that could be turned into wall plaster, so that even the walls of the hotel had planking over their entire surface. As for the hut, its walls were made of two layers of cheap reed screen, such as charcoal is sometimes wrapped in, with loose straw sandwiched in between.

'Yessir, this here house would make a real feast for the horses and cows, that it would', said Haru is a very serious voice. We all laughed.

Twilight on the mountain always puts one into a mellow wood, especially after a rainfall. And whom, as now, we had been working and paused to observe our day's work while having a smoke, a fleeting kind of joy arose between us.

On the day before it had also cleared up in the afternoon and the twilight had been beautiful. It was made all the more beautiful by a great rainbow that extended all the way from Torii pass to Black Cypress Mountain. We had lingered near the hut for a long time. For a long time everyone had lingered the hut. It was placed among a grove of oaks and we couldn't resist climbing them. Even my wife had wanted to climb up to have a good look at the rainbow, so K. and I had helped her climb to a height of more than twenty feet.

K., my wife and I were all up in one tree and S. was in a tree beside us. S. and K., competing with each other to see who could climb the highest, worked themselves up to a height of thirty-five or forty feet.

'It's as comfortable as an armchair', K. had shouted down to us. He lay face up in a fork of high branches that were conveniently wide-spread and, puffing on a cigarette, he set the branches swaying like great waves.

Finally Ichiya, a feeble-minded boy whose head seemed too big for his body, came up with K.'s second child slung over his back to tell us that it was suppertime. We all climbed down from the trees. By this time it had grown so dark at ground level that, without a lamp, we couldn't search for a comb that had fallen from my wife's hair while she was up the tree.

Remembering what a pleasant time we had had together the day before, I suggested to the others that we should go boating on the lake that night. They all readily agreed. Having gone our separate ways to eat supper, the four of us not later in front of the big sunken fireplace in the hotel lobby. K. dissolved some condensed milk for his baby in a large kettle hung over the fire, then went into the ice room and emerged carrying a thick a thick oak plank.

We passed through the dark precincts of a Shintō shrine that was hidden among tall fir trees. When we came to the front of the ceremonial hall, K. spoke in a friendly manner to a man who was selling good-luck charms: 'Say, the hot water's ready if you feel like a bath.'

We could see the silvery glitter of the lake's surface between the trunks of two stout fir trees.

The boat was half drawn up onto the beach. While K. drained off the water which had collected from the afternoon rains, the other three of us stood waiting on the sands, which had turned black from the wet.

'Please get in', said K., placing the thick plank he had brought with him across the boat. My wife boarded first, then S. and I. K. pushed the boat off.

It was a tranquil evening. Some faint after-glow of the sunset still remained in the western sky. But the mountains on all sides were black, and I thought they resembled the backs of crouching water lizards.

'Black Cypress Mountain looks very low, doesn't it', said S. from the prow of the boat.

'Yes, mountains seem lower at night', answered K., who was sculling quietly at the stern with his single oar.

'Someone's made a bonfire', said my wife. We which led to the bark of Bird Island. Reflected as it was in the calm water, we saw it double.

'Strange at this time of night', said K. 'It might be a bracken-gatherer camping out. There's an old kiln for charcoal-making over there and he might be sleeping in that. Shall we go see?'

Putting more force into his scudding, K. pointed the bow of the boat towards the fire. He told us of the time he had once swum alone from Bird Island to the Shintō shrine. He had been startled to pass a snake that was also swimming across the lake.

As K. had surmised, the bonfire was burning outside the entrance of the charcoal burner's kiln.

'Is there really someone inside there, K.?', asked S.

'Probably. But if there isn't, we shouldn't leave without putting the fire out first, so we'd better go and check anyway'.

'I'd like to go and see too', said my wife.

We reached the shore. S. jumped out first, holding a rope, and pulled the boat up between two rocks.

K. squatted down in front of the kiln and kept peering inside. 'He's asleep'.

It was quite chilly so everyone was glad of the bonfire. Scraping some embers out of the fire with a fallen branch, S. lit a cigarette on one of them.

Inside the kiln there was the sound of rustling leaves and of someone groaning in his sleep.

'It must be very warm sleeping in there', said S.

'But the fire will go out eventually, so if he sleeps right through he'll be pretty cold towards morning', said K., building up the fire with fallen branches.

'Won't he suffocate, with the fire so close to the kiln?'

'It's alright as long as the fire's not actually inside', said K 'But what does happen with these kilns is that when they get too old they sometimes cave in, They're especially dangerous after it rains'

'How terrible! Perhaps you should warn that man inside', said my wife. 'Yes, we'd better warn him', added S.

'No need to bother', replied K. with a laugh. 'We've been talking in such loud voices that I'm sure he's heard every word we've said.

The sound of dry leaves being rustled about came again from inside the kiln. Everyone burst out laughing.

'Shall we go', said my wife suddenly in a somewhat uneasy voice.

When we got back to the boat, S. boarded first. 'This time I'll row', He said.

From Bird Island to the mainland, the water was especially calm. Looking over the sides of the boat, we could see below us a perfect mirror image of the clear, star-filled sky.

'Shall we make another bonfire on this side?' asked K.

Characteristically, S. whistled the 'Blue Danube' as he rowed.

Where should we land?' he asked K.

'Keep going straight ahead'.

For no particular reason, we all remained silent for a while. The boat moved forward quietly.

'Can you swim from here to shore?' I asked my wife.

'I wonder. Perhaps I could.'

'Can you swim, ma'am?' asked K., seemingly surprised. 'About what time of year can go swimming around here?' I asked K.

As long as it's a fairly warm day, you can go swimming even now. In fact, I went swimming about this time last year.'

'It seems a little cold', I said, dipping my hand into the water. 'But when I spent a few days viewing the autumn leaves around Ashino Lake a while ago, I went swimming there early one morning and it wasn't as cold as I thought it would be. I have even gone swimming there in early April'.

'My, you were really something in the old days', said my wife teasingly, knowing full well how I am usually so sensitive to cold.

'Would it be alright to land here? S. asked.

'This'll be fine', replied K.

S. put three or four times more strength into his rowing. There was a scraping sound as the bow of the boat touched the sandy shore.

We all stepped out and stood on the beach.

'With everything so wet will we be able to make a fire? asked my wife.

'We'll use white birch bark as kindling', answered K. 'Even if it's wet it burns well because it has oil in it. I'll go collect some firewood , so why don't the rest of you gather up some bark'.

To collect materials for the bonfire, we all entered the dark forest. There was everywhere a luxuriant growth of ferns, wild plants, yellow-flowered shrubs and so on. We all went our separate ways but, whenever K. or S. puffed on a cigarette, we could see where they were by the small red glow.

Where the old bark of the white birches was already peeling, its rough edges turned out, it was easy to tear off. Every now and then, the sound of K. snapping off a branch broke the deep silence of the forest.

When we gathered as much as we could handle, we carried it back to the beach. It made quite a pile.

As if frightened by something, K. suddenly came dashing out of the forest. We asked him what was the matter.

'There's one of those worms in there, the ones with the shiny rear-ends, that wiggle their tails like this. They give me the creeps'. K. obviously had a great dread of inchworms. He was breathless. We all went back into the forest to take a look.

'Around here? asked S. from the front, looking round at K. who was now hanging back behind us.

'Don't you see anything shining over there?' asked K.

'Oh yes, I see it now', answered S., striking a match and looking by its light. We saw a more than inch-long caterpillar which was slowly wriggling its relatively large rear-end. Its front part glowed faintly blue.

'Is this really so terrifying?' asked S.

'From now on, because I know those things are around, I won't be able to feel at ease', answered K. and then: 'Everything looks more or less ready, so why don't we light the fire?'

Everyone came out again onto the beach.

When we set fire to the birch back, wet as it was, there arose a smoke as jet-black as lamp soot and then the bark burst into flames.

K. fed the fire with twigs first then gradually added larger branches so that a full-fledged bonfire was soon blazing away. The area around us suddenly grew bright. The firelight was reflected across the water and even onto the trees opposite us on Bird Island.

K. carried the thick oak plank from the boat and placed it down for us sit on.

'Even a man who has grown up in the mountains can be afraid of insects then', said S.

'That's right', said K. 'If I know they're there from the beginning, I can prepare myself. It's when I come upon them unexpectedly that I get a real shock'.

Are there any really dangerous things in these mountains?' asked my wife.

'No, nothing at all', replied K. 'No big snakes?'

'None'.

'How about adders?' I asked.

'I sometimes see them when I go down to Minowa, but I haven't see any up here'.

'Were there any wild dogs about in the old days?' asked S.

'As a boy I often heard them', answered K. 'Sometimes in the middle of the night I heard them howling in distance and I remember it gave me a terrible feeling of loneliness'.

He then told us a story about his father, now dead, who had liked to go night-fishing. One night the wild dogs had surrounded him and, to escape them, he had had to make his way home through the water along the shoreline. And the year when they had first put their horses out to graze on the mountain, he had seen one of them that had been attacked and half-devoured by the dogs.

'That year we put out some meat stuffed with dynamite and, within a week, all the dogs were wiped out'.

I mentioned that, four or five days before, I had seen the skull of a small wild animal towards Hell Valley.

'Must have been a badger', said K. 'It might have been eaten by an eagle or something. A badger is a defenseless creature, you know'.

'So, there's nothing really dangerous on this mountain then'. my fainthearted wife said with emphasis.

'Well, ma'am, I once saw a giant', answered K. with a laugh.

'I know all about that', said my wife in a triumphant tone. 'Wasn't it your own shadow reflected in the mist?'

My wife herself had had this experience early one morning when we went to view the 'sea of clouds' below Torii Pass.

'No, it wasn't that'.

The story was that K., as a child, was coming home from Hebashi one night when he saw this thing in a large pine grove about eight kilometers past Kogure. An area about three hundred meters in front of him glowed with a vague light and a black figure over two meters high moved within it. But when he walked further on he came across a man with a large pack on his back resting by the roadside, and he realized that it had been this man , occasionally striking a match to light a cigarette as he walked along, whom he had taken for the giant within the halo of light.

'Mysteries usually turn out that way, don't they?, said S.

'But I think there are some real mysteries', said my wife. 'I don't know about giants and such but I believe, for instance, that things are sometimes revealed to us in dreams'.

'Well, that's something else again now, isn't it', said S. And then, as if suddenly remembering something: 'Say, K.-san, that story about when you were trapped in the snow last year, that's pretty mysterious, isn't it.' And, turning around to me: 'Have you heard about that yet?'

'No, I haven't'.

'Yes, that was really quite strange', said K. And he proceeded to tell the story.

That previous winter, at a time when two or three feet of snow had piled up on the mountain, K. had received news of the serious illness of his elder sister in Tokyo, and so had suddenly to go down the mountain. But it turned out that his sister's illness was not so bad as was thought, so K. stayed with her only three nights and returned home earlier than expected. When he arrived at Mizunuma, it was only about three o'clock. He had planned to climb the mountain the following day but, since it was a were ten kilometers home, he didn't really feel like staying the night and soon changed his plans. Thinking that he would go as far as the foot of the mountain anyway and then decide whether to climb or not, he left Mizunuma.

Dusk had just settled as he approached the second of the series of Shintō archways at the foot of the mountain. There was ample moon light and he left no tiredness in either body or mind. He decided to climb.

But the snow grew deeper and deeper the higher he climbed. It had grown to abut twice the depth it was when he had descended the mountain a few days before.

In a place where people often walk, even if there is deep snow, the surface hardens so it's not such a problem. But no-one at all had walked here and K. soon found himself waist-deep in soft snow. What's more, it was difficult to know where the trail lay under the uniform surface of the snow, so that even K., who had grown up on this mountain, gradually got lost.

He could see Torii pass just above him in the moonlight. In the summertime this was a thickly forested area but it was winter now and the pass looked very close to him through the bare branches. The snow also made the distance seem shorter. He didn't feel like turning back now, after coming so far, and he crept forward like some tenacious ant. But, in reality, it wasn't so easy to get to that place that seemed close enough to reach out and touch.

If he tried to backtrack now, it would be fine if, by good luck, he was able to retrace his footprints; but if he strayed from these, he would just end up lost again.

When he looked upward, the pass seemed very close. He continued climbing, urging himself on step by step. He didn't feel especially afraid or uneasy. But he felt a certain vagueness encroaching upon his mind.

'Thinking about it now, I know I was in real danger', said K. 'People who die in the snow usually get that way and then they fall asleep. They end up dying in their sleep'.

Strangely enough, even though he had known all this, K. hadn't felt the slightest uneasiness at the time. He had simply resisted the sense of vagueness spreading within him. He was a strong man physically and, as a mountain-dweller, he was used to the snow.

And so, after more than two hours, he finally managed to work his way up to the top of the pass. The snow was even deeper. But from here on he would begin to descend. And once he was down, it would be flat ground all the way home. Glancing at his watch, he saw that it was already past one.

Suddenly he noticed two lanterns shining in the distance. He thought it strange that anyone would be out at this hour. But he was glad to meet up with them in so lonely a place, even if it was only just to pass them by. He roused all his energy and proceeded downward

He met up with the lantern-carriers in the area of the Kakuman pond. It was his brother-in-law, U., and three ice-cutting men who were staying at K.'s inn at that time.

'Welcome back. It must have been rough going', said U. 'Were are you all off to at this time of night?' asked K.

'Mother got us up and told us to come out for you', answered U. in a matter-of-fact tone, as if there was nothing at all strange in this. K. felt a chill run down his spine.

'I hadn't told anyone that I was coming back that day. When I asked for an explanation later, they told me that mother had lain dow n to sleep that night with Mii-chan, my oldest child, in her arms, and perhaps hadn't fallen asleep but, anyway, she had suddenly gone and woke up U. and begged him to go out and meet me, as I was coming back over the mountain. She told him that I had called out to her. She spoke so clearly and firmly that U. hadn't thought to question what she said. He had quickly roused the ice- cutting men and they had all got ready and set out. When I asked about it, it turned out that this was exactly the time when I was most weak and had that slight feeling of vagueness. On the mountain we go to bed early, at seven or eight, so it was just around that time when everyone had fallen into the deepest sleep. Even so, my mother woke up four men and sent them out into the night – so I think she must have heard that call very clearly.'

'And did you in fact call out to her?' asked my wife.

'No, I certainly didn't. Because no matter how hard I had called from the other side of the pass, no-one would have heard me'.

'Of course', said my wife. Obviously she had been very moved by the story. There were tears in her eyes.

'She must have been very sure of what she was doing, to get everyone up like that in the middle of the night and send them out into waist-high snow', continued K. 'Just to get ready on a night like that is quite some trouble. For instance, if you don't roll on your puttees properly and one of them comes loose, it will soon freeze solid like a stick and you won't be able to roll it back on again. So, no matter how they hurried, it would have taken them at least twenty minutes to get ready. During all that time, Mother expressed no doubts at all but just went ahead and made some rice balls and lit the fire'.

If one knew about the relationship between K. and his mother, one was even more deeply moved by this story. I didn't know him very well but K.'s dead father, who was nickname 'Ibsen' because of his resemblance to the playwright, didn't seem a particularly bad man but, to say the least, he didn't amount to much as a husband. They say that he lived most of the time around Maebashi with his young mistress and, come summer, he would bring her with him to the mountain, pick up his earnings from the inn and them leave. K. was deeply upset by his father's behaviour and often clashed with him. And this made K. all the more deeply attached to his mother and his mother all the more deeply attached to him.

For some time now the calls of an owl had been reaching us from Bird Island. 'Go-ro-ske!' it said and then, after a short interval, 'Ho-ko!'

The bonfire was now burning low. K. took out his pocket watch and glanced at it.

'What time is it?'

'It's past eleven'.

'Shall we start back them', suggested my wife.

K. picked a well-charred branch out of the fire and hurled it with all his might far out over the lake. Red sparks scattered from the branch as it went flying through the air. In simultaneous reflection, a branch scattering red sparks went flying through the water. The upper and lower branches described the same arc, one through air, the other through water, until, the instant they came together at the water's surface, they sizzled out and the surrounding area fell back into darkness. The effect was fascinating. The rest of us also began to pick up smoldering branches and hurl them out over the lake. Using the oar, K. skillfully splashed water onto the remaining embers of the bonfire until they were all extinguished.

We boarded the boat. The bracken-gatherer's bonfire across the lake had now also died out. Our boat rounded Bird Island and glided quietly towards the woods around the Shintō shrine.

The calls of the owl grew more and more distant.

MANAZURU

It was year-end on the Izu Peninsula. The sun had set and it was the time of day when the whole of nature seemed tinted blue. A boy of eleven or twelve, a thoughtful expression on his face, was leading his younger brother by the hand along a coastal highroad that overlooked a deep sea. The younger brother was exhausted. Although he was only a child, an ill-tempered frown wrinkled his brow as he trudged reluctantly along. But his older brother was lost in his own reflections. He was agonizing, at that moment, over 'love', although he didn't really know what the word meant.

A strange thing had happened to him once when he was walking along a street behind two teachers from his elementary school. One was a male teacher and the other a young female who had just recently arrived at the school. Suddenly the male teacher had turned around to him:

'Say there, do you understand the meaning of the poem: "My love is a small boat adrift on an ocean of a thousand fathoms / Without haven and tossed about by countless waves"?'

Having said this, he laughed and cast a sideways glance at the lady teacher. She glanced down and remained silent, but her face reddened noticeably.

The boy also had felt strangely embarrassed. It was almost as if the poem referred to him or as if he himself had recited it.

'Well, do you understand or not?' he was asked a second time and, as the lady teacher had done, he just stood there quietly with his head bowed. Then for no particular reason, the image of a small boat swaying gently back and forth in the middle of a vast expanse of ocean appeared like a picture before his mind. But, of course, a boy who did not even know the word 'love' could not understand the meaning of the poem.

He was the son of a fisherman of Manazuru and had a dark complexion and a rather large head. On that large head he was wearing today a sailor's cap so disproportionately small that it looked like a pill-box hat. His flesh was pinched tight by the cap's elastic chin-strap. That a lad of his appearance should have assumed the role of someone 'in agony over love' was certainly strange and incongruous. But to him, no matter how strange or incongruous or even laughable all that was, the sailor's cap itself was not something to be made light of.

He had received some money as a New Year's present from his father today and set out for Odawara with his younger brother to buy wooden clogs for both of them. But before reaching the shop where clogs were sold he had chanced upon a foreign goods store where the sailor's cap was displayed in the window. He had decided on the spur of the moment that he must have it. Without any thought of consequences, he had entered the store and spent all his money.

An uncle of his who had once been a stonecutter at Nebukawa was now a warrant officer in the Navy. The boy had often heard stories of navy life from him. So he was determined to be a sailor himself when he grew up. His uncle had once made fun of the train that went to Atami that looked like it had a small round oven fitted on top of its smokestack:

'What do you think of that', he laughed. 'It's such a small boiler, it's exactly like our kitchen stove at home'.

Since he himself had never laid eyes on any other train, this alone was enough to impress the boy with his uncle's worldly knowledge. And so his sea fever grew all the more intense.

For this reason, there could be no greater joy for him than to own a proper sailor's cap. At the same time, he did feel some remorse. He was sorry for his younger brother who had eagerly come along all that way in the expectation of getting a new pair of clogs. And his spirits sank when he thought how his short-tempered father would react on learning that he had spent all the money on himself alone. Still, he had forgotten about all this when he was walking through the busy, festive town with its New Year's decorations. The two brothers had intended to visit the Ninomiya Santoku Shrine, which they had often heard about, but, while making their way in that direction, they had come upon a boisterous troupe of strolling players at a street corner.

There were three entertainers in all. A half-blind man of about forty was playing a miniature *koto*. A woman who looked to be his wife, her face and hands painted snow-white, was singing in a strangely shrill voice and plucking on a moon-shaped lute. Finally, a girl about his own age, whose face was also marred with thick patches of make-up, was striking small wooden clappers and singing in a high, wailing voice.

The boy was fascinated by the woman playing the lute. Her eyes, already pulled up by her headband, were made to seem even more turned up by the makeup she had applied around the corners. Her narrow, dirty sash of white crepe was fluffed up at the back, tied around as it was by a cord to keep her long sleeves from flapping. He had never known a woman so beautiful or of such sheer whiteness of complexion. He was utterly enraptured and, from then on, followed the troupe wherever it went. Even when they entered some back-alley café, he stood waiting out front like a faithful dog, holding his younger brother's hand.

Out across the open sea the low, lengthening form of the Miura Peninsula now seemed to float in mid-air away from the distant horizon which shone brightly through the dusk. The surrounding land fell into ever darker shadow. A single fishing boat was moored by line ten or twelve yards off-shore. A red beacon burned brightly at its bow as the boat swayed back and forth on the gentle swell. He could hear coming from below the quiet sound of waves washing the shore – and he couldn't help but hear in this the sound of the troupe's *koto* and lute. Of course, if he tried consciously to hear the sound of the waves as nothing but the sound of waves, he could do so for a while. But it was just as if he was half-asleep, trying to wake up, and at some point he was drawn back into his dream and the sound of the waves soon changed again into the sound of the *koto* and the lute. And once more he could hear quite clearly in those dream-like depths the voice of the woman as if she were actually there. 'Plum blossom, plum blossom' – he could even make out some of the words she was singing.

'This is a standard-bearer' – as she sang these words she went through the ceremonial movements of a standard-bearer in a feudal procession: she stretched her arms down in front of her, with her fingers clasped as if around a standard, and, crouching down with her knees spread apart and her head swaying, she stepped forward two or three times. Or else she went through the motions of the *Foundling's Dance*, raising her white-painted hand to cover her eyes in the traditional 'weeping' gesture and pressing a rag doll to her cheeks. As all these images flitted once more before his mind, the boy felt strangely aroused.

Turning back now, he could see the coast of Odawara far behind him through the evening haze. He felt with renewed intensity the distance that lay between the woman and himself. And he wondered what she might be doing at that moment.

He could not imagine anyone whose life he envied more than the young girl who had sung in that shrill, wailing voice. Not that he had felt friendly towards her. When he had stood exhausted outside the café, she had occasionally thrown a sharp, scornful look his way. And finally, while staring in his direction, she had said something malicious about him to the woman, who was at that moment engaged in drinking *saké* with the man. The boy had trembled – but the woman had just glanced his way with a look of complete disinterest and immediately resumed talking with the man. He had felt greatly relieved.

Night was closing in. The beacons burning on the fishing boats began to be visible here and there on the open sea. The whitish half-moon hanging high in the sky had at some time grown brighter. Manazuru was still a good three miles away. Just then the small train to Atami came chugging past the two boys, spewing out sparks the size of large rain-drops. The lamplight that shone dully out of the windows of the two passenger cars flickered across the boys' faces, lighting up their profiles.

After a while the smaller boy, who was dragging his feet a step behind, clutching his older brother's hand, finally piped up and said:

'Those street musicians we saw today, they were on that train'.

The boy heard his own heart thump. He, too, imagined now that he had caught a glimpse of them – but the train had already rounded the tip of the peninsula and he could no longer even hear it.

At this point he finally noticed how exhausted his younger brother was, and he felt a wave of pity for him. He asked him if he was tired, but the younger boy would not answer. He offered gently to carry him piggyback but, instead of answering, the younger brother turned his face away and stared far out over the sea. Somehow he seemed to feel that if he opened his mouth to say anything, he would immediately burst into tears. When he was spoken to in such a gentle manner, he obviously felt this all the more.

'Alright, climb on my back', the boy said, letting go of his younger brother's hand and squatting down in front of him. Without a word, his brother collapsed onto his shoulders.

Fighting to hold back his tears, he pressed his cheek against the older boy's neck and closed his eyes.

'Aren't you cold?' the boy asked.

The younger brother shook his head almost imperceptibly.

The boy began to think of the woman again. When he thought of her being on the train just now, his imagination raced wildly. The train would derail while rounding the sharp curve of the peninsula and go tumbling over the cliff. The figure of the woman lying there, her head smashed against the jagged rocks, arose clearly before his mind. Then he began to imagine that the woman would suddenly rise up before him at the roadside. And he became convinced that she was actually waiting for him somewhere.

His younger brother had at some time or other fallen asleep. He repeatedly shifted upwards the dead weight of the small body on his back, which had suddenly grown much heavier. It became more and more of a strain just to continue walking. His arms felt like they might fall off, but he bore the pain bravely. He felt that it would be wrong not to patiently carry on, although he didn't understand clearly why this was so. He just stuck out his neck like a young turtle and plodded on, step by painful step.

At long last he came to the tip of the peninsula – but nothing happened. As he rounded the bend, though, he suddenly saw a woman holding a lantern and walking towards him. He gasped. The woman spoke to him. It was his mother. Worried that her two boys were so late in returning home, she had come out to meet them.

The younger brother was fast asleep. When the boy went to transfer him to his mother's back, he suddenly opened his eyes. When he saw that his mother was there, all the feelings of self-pity and anger which he had suppressed up to that point suddenly burst forth, and he exploded into an unintelligible tirade of complaint. His mother scolded him but his frenzy only grew wilder. Neither the mother nor the older brother were able to control him. Then the boy suddenly remembered something. He took off his sailor's cap and put it on his younger brother's head.

'Alright, alright, quiet down now. I'll let you have it.'

The boy did not feel so bad now about having bought the cap.

KAKITA AKANISHI

Long ago, a *samurai* going under the name of 'Kakita Akanishi' came as a new retainer to Lord Hyūbu Daté's mansion in the Sendai Hill area of Edo. He was said to be thirty-four or five but anyone would have taken him to be past forty. His looks were on the ugly side and he spoke with a strange provincial accent; he was, in fact, a 'country *samurai*' down to his fingertips – one could almost smell the mud of the rice-fields on him. His accent was not that of Sendai, so everyone thought he was probably from the more northern province of Akita. Actually, it appears that he was born far to the south of this, at Matsue in Unshū Province.

Kakita was a serious worker and would plod along industriously by himself, so that his reputation was generally good. Since his appearance belied his industriousness, however, the younger *samurai*, who were all rather too clever for their own good, made fun of him and used him for whatever purpose they pleased. At such times Kakita did not resist but placidly allowed himself to be used. As the young *samurai* were not so stupid, they sensed that Kakita could see through them and they were not very happy about this. He seemed to know that by agreeing to be used he would make them lose interest. And, sure enough, they all gradually stopped taking advantage of him.

Kakita lived by himself, without servants, in a single room of the *samurai* barracks. He didn't drink or play around with women, so people thought he must be hard put to amuse himself on his days off. As a matter of fact, though, the man was never bored. Rather than drink *saké*, he ate pastries. Whenever the pastryman sought out Kakita, carrying a stack of innumerable shallow boxes piled high on his back and bound together with braided rope, his journey was never in vain. Nevertheless, Kakita was not exactly open-handed, even when buying pastries. He would ask the price of every single item, using his fingers like chopsticks to point first to one, then another, in a confused and unsightly manner.

'My cakes are always the same but this fellow never remembers the prices', the pastryman would think to himself. On days when he was in a bad mood, he would become nauseous with rage. But even if Kakita did know the prices, somehow he didn't feel satisfied unless he asked them at least once again.

The pastry-loving Kakita suffered from stomach and intestinal disorders. As a result, he kept himself well-stocked not only with pastries but with the medicinal plant, green gentian. The odour of this plant always drifted about his room.

Besides pastries, he had one other pleasure in life: *shōgi*, a form of chess, and in this he was uncharacteristically skillful. Even though he was rather circumspect in buying pastries, in playing *shōgi* he would often astonish his opponent with his boldness. Some aspects of his technique were quite sharp – indeed, his opponent would often be made to feel that this couldn't be the same Kakita he had always known. Much as Kakita liked *shōgi*, though, he had no desire to play with anyone else. He preferred rather to play with a book of tactics open on his lap, lining up all the pieces on the board by himself. Placing a paper lantern on the opposite side of the chess board, he would play far into the night. If anyone glanced into his room, it looked for all the world as if he were playing *shōgi* with the lantern. Some of his comrades would poke fun at him by asking: 'Who won at *shōgi* last night, you or the lantern?'

In the Atagoshita area of Edo there was the mansion of another lord from Sendai, one Kai Harada, who kept as his retainer a young *samurai* by the name of Masujiro Ginzamé. He was a lively fellow, as clever as he was handsome, and he had a marked fondness for the pleasures of both wine and women. In appearance and tastes he was very much the opposite of Kakita, but they did have one thing in common – a love for *shōgi*.

One day Kakita had been sent on an errand for his lord to Atagoshita and the two men, apparently having met by chance and having discovered their common interest in *shōgi*, became close friends from that time on.

When people saw the friendship which had sprung up between these very different men, they made remarks such as: 'It's strange what kind of people are attracted to each other'. But really these people did not think it was all that strange.

More than a year passed and nothing out of the ordinary happened. During that time the two friends invariably got together every ten days or two weeks for a game of *shōgi*.

145

Then suddenly a strange rumour arose concerning Kakita. It was said that he had attempted to commit '*hara kiri*'. When people went to see for themselves, sure enough there was Kakita laid out on his back looking only half alive. His good friend Masujiro was beside him, but even he didn't know why Kakita had done it. The doctor said it had taken more than ten stitches to sew his entrails back in.

'He always has nightmares because of his indigestion', someone said. 'Maybe he was having one when he did it, the stupid fellow'.

'That could be. Or he might just have gone out of his mind', someone else said.

Later, the true story of Kakita's attempted suicide was secretly related by a masseur named Anko in the room of an old lady named Ezogiku.

One evening Anko had been called to Kakika's room. He found him lying all curled up like a prawn, groaning in agony.

'I can't bear the pain in my stomach any longer. I don't care if it's massage or acupuncture, but do something fast', he moaned.

Anko applied five or six acupuncture needles right away but it didn't seem to relieve Kakita's suffering at all. He concluded that Kakita must be having stomach cramps, so he tried applying some needles in the area of his solar plexus. But Kakita told him that the pain was more in his lower abdomen. When Anko pressed this area, he said it was more to the right. And when Anko pressed to the right, he said it was more to the left.

'Anyway it hurts all over so you can massage anywhere – but do it as hard as you can', Kakita begged.

Anko began to massage his abdomen gently. He felt some kind of strange swelling – and thought to himself that this sort of thing was not in his line of business.

'It won't do any good unless you press harder', said Kakita angrily.

'It's dangerous to put too much force into an abdominal massage', replied Anko. 'It might even cause volvulus'.

'Volvulus? What on earth's that?'

'That's when a twist develops in your intestines', replied Anko, putting a little more force into his massage. Inexplicably, Kakita's stomach grew more and more bloated. Then his face turned white and he groaned strangely every time he breathed out.

Anko was panic-stricken. Indeed, he had reason to be (although he left this out in relating his story to Ezogiku). When he was young he had once caused a man's death by volvulus because of an ineptly administered stomach massage. The day after he had given the massage he had gone back to see the patient and the man looked then much the same as Kakita looked now. Once things had reached this point, he thought that, even if he sent for a doctor, Kakita wouldn't recover. But he also felt helpless to do anything himself.

'Anyway, this is all a terrible mess', he thought. 'I don't know whether he got this way before or after I started on him but, either way, I'm sure that, from now on, no-one's going to call on me when they need a stomach massage'. Trembling with fear, he then advised Kakita to send for a doctor.

'So I've developed volvulus?' asked Kakita, apparently still in great pain.

'I'm afraid it looks like it', answered Anko.

Kakita glared at him threateningly. Anko was startled, but when Kakita spoke to him it was in a rather gentle voice.

'I want you to tell me the truth, however bad it is'.

Anko nodded.

'This sickness of mine isn't going to be cured even if a doctor treats it?'

Even the usually talkative Anko couldn't bring himself to answer. He said nothing.

Having told the story up to this point, the chatterbox masseur suddenly fell silent. He appeared uneasy for some reason and continued with only a rough sketch of the story, as if holding something back. The gist of it was that Kakita, saying something to the effect that 'it can't be helped', had finally proceeded to cut open his own abdomen and, with Anko's help, had managed to straighten out his own twisted intestine.

(If she had known anything at all about medical science, the old lady would have interrupted at this point to ask how they had managed to deal with the bleeding. But the old lady possessed no such knowledge. Even if we were to suppose that she did know something about it, perhaps she admired Kakita's bravery so much that she didn't think to raise such a question at that particular moment. At any rate, as you will find if you read further, Kakita somehow managed not to develop peritonitis.)

'I've never known such a stout-hearted man', said Anko. And before taking his leave he repeatedly urged the old lady under no circumstances to tell anyone what she had heard, because Kakita had strictly forbidden him to speak of the matter.

One morning two or three days later, the corpse of Anko the masseur was discovered in a place just below Sendai Hill. The wound on his neck indicated that he had been killed by one sword-blow from behind.

On an afternoon a few days after that, Masujiro visited Kakita's bedside. His friend had been progressing well and was now able to speak a little. Lying flat on his back, Kakita looked straight up into Masujiro's eyes and asked in a weak voice: 'Was it you who killed Anko?'

'Of course not', answered Masujiro with a sly grin.

'The poor fellow', said Kakita and, seeming very weary, closed his eyes.

More than a week later, Masujiro came again to call on Kakita and the talk turned once more to Anko's murder. Kakita now seemed much livelier and so Masujiro felt free to speak his mind.

'What a fool you were, revealing the whereabouts of a secret document to a chatterbox like that', he chided Kakita with a smile.

'Don't say that. It was only that I couldn't bear the thought of dying without first delivering my report to our lord in Shiroishi. Death is death, I suppose, but it would have been terrible to have died so fruitlessly. It has taken me almost two years to put together that report. I couldn't leave it to rot in the attic along with all the mouse shit!'

'Perhaps you have a point there, but was it right to confide your secret to a fellow like that, of all people?'

'Well, given the situation I was in, who should I have told then?'

'But why did you have to reveal your secret at all? Don't you think I'm capable of doing my job? If I had heard that you had died, I would have rushed over here immediately and, when no-one was looking, somehow or other I would have found your report by myself.'

'Well, if that's so, can you guess right now what part of the attic it's in and how it's hidden?'

'Why do I need to guess? That masseur gave me all the details. By that time your recovery was assured, but still he told me everything. He talked glibly as if he were revealing some great secret and with a smug expression on his face as if he were performing a great service. He talked on and on like he had verbal diarrhoea – there was no stopping him. I thought to myself that if I allowed this fellow to live, he would certainly blabber to other people in the same way – really I had no choice in the matter. Even if you had died and he had carried out your last wish by bringing me your report, I couldn't have let him live, you know'.

'Perhaps you're right'.

'You say "perhaps" and I know you don't really think so now – but if you had died and he had come to me with your report, I would naturally have assumed that you wanted him killed afterwards'.

'I had no such intention. I trusted him to some extent. I knew he was a blabbermouth but I thought he would keep our secret at least until our mission was finished. If only because it was my dying wish'.

'Ah, you're the true gentleman as always', said Masujiro with a somewhat pained expression on his face.

Kakita remained silent. Masujiro, on the other hand, was not the type who could keep quiet on such occasions.

'You're too much of a gentleman for your own good. The fellow almost killed you but still you defend him'.

'But there was a twist in my intestines before he ever laid hands on me. The doctor told me so. He said it's not the sort of thing that can happen so readily during a massage'.

'But probably it got worse much faster because of his incompetence'.

Kakita again fell silent. This time Masujiro also kept quiet. But only for a while.

'Anyway, we've accomplished our mission for the most part, so, if you're feeling better, we should take the first chance we get to report back to Shiroishi'.

'Yes, let's do that'.

More than two months went by. It was the day of the autumn equinox. By this time Kakita had fully recovered. Masujiro was off duty that day so they rented a boat at Tsukiji and went out fishing for mudskippers. In addition to lunch Kakita brought along some cakes and Masujiro some saké. They managed to catch quite a few fish alongside the stone wall of Ohama Palace. However, there were many other boats in the same area so they weren't able to talk freely.

'Well, what do you say, have we caught about enough? Shall we row further out on the lake a little and have our lunch in a more open area?' asked Masujiro, beginning to reel in his several lines.

'Yes, let's do that', answered Kakita, raising up his rod. 'See that mountain over there, the one that looks so high and heavily forested, that's probably Mount Kano'.

'Is that so? If one sips *saké* while viewing such scenery it seems to take on a special flavour. It's too bad my companion is the sort of fellow who prefers to munch on cakes while sightseeing'.

Kakita just laughed.

'But if you don't exercise moderation in eating cakes it could prove fatal, you know. What kind did you bring today? If you eat too many you'll just injure yourself again'.

'Today I've brought some rice crackers'.

'You're just a big baby', said Masujiro and laughed loudly.

When all the fishing gear was packed away, Masujiro rowed the boat out to open water. They tied up to one of the piles that marked out a channel for ships. There were no other fishing boats in the area. In a carefree mood, each man opened his own lunch box.

'By the way, I suppose you're well enough to travel now?' said Masujiro.

'I think I'm recovered, more or less'.

'You didn't feel weak when rowing just now?'

'Not particularly'.

'Well, what do you say, then – shouldn't we start getting ready to return to Shiroishi? My own report is pretty well ready'.

'If your report is ready, perhaps you should return ahead of me – although mine is almost ready too'.

'But perhaps I should stay and observe Harada's activities a while longer'.

'Maybe so'.

'Anyway, once you've decided on the day of your departure, I'll bring you my report shortly before you leave'.

'It's alright to travel but what excuse should I give for taking time off?'

'If you formally ask for time off, they might raise objections'.

'Well then, should I steal away in the night? But it would be dangerous not to give them some reason for my departure. It would be risky for you, too, who would be left behind here'.

'In any case, the trouble is that Harada's a clever fellow. It would be a disaster if we were to give him the advantage by our own bungling.... The problem is how to make your night-time escape look more natural'.

Kakita didn't feel that such detailed planning fell within his sphere. Having decided that he would leave all that to Masujiro, he didn't think about it too deeply.

'Anyway, you'll have to do something that will compromise your honour, something that will make you ashamed to face other people', said Masujiro, glancing at Kakita with a malicious smile.

'You mean something that will sully my honour as a *samurai*?'

'Yes, I mean something that will sully your honour as a *samurai*', repeated Masujiro cheerfully.

'Don't tell me I have to become a thief – anything but that'.

'Yes, perhaps thievery would do the trick'.

'If anyone chased me I'd soon get caught, you know'.

'It wouldn't be so bad if someone chased you, but you'd probably get caught before you even laid hands on anything'.

They both laughed.

Kakita ate his lunch in silence. Masujiro, on the other hand, fell into deep thought – while sipping his *saké*, popping salty tidbits into his mouth and occasionally pausing to admire the wide sweep of scenery.

'How's this?' he suddenly burst out enthusiastically, slapping his thigh. 'You'll send a love letter to some woman. Understand? Anyone's fine but the more beautiful the better, and also it would work better if she's haughty and proud. You'll send a declaration of love to her. Unfortunately, of course, you'll be rejected. You'll be the laughingstock of everyone. Having lost face in such an embarrassing way, you'll find that you're unable to remain at the mansion. So you'll escape in the night.... Perfect, isn't it? If we base our plan on your losing face, we're sure to succeed. How does the idea strike you? Probably you know someone among the ladies-in-waiting. But remember, an old one would be useless for our purposes. Old ladies sometimes have eccentric tastes or even lack a sense of shame – if she's that sort our plan might backfire. At any rate, she has to be a young one with a taste for higher things'.

Kakita thought to himself that here was a man who said some pretty indelicate and uncouth things. But he wasn't angry.

'Well, I suppose it would be better than stealing', he said in an indifferent tone.

'It's not just "better" – I assure you that you won't find a more brilliant idea. Anyway, can you think of an appropriate woman? I know you're usually rather backward in that area but. . . .'

Kakita did not answer.

'There must be some girl who's often gossiped about among young people'.

'Well, there's a very beautiful lady-in-waiting by the name of Sazaé'.

'Sazaé? If you've been eyeing her, you're not quite so backward as I expected. Hmm, I see. Well, if you choose Sazaé, there is even less doubt that my plan will succeed'.

Kakita had not harboured any feelings of love for Sazaé up to that point. But he was aware of her beauty. And he was also aware that hers was a very pure kind of beauty. He felt that for him now to send her a love letter, even as a means to some serious end, would be a perverse and terrible thing to do.

'Let's choose some other lady-in-waiting, not Sazaé.'

'No, that wouldn't do. That wouldn't do at all. Don't give in to sentimentality, now.'

Kakita wasn't sure what Masujiro meant by 'sentimentality', but he was sure that to write such a letter to Sazaé would be a perverse thing to do, like putting a stain on something perfect, and he didn't feel like doing it at all. However, if a young and beautiful girl was necessary for the success of Masujiro's plan, he could not think of any but Sazaé. So finally he became resigned to the inevitable and agreed to use her.

'Alright then', he said, 'will you make me a draft of the love letter?'

'No, you'll have to write it yourself. If I write it, it'll be my love letter. Since it'd be Sazaé I was writing to, I couldn't help but put too much of my own feeling into it, and the girl might easily be won over.'

Kakita smiled wryly. And thought to himself that if he, rather than Masujiro, wrote the letter, perhaps he might be able to finish the whole business without sullying Sazaé.

A wind was blowing up so they took the boat back in. As the Sendai mansion was right on his way home, Kakita stopped off to visit with Masujiro. The two men matched wits over a game of *shōgi*, their first in a long while.

152

It was the first unusually cold night of autumn. Kakita sat in his own quiet room, warming his hands over the meager heat of an *hibachi*, and, with a sheet of cheap writing paper spread before him, thinking on into the night. He wore a deadly earnest expression on his face and now and then, as if deeply perplexed, he scratched the shaven part of his pate with the hand which held his writing brush.

He began to write. But, however hard he tried, he couldn't seem to make a good job of it. His calligraphy was excellent but the sentences themselves were no good. They had a strange kind of sincerity but were totally lacking in grace or style.

'There's never been a love letter like this one', he said to himself, smiling wryly. He tried to remember how love letters were written in illustrated romances, but couldn't remember the exact phraseology. He couldn't think what else to do, so he tried to imagine himself as a handsome *samurai* of about twenty as in the pictures in those books. He closed his eyes and applied all the force of imagination at his command . . . and he did manage to get a little of the feeling. But as soon as he opened his eyes again he saw before him his own dark, hairy, uncouth hands. He was stumped.

Still he found it difficult to write. He guessed that if he were writing to any other woman than Sazaé then perhaps he might have been able to write with great fluency. Then it occurred to him that he might give up the idea of writing a love letter and talk to her directly. But that seemed to him even more difficult. And he thought to himself that it would have been far better, after all, if he had been able to persuade Masujiro to write the letter that afternoon in the boat.

His spirits sank when he imagined Sazaé's surprise and discomfort on receiving a love letter from him. But he reproved himself for harboring such feelings and set to work on a new draft. It still didn't satisfy him. It sounded too bluntly honest and wouldn't give anyone the impression of a man agonizing over love. Here, thought Kakita, was the real conundrum.

In any case, he should not cling to the idea that he was trying to fabricate a fictional love letter. Rather, he should be able to write directly from the heart, with deep, spontaneous feeling. Having so concluded, he tried, regardless of how impossible it seemed, to induce in himself a feeling of love towards Sazaé. He tried to submerge himself completely in the role of a man burning with passion for her. Finally he managed to achieve such a state, more or less. Before he had a chance to cool down, he quickly let loose with his writing brush.

But he had only written a little when his ardour began to cool and he was stumped again. Nevertheless, the parts of the letter in which he appealed for sympathy for his own ugliness were not based on any falsehood and so had a true feel about them. Anyway, he had written a kind of love letter and he was sure that he could do no better. He read it over once more, then rolled it up carefully, sealed it and, as if it were some important document, hid it away in his desk drawer. Then finally he was able to go to sleep.

Next morning he went up to the mansion earlier then usual. Trying to be as inconspicuous as possible, he stood in the main hallway, in a state of great perturbation, waiting for Sazaé. Though he couldn't understand why, he felt a strange palpitation in his chest. Even though he wished to suppress it, he didn't know where to apply force in order to do so. As soon as he spotted Sazaé, and before the chance escaped him, he would have to hand her the letter. He buried his hand that was clutching the letter between the folds of his *hakama*. He could feel it getting wet from the sweat of his hand.

He felt extremely nervous, as if he were waiting to meet some powerful, intimidating person. He tried to convince himself that such was not the case, and that he must face up to this as a mission which it was his duty as a *samurai* to accomplish. But he couldn't help thinking that Sazaé's beauty, in contrast to his own ugliness, definitely put her in the stronger position and him in the weaker one. In relations between the sexes beauty and ugliness easily become the equivalent of strength and weakness, and Kakita in particular felt the reality of this very deeply. The resulting pressure seemed unendurable to him. Unable to calm down, he kept walking in and out of a vacant side-room off the hall.

At last the moment arrived. He felt a jolt through his whole body. Then, surprisingly, he became quite calm. He behaved not at all like someone handing a letter to his love.

'Please have a look at this', he said and, staring with a stern expression straight into Sazaé's face, handed her the letter.

Sazaé was somewhat startled but took the letter anyway. 'Does this require an answer?' she asked.

'Yes please', answered Kakita, although he didn't really expect one.

Sazaé bowed and walked on. Kakita breathed a sigh of relief. The thought that he had now accomplished his mission put him into a rather cheerful mood. He wondered whether things would come to a head today, or perhaps tomorrow, and thought that he would soon have to make ready for his escape. But the day passed and nothing happened.

The next day arrived. As Kakita didn't really expect an answer, he didn't particularly seek out an opportunity to receive one: so again the day ended with nothing having happened. He thought this strange. He worried that perhaps Sazaé, in order not to expose his shame, had crumpled up his letter and thrown it away, pretending that it was nothing. Since she was, in fact, mature beyond her years, this might well have happened. If so, thought Kakita, it would present a problem.

The third day also passed in this way. He still had found no chance of meeting with Sazaé alone. He recognized later that he had, in fact, unconsciously avoided such a chance. He had met Sazaé in front of some other people but she behaved as if nothing at all had passed between them. In the depths of his heart, Kakita was impressed by this. But he thought that he could not allow things to go on in this way.

So he conceived a new plan which, much to his regret, required him to write another love letter and drop it somewhere where someone would find it.

That night he sat down to write again. He tried his utmost to write in such a manner as to cause Sazaé the least possible amount of pain. He explained that he understood her refusal to answer as an act of kindness, an attempt to save him from being shamed: 'Confronted by such a fine compassion, I feel that I cannot allow myself to write you yet another letter of this kind. But I find that, however I try, I simply cannot give up the idea', etc. etc. Kakita broke into a cold sweat when he thought how the young *samurai* would laugh on reading this.

When he entered the mansion the following day, he immediately went and dropped the letter beside a paper lantern in a corner of the main hallway. More than an hour later he casually passed by again to take a look. The letter was gone. Feeling a strange mixture of relief and misery, he had just turned to go when he saw Sazaé coming towards him alone. Automatically he lowered his eyes. Trying to slip by as if he hadn't seen her, he felt a touch on his hand. Suddenly he was holding something. It was a thick letter.

On returning to his room that evening, he hurriedly turned up the wick of his lamp and opened the letter. He had not expected an answer at all. There were two letters, one of which she had written on receiving Kakita's first letter, but had found no chance of giving to him. Its contents were roughly as follows:

> I cannot say that I have ever felt any love towards you but I have, for some time, held you in the highest regard. It has occurred to me that, before long, the question of my marriage would arise but I have not thought of it in regard to any one of the young *samurai* who presently reside at this mansion. And, up to now, I have not thought of it in regard to yourself, either. This was because I could not associate you with the idea of marriage. I hope you will not understand this in a bad sense.
>
> I am a merchant's daughter. Within a year or a year and a half, I shall be expected to return to my parents' house. I have always assumed that eventually I would have to marry into another merchant's family. But now, having received your letter, I am confronted by a new problem. I have thought much about it. A new feeling has arisen within me. I have always felt a certain respect for you. Now this has suddenly become clearer. I have become aware, for the first time, that what I have always unconsciously wanted in a man are those qualities to be found in you. I have also come to understand that the reason why I was somehow dissatisfied with the so-called 'handsome young *samurai*' was that they lacked those qualities. When I received your letter my own preferences became clear to me for the first time. Now I am happy.
>
> However, you seem to do nothing but worry about your appearance and so forth – this is unworthy of you. Certainly I do not think badly of you for this, but really such worries are groundless. I beg you not to speak of such things anymore. I feel a great happiness in my heart....

And so on and so forth. This was roughly what she wrote, but her own words were more beautiful and written with more alluring womanly sentiment.

In the second letter, written later, she said she didn't understand why he had avoided all opportunities of receiving her answer and she repeatedly chided him for this. After that she wrote in detail of such practical questions as what should be their next step, etc. And she said she was thinking of revealing everything to her parents on her next day off, which was coming quite soon.

Kakita's face reddened. His heart-beat quickened. He remained, for a while, in a kind of trance. He couldn't make up his mind whether or not to believe what he had read. A strange new feeling had arisen within him, one that he had not felt until five minutes before. He no longer knew how old he was. The reason was that he had once felt the same kind of strange feeling when he was twelve or thirteen years old and living in Matsue. At that time the girl had responded with a derisive laugh and he had ended up miserable and disillusioned. Since then he had lost all confidence in himself – though Kakita would simply say that he 'knew himself' – and until today he had not been visited again by such a feeling.

He began to feel as if he were in a dream. But then he remembered the love letter he had dropped that morning – and felt a jolt. He asked himself what he should do. He felt that he could no longer endure all this strain. He considered himself a complete idiot. Though he could try to excuse himself by saying that his motives were good, still the fact remained that he had taken advantage of the highest human feelings in order to fabricate a ruse. How had he forgotten his respect for such higher things? And how could he compensate for what he had done? Puzzling over such questions, he grew extremely heated.

The night grew late. Kakita went to bed but couldn't sleep. He still kept asking himself how he had got into such a mess. He concluded that it could no longer be helped. Having already dropped the letter in the mansion hallway, he decided that he could do nothing but wait and see what happened next and be guided by that.

Gradually he calmed down. He reminded himself again of his duty as a *samurai*. He felt as if he were waking from a dream. It would be inexcusable, he thought, for him to become preoccupied with his own personal affairs in an important case like this, when the destiny of the fifty-four counties of the province of Sendai was at stake. Now was a time when he must harden his heart. At any rate, he must carry out his mission to the end. Sazaé too would understand this later. It was not as if he wouldn't be able to set things right with her and revive their relationship once everything turned out successfully. If such a happy time did come, then she would understand everything.... Though he tried to reassure himself in this way, Kakita still was left with a somewhat desolate feeling. But he lay feeling this way only a few moments before falling asleep.

Next morning he went at his usual hour to attend to his duties at the mansion. His face was paler than usual. He felt somehow unwell. And yet he felt excited.

After a while a message came from the old lady, Ezogiku, asking him to come to her room for a moment. Kakita went, looking thoroughly depressed. Since this seemed entirely appropriate to the situation, he didn't try to put on a cheerful front.

After clearing her maid servants out of the room, the old man handed Kakita his letter. The seal had been broken.

'You're lucky it was me who picked it up. What would you have done if someone else had found it?' she said in a scolding tone.

Nevertheless, the old lady too had a soft spot for Kakita. Especially since his 'attempted suicide', her admiration for him had grown even more, so that she honestly felt that it would be regrettable for such a *samurai* to be hurt by such a thing. She softened her tone and, telling Kakita that she would forget that she had ever found his letter, she implored him to continue working diligently as he had always done. She herself would, without fail, get the other letter back from Sazaé when a good opportunity presented itself. And she admonished him even more earnestly about his future.

Kakita didn't utter a word. He wondered why everyone he met with was so good, not realizing that his own good character was reflected from their hearts. Lord Hyōbu himself was a bad man but there were good people living in his mansion and when Kakita thought how he must work for their downfall he was left with a rather desolate feeling.

Excusing himself by saying he was sick, Kakita returned to his room. It was too late now anyway, he thought to himself, to alter the course of events. He wrote a note to leave behind for Ezogiku:

> Forgetting my own age, I have succumbed to a foolish infatuation. I am truly ashamed of myself. Having lost so much face, I cannot bring myself to meet you again. Things have reached the point where I can neither forget Lady Sazaé nor continue to carry out my duties in the usual manner. In truth, I can no longer put up with myself.

This was roughly what he wrote.

Kakita then removed his own and Masujiro's secret reports from the attic and hid them within the folds of his *kimono*. He waited until late that night and then slipped quietly out of the mansion. Then he hastened towards Shiroishi.

His note came into Ezogiku's hands on the following day. She thought it unfortunate that he should run away but that it was too late to do anything about it. She couldn't just leave things like that though, so she went and showed the note to Lord Hyōbu. He had a great laugh over it and some *samurai* who happened to be present joined in his hilarity. To them the most humorous thing of all was the contrast between Kakita and Sazaé. It was a funny story indeed but, as a matter of fact, people had been wondering lately why Sazaé seemed so noticeably tired and troubled.

Sazaé herself was puzzled by Kakita's behaviour. But she was not stupid. She guessed that there must be some reason behind it all. She bore her heart's suffering alone, not revealing her secret to anyone. When Ezogiku asked to see the first letter Kakita had written to her, she replied that she had already burned it. Soon after she actually did throw it into the fire. So the affair of Kakita and Sazaé was only enough to provoke a moment's laughter and that was all that remained of it.

One day a short while later Kai Harada came to visit the mansion. He and Hyōbu retired to a teahouse in the garden and had a confidential talk together, away from public view. When their business was finished they both returned to the main house and joined everyone in a drinking party. Then, just to make small talk, Hyōbu told the story of Kakita and Sazaé. At first Harada laughed along with Hyōbu. But gradually his face clouded over. Finally he seemed to be in an extremely bad humour.

He asked Hyōbu to come with him again to the teahouse. The two of them went out for another tête-à-tête. After a while they called in Ezogiku and Sazaé. Sazaé was ruthlessly interrogated by Harada. She thought that now she had no choice but to tell the truth and she calmly proceeded to do so. Harada's expression grew more and more sullen.

Sazaé was immediately sent back to her parent's place, where she was kept under close watch. Ezogiku was retired from service at her own request.

Shortly after there occurred the so-called 'Daté Family Feud' of the sixteen-sixties and 'seventies. The troubles lasted a long time and finally ended, as is well known, in the defeat of Kai Harada and his fellow conspirators.

After things had settled down again, Kakita changed back to his real name and went looking for the man whose alias had been Masujiro. He couldn't find the slightest trace of him and so assumed that his friend had been secretly assassinated by one of Harada's henchmen.

It would be satisfying to be able to write how the love story of Kakita and Sazaé finally turned out, but it is difficult to investigate ancient matters in modern times. So it remains a mystery.

THE DIARY OF CLAUDIUS

–day

He is a man of rare talents. Not only does he possess a wide and deep understanding but he is also a poet. Before long I must talk everything over with him, so that I may win him over to my side. I won't mind revealing everything to him. But it is not yet the time. At the moment he is too upset. And of course it is the same with me. Having married my older brother's wife and assumed his crown so soon after his death – if only because of such a drastic change in my life, somehow I cannot yet return to the rhythms of normal everyday living. Still more because a love cherished for so long, and the joy which arises from that love – a love for which I had given up all hope – also makes it difficult for me to maintain my composure.

At the moment, I am trying hard to hide these feelings of mine from others. This is not because I'm ashamed of what I feel or of what I've done. It is simply that I realize that there are people who disapprove of my feelings. Not only do I realize this, but I can also sympathize with them.

Besides, he himself is the first among those people. It's a great pity that he seems somehow so melancholy and out of sorts lately. Not only that, but he seems to disapprove of me in some way. I can sympathize with that also. My ability to appreciate the feelings of others is my one and only hope for reaching an understanding with him. I must be as careful as possible not to lose this capacity.

–day

I do not feel at all ashamed of what I've done. But from a conventional point of view, it really wasn't a very respectable thing to do. During the next few months at least, I shall be tossed continually between joy and sorrow.

161

There can be few people whose moods are more governed by external circumstances than mine. When I try to control this tendency, I always fail. Rather, I have no choice but to surrender to it, all the while trying to manage my affairs as best I can.

In any case, this isn't the time to talk things over with him. I'm not in the mood yet. If our talk went badly now, the split between us would become forever irreparable.

When I met him a while ago, he had a very strange expression on his face. 'Aren't you well?' I asked. He answered in a most unpleasant way. He's a rather childish man. He displayed his hostility towards me in a really childish, vulgar way. I must always beware not to be drawn into that kind of childishness myself. In any case, I'm glad he's given up the idea of returning to the University of Wittenberg. Parting under these circumstances would probably widen the gap between us until finally it became unbridgeable.

I can't possibly love him the way his mother does. It's only natural that I don't wish to do so. Even if it were possible, he is no longer the sort of person who would accept such love – and, anyway, that doesn't matter. What matters now, rather than love, is mutual understanding. If we could only understand each other, then love might follow.

–day

... I sent for him two or three times but he didn't come. Of course, we didn't put on tonight's banquet just for his sake, but when I saw that the seat prepared for him next to me was vacant right to the very end, I began to imagine all kinds of things and, no matter how much I drank, my spirits sank lower and lower until I could hardly bear it. When old Polonius tried to cheer me up, all it did was make me feel even more depressed. How bravely I sat through to the end, enduring that empty seat!

'It is better to violate rather than respect this custom of having banquets. Foreigners call the men of this country pigs because they wallow in such customs' – he is reported to have said this before going off somewhere with his friends. Even though he declined my invitation to tonight's banquet, the first of my reign, with such rude remarks, I must not show any anger. But this need to suppress my anger has made me feel even more depressed. Still, I must not take too seriously words which only express his present bad mood. Perhaps, for instance, he is disgruntled because his father's funeral was not mounted with sufficient pomp.

Anyway, we must talk everything over together before long. I mustn't hold anything back, even the fact that I have loved his mother since before he was born. Undoubtedly this will not make him happy. But I must tell him everything in order to clear up all misunderstandings. For this also the time must be right. Otherwise he won't understand half of what I say. I'll wait for the right moment.

My wife seems to want to give him some advice. But whatever one says to him now, one is only argued into silence. He is far more grown-up than my wife imagines.

–day

All last night I felt somehow uneasy. However hard I tried, I couldn't get to sleep – even though I was dead tired. Even now I have an unpleasant sensation in the pit of my stomach. Perhaps I've been putting too much strain on my mind again. Without my realizing it, my mind has been overworking lately. This has probably worn out my nerves. But last night even the weather too helped to create a sinister atmosphere. A violent wind kept shaking the windows. I had drunk too much and my head was throbbing with pain. Thinking to cool it off, I got up and opened the shutters. The instant I went to open them, I noticed through the crack between the two shutters a small sphere shining vaguely white and drifting off with a puff into the night. I imagined that this was caused by my suddenly looking out into the darkness from a bright room.

It was so cold outside that I couldn't stay at the open window for even thirty seconds. It was also so windy that my lamp seemed about to be blown out. I closed the shutters. Suddenly I saw the same luminous object as before – or rather I felt it more than saw it. The thing that had flown away flew back again with a puff, right up to the crack between the shutters, and hovered there, peeping through into the room. That's what I felt, and it was somehow a weird and dreadful feeling.

Recently I feel as if I have been placed under some kind of curse. No doubt this is all the product of my own physical condition. In any case, I have my work to do. I can't afford to bother about such things. I can't go anywhere as yet but soon, I think, I might want to go hunting wild boar.

–day

This morning Polonius came, as if on some urgent business, to inform me that the prince seems to be in love with the old man's daughter, Ophelia. He told me that I wasn't to worry about it, as he had lectured his daughter at great length about the dangers involved.

I too have sensed that he is in love with the girl. She is such a feminine, intelligent girl that I have even felt attracted to her myself. It wouldn't be wise for me to oppose the match as steadfastly as the old man does. I didn't say anything about it today but, to be honest, I hope he feels that love profoundly, in the depths of his heart. If he does, then I expect that out of that experience will grow some degree of understanding of my own love for his mother.

The old man takes the prince's love as a rather frivolous thing. That's a pity. Without much grounds for thinking so, the old man is under the illusion that he has tasted all the joys and sorrows of life. And so, whatever the problem is, he thinks he can quickly understand it and quickly solve it all by himself. But really he is not an understanding sort of person at all. Moreover, the prince is not the frivolous youth the old man takes him to be.

My health is usually fine during the winter but this year it's a little strange. The changes in my life have no doubt upset me both mentally and physically. Considering this, too, I think I should try to come to an understanding with him as soon as possible.

My good wife's attitude towards me is exactly the same as it was towards my older brother when he was alive. Only a bad person could feel dissatisfied with such a peaceful, feminine nature. I have often thought recently that I would like to make that peacefulness of hers reign all through my house.

Polonius came to me again just now with the following story: his daughter was doing some needlework in her room yesterday when the prince entered pale-faced, hatless, with his coat open at the chest. Suddenly he grasped the girl by her wrist and gazed long and hard into her face. He shook her arm lightly and nodded his head two or three times. Then he sighed deeply and made his exit without a word, all the while looking back towards the girl. The old man described all this with theatrical gestures, as if he had been present himself, and offered it as conclusive proof that the prince has been driven mad by love.

But somehow I can't believe it.... And yet, perhaps something of the kind did happen. Indeed, in some ways the prince has more of a tendency towards melodrama than the old man, so that whatever did happen was perhaps merely a display of this.

–day

The old man came to show me a letter written to his daughter by the prince. He seems, as always, determined to attribute the prince's disorder to love. Still more he seems determined to convince me of his own astuteness, chattering on glibly about how his daughter has obeyed his will by completely repulsing all the young man's advances. But there are reasons why I can't accept his version of the story at face value. First among these are the extremely disgruntled looks the prince has been casting my way for the past two or three days. They were somehow the looks of a man harbouring some secret, malicious design. While those eyes stared at me fixedly as if placing a curse on me, I felt as though I were losing my very inner freedom. Suddenly I remembered that small luminous object which had peeked through the crack between the shutters into my room last night.

They were definitely not the eyes of a man in agony over love. I have noticed that he sometimes directs the same kind of look at his mother. Perhaps I am wrong but his mother seems to regret that she married so soon after his father's death. If my suspicion is correct, then those looks of his no doubt caused her much distress. My wife seems to believe that this is the reason for his madness. To think of this now causes me intolerable anguish.

But I don't blame her. I am well acquainted with her good and vulnerable nature. I have no choice but simply to resign myself to our misfortune as a *fait accompli*. All will be well if I simply cling firmly to the conviction I've had from the beginning, that I have no reason to regret what I've done.

As I cannot accept the old man's story at face value, he has suggested that we try to arrange for the prince and his daughter to meet as if by chance in a passageway off the Great Hall when there is no one else about. Eavesdropping is not really to my taste but I have agreed to his plan for now.

–day

I am not at all ashamed of my present marriage. If I had felt even the slightest shame, my character is such that I couldn't have gone through with it. However much I loved her, if I had married her without being convinced that it was the right thing to do, I would have been little better than a criminal. And I would have been a fool too. But my heart felt more than ready for what I was about to do. I was able to so boldly propose marriage exactly because I felt this way, and, when I was accepted, to announce it so quickly to the whole world. And even when I made the announcement, I added no apologies, as this would have just given an impression of irresolution. I felt that I myself could see in this my own impregnable self-confidence. But perhaps there was a point of weakness here somewhere. It was a mistake to try to measure my own strength so precisely. As things have turned out, it is precisely at this vulnerable point that he has attacked me. Nevertheless, I never expected him to attack me in such a crude and vulgar manner, with no trace of sympathy or understanding. He views my relationship with his mother more or less as he would some adulterous back-street affair. He doesn't permit himself to have any doubts about his own viewpoint. Despite my inner resolve, I was not prepared for his determination to see our behaviour in the worst possible light.

The rightness of my marriage is something I must defend to the bitter end.

In spite of this, today I suddenly felt within me the presence of a still more terrible weakness. It is as though I have suddenly encountered it after so long a time.... It is a cheap, conventional thing, what is called conscience, which is still lying dormant somewhere within me. That's what is betraying me.

Polonius said to his daughter: 'Pious-seeming faces and apparently commendable behaviour, fiendish natures clothed in garments of the best taste – such phenomena are to be found anywhere and everywhere'. Standing beside them, I suddenly had the feeling that he was talking about me. Inexplicably, I felt a sharp stab in my heart. Then I started, surprised at myself. I reproached myself and tried thinking clearly again about whether any part of me felt guilt. While considering this, it suddenly occurred to me that perhaps I had to believe there was no shame, simply because I couldn't bear to think otherwise, so that really I couldn't be sure there was no shame in the depths of my heart. In the end, I succeeded in making myself feel extremely uneasy.

My great weakness is that I allow some trifling feeling to permeate my whole being and finally cause me to lose my inner balance. It often happens that I lose my equanimity for a whole day just because of a dream I've had in the morning.

I do not fear in the least what other people think of me – as long as that's all there is to it. I'm well aware that I have no shortage of enemies. I know who they are, more or less, but as long as this remains just an objective fact it doesn't affect me. I'm not very nervous about such things. But the problem is that something in those people who hate me draws me in and exercises a power over my heart which becomes the most dreadful thing of all.

While I was hiding behind some curtains with Polonius, the prince came along with his head bowed as if deep in thought. His expression was calm and dignified. Concealed as I was, I felt rather contemptible.

When he saw Ophelia standing by herself, he began to talk to her. He told her that he was basically an honest man but also proud, revengeful and violently ambitious; if he were to allow himself free reign, he would be capable of some terrible crimes. The only thing that was holding him back was that he lacked the forethought to plan these crimes, the imagination to give them shape and the time and chance to act them out.

And he repeatedly told the girl that she should retire to a nunnery.

If I regard these words of his as merely revealing his character, then I can have interest in and sympathy for him. But he seemed to be scheming about something. And while he was scheming those thoughts came into his mind. Whatever it is, undoubtedly it has something to do with me. If these dark thoughts of his hatch out, I don't know what he might do. And what should I do? If I am to talk things over with him, then I should do it right now. If, however, those dark thoughts are a symptoms of the state of his health, then another possibility would be to send him to England.

My wife said to Polonius' daughter: 'I pray that my son's madness has been caused by your great beauty. If so, we can hope that he will be restored to sanity again by your good nature'.

When she spoke like this, it was almost like she were posing a riddle. I don't know a more feminine, gentle, pure-hearted woman than my wife. For her sake too, I don't want to dislike her son. And I still do love him for his rare character and his superior talents. In any case, we urgently need to come to an understanding with each other in the near future.

167

He says he's going to stage some kind of play. If his heart really is set on such amusements now, then I am glad.

–day

When did I poison your father?

Did anyone witness such a thing? Who was the witness? Was there even one? Whatever made such an idea enter your head? Did you come to know of it yourself? Did you imagine it? In all the world there cannot be anyone with more of a taste for melodrama than you. Oh yes, everyone is in league to drive me out of my mind. I've never had such a dreadful experience.

What satisfaction does it give you to intimidate me and portray me as a criminal who has murdered his own brother? These thoughts of yours reveal an imagination blacker than Vulcan's smithy! Has it never occurred to you to doubt them? Your vivid imagination springs solely from nothing but the evil spirit of sensational literature. Have you never doubted the picture of life it gives you?

There is no-one with a stronger taste for melodrama than you. Do you want so much to become the hero of a stupid tragedy?

That wouldn't be so bad if you acted it out all by yourself. But you are trying to force me to play the villain's role – a role that has nothing to do with me. Yes, you are forcing me to play this role – and I won't allow it.

There cannot be a more presumptuous, affected fellow than you, nor anyone more crazy about stories and dramas, nor – on top of all that – anyone who is more of a blabbermouth.

You asked the old man what role he performed long ago when a play was staged at the university. He answered that he played the role of Caesar, who was assassinated. Why, at that moment, did you steal a glance at my face? How much do you believe you were able at that moment, just by glancing at my face, to read into my heart? You noticed that I began to lose my composure, didn't you? But you are not the sort of fellow who would probe deeper and ask why exactly I lost my composure. This is because you do not try to look any deeper than those things which fit in with the plot you have already hatched.

I felt immediately why you stole a glance at me at that moment. And because I felt this instinctively, at that same moment all the cheap literature that lies hidden somewhere in my heart committed treachery against the former king, my brother. The more I tried to remain calm and detached, the more I seemed to lose my composure. Finally my face took on an expression which seemed to justify all your suspicions. It was nothing more than this that you took as welcome evidence of my guilt. Still, that much was tolerable. But what about that play of yours, *The Murder of Gonzago*! For someone like you, who is supposed to detest the cliché and the commonplace, what a crude and over-obvious plot! And furthermore you tried to use it shamelessly to put pressure on me. Despite the fact that you like to pose as a skeptic, you were gullible enough to believe in these fantasies of yours, and so were able to calmly impose your fantasies on me. And because I myself am all too sensitive, I couldn't help but be ensnared by your calm audacity. Indeed I was beautifully ensnared. But surely this does not constitute true evidence of my guilt!

During that mime scene, when the actor playing Lucianus poured poison into the sleeping king's ear, how I had to struggle with the devil within me! It was then that I found I could stay no longer. But when I thought of the danger of my seeming to run away, I couldn't stand up. I don't know how many times I repeated to myself: 'Calm yourself, calm yourself'. But Horatio continually stared at my face with his irritatingly calm eyes. And finally I myself became nervously aware of the slight twitching spasms of my cheek muscles.

Then something that the king in the play said made me feel that it was really your father standing there talking. And I myself began to feel that I was a terrible villain – yes, what do you make of that? Does that amount to any kind of real evidence?

Oh, what terrible plots you are hatching against me! What hateful designs! Whichever direction my feelings take, you are hiding there with your plots to ensnare them. Unfortunately, my mind can't help but continue to be aware of these emotional traps of yours – and I end up falling into them.

I've long been aware of your true intentions in regard to me. But up to now I've looked at them from every possible angle, trying to see them in a good light. I have also tried as much as possible to suppress any hostile feelings towards you which have arisen within me. I have done likewise with any such feelings I have had towards your good mother. But I can no longer live in such a state of emotional ambiguity. I can no longer tolerate the risks to my own sanity involved in this. I refuse to put up any longer with the foolish and painful struggle involved in trying to force down into my heart's depths feelings which, with a tremendous force of their own, keep rising to the surface again and again.

I hate you from the bottom of my heart! Yes, I can freely hate you now from the bottom of my heart!

–day

Murder by poisoning – how could such a thing be kept secret? Among all the inquisitive eyes of the world, how could it possibly be kept secret? And if there were even a single witness, regardless of how much I tried to pressure him into keeping quiet, wouldn't it get whispered somehow from ear to ear until finally everyone knew about it?

Do you know even one person who has actually heard such gossip? Is there anyone? Have you managed to obtain even one piece of objectively witnessed evidence?

In the first place, if I were the kind of clever villain who could so skillfully conceal such a heinous crime, I would not have gone along so easily with your play – the purpose of which was transparent to me from the beginning. What's more, I wouldn't have married my brother's wife so soon after his death. The very fact that I could do this means that I had the self-confidence of an innocent man.

There's going to be trouble if you don't spend more time in deep thinking rather than in making witty remarks. And there's going to be trouble if you don't go about things more openly. There is nothing more ugly than barefaced deviousness. If you contrive to be devious about something that would soon be understood if presented openly, then you may well end up creating a real misunderstanding.

Whatever else one may say of you, you are, nonetheless, the beloved child of my beloved wife.

Because of what you have done, I can now no longer speak my mind freely even to my wife.

I feel very calm today. I wonder if we'll have a chance to meet each other soon to talk everything over and reach a mutual understanding. I pray in my heart that nothing serious happens before that chance comes along.

Now he has murdered Polonius! They say he ran him through with a sword. He's insane! A mad devil!

–day

He has finally succeeded in causing his mother to feel remorse. The fellow seems to have come into this world just to act out a tragedy. The sole purpose of all his education was to enable him to construct the plot and of his philosophy to make it seem meaningful. His circumlocutions and his shallow cynicisms are intended only to vary the tone and rhythm of his speeches. That's all they're for. And he assumes the good role of hero himself and casts me in the hateful role of villain. Regardless of who plays the part, the hero of a tragedy always causes grief to a woman. He has imposed this female role on his own simple and innocent mother.

His mother tells me that, while he was berating her in her room, he seemed suddenly to see the ghost of his father. He became enraged when she suggested that it was merely an hallucination caused by his present mental instability. Because I can't imagine a more outlandish performance than this, I think perhaps he really has gone mad. And if he does have the strange idea that his father was murdered, perhaps he got it from that ghost.

In any case, he is no longer a sane human being. If he were sane, he wouldn't so calmly indulge in such obvious self-contradictions. Once he had filled his head with such outrageous imaginings about his father's death, he didn't spare a thought for the children of Polonius – even though he had run the old man through because of a mistaken identity. He simply said: 'It's the natural outcome of his misdeeds'. And I'm told he also said: 'It's an unfortunate thing I've done but it's Heaven's will. Heaven punishes me in this way and also uses me as a temporary instrument to punish these people'. All things considered, did Polonius ever commit a crime for which he deserved to die? And what should Laertes and Ophelia do, whose father has been killed?

My wife said: 'I bitterly regret that he killed someone in his present fit of madness' – but I myself no longer believe it. After all, he went and hid the old man's corpse somewhere.

Anyway, I can no longer stand to have him here beside me.

–day

With his facile talk and the clever look in his eyes, he has won the respect of a certain section of the people – so it would be impossible to punish him in this country. But his derangement has reached a critical stage. I cannot possibly leave things as they are. I cannot wait any longer for such a slow, leisurely thing as 'mutual understanding'. I must apply some dangerous and drastic measures.

I am thinking now of sending him to England.

It will be more of a true tragedy, after all, if the hero dies rather than the villain. . . .

–day

The gentle Ophelia has lost her wits. I would never have imagined that a single chance idea, suddenly appearing in one man's mind, could cause so much unhappiness to so many people. I curse him now from the bottom of my heart.

–day

One misfortune is always followed by another. Because he buried the old man's body somewhere secretly, strange and groundless rumours have begun to spread among the ignorant masses. These rumours have even had their effect on Laertes, just back from France, who seems to suspect me

–day

Isn't it only natural that I couldn't mourn my brother's death from the depths of my heart? To say that it is 'natural' is an excellent justification. It is indeed an excellent justification -if only for myself. But he has tried to destroy all that. Even this I could bear – but what is so hard to bear is that he is someone who has been living in my own home.

Really it doesn't give me any pleasure, even now, to think of the events of that time. I really was sad to lose the brother I had grown up with. But, nonetheless, an even greater feeling of joy arose within me. My heart is free – and I cannot control it with my mind. This certainly did not please me, but was there anything I could do about it? My heart's freedom often gives me solitary pleasure but, at the same time, it also causes me to suffer greatly. In this respect, for me there is nothing less free than my own heart. At this very moment, I am really more afraid of my always-vacillating 'free heart' than of he who is planning to kill me. There is almost no boundary at all within me between 'think' and 'do'. (Doesn't this mean that I immediately act out whatever I think?) Nevertheless, I can say clearly that I have never, at any time, thought of killing my brother. I cannot remember entertaining such an inhuman idea even once. But isn't it true that one cannot do anything about an idea which arises spontaneously and unexpectedly within one?

My brother began to have suspicions about his wife and me more than three years ago. But she herself never noticed my love for her and so did not even dream that her husband had begun to suspect her. Because of our love for the same woman, my brother and I sometimes waged secret emotional wars. From about this time too he never left me behind when he went somewhere away from home. Whether he went hunting or touring, he always invited me along. But I never expected it to be a very pleasant hunt or trip for me. In the first place, I found it very provoking that my brother watched me closely all the while to see if I would betray myself. From my present perspective, though, I think that this was rather fortunate – because it gave me all the more courage to propose marriage to his widow.

It was a cold night with an autumn moon in the sky. The hunting dogs, tied up in their kennels, bayed on and on. Not being used to sleeping on a hard bed while out hunting, I couldn't get to sleep for quite a long time. A dim lamp cast a faint, gloomy light over my brother's bed and mine, which were placed side by side. Worn out by fatigue, thinking I know not what thoughts and feeling myself to be half-dreaming, half-awake, gradually I was as if sucked down into sleep. But before I had fallen completely asleep, I was suddenly startled awake again by a strange voice. Opening my eyes, I saw that the lamp had at some time blown out and I heard my brother groaning in the darkness. I soon realized that he was having a nightmare. He was moaning in a ghastly way, as if he were being strangled. I myself began to feel uneasy. Thinking to rouse him, I had risen half out of my bed when suddenly, inexplicably, a strange idea floated into my head, surprising even me: it was me who was strangling my brother in his dream. And then my own dreadful form rose up clearly before me in the darkness – and, simultaneously, there arose within me the state of mind of this apparition. . . . How savage I looked! What an atrocious thing I had done! Thinking that the deed was already done, I became almost crazed and tried to strangle him more and more violently – I saw myself doing this very clearly.

My brother's howl-like moans continued. I didn't know what to do.

If there had been a bright light, I never would have been troubled by that terrible vision. As such things do happen to me at times, I am always prepared for them when I sleep in my own room. I keep a bright lamp by my bedside which I can quickly light when the need arises. Whether I have just awoke from an unpleasant dream or have just become absorbed in an unpleasant fantasy, if these involve the sense of sight, when I light the lamp they are easily dispelled. Furthermore, to make my room even less conducive to such visions, I have hung on the walls two or three landscape paintings rendered in the most cheerful colours. When I look at them by a bright light, my state of mind soon changes. I am soon freed from any unpleasant feelings. Because I almost always dream when I sleep, I never forget to make these preparations before going to bed. But on the hunting trip, sleeping in a farmer's house, I wasn't able to do so. My eyes, opened widely in the darkness, reflected only the imaginary scene of my brother's strangulation. And I couldn't set right either my eyes or my mind.

I buried my face in my pillow and held my breath for a while. I told myself that I must distract my attention from the vision by means of some other sensation. I tried biting hard into my arm. Meanwhile, my brother had fallen into a deep, peaceful sleep.

The following morning I felt somewhat uneasy but my brother, seemingly unaware of his nightmare, talked over with me his hunting plans for that day. I was much relieved by this. But ever afterwards that dreadful vision would sometimes be recalled to my mind – suddenly, inexplicably – and I was caused intense suffering each time this happened.

–day

He must be arriving in England about now. Somehow I seem to have become exceedingly tender-hearted of late. But still I don't think it's wise to feel pity for someone who's planning to kill me.

–day

When I think of the moment the news of his death arrives, I feel a very troubling apprehension. I find it intolerable to think of how both my wife and I will react to the news. There is nothing more unpleasant than this mood of patient waiting for something terrible that you know is going to happen. Time will naturally bring that dreaded moment near. I must suppress my tender feelings and just keep my eyes tightly closed....

[Author's note: The diary cuts off here. But it should be noted that the eventual fate of this Claudius is not necessarily the same as in the play *Hamlet*.]

RECONCILIATION

Part One

This July 31st. was the first anniversary of the death of my first child, who died last year fifty-six days after her birth. It had been a long while since I had come up to Tokyo from the town where I was now living, Abiko, to visit her grave.

From Ueno Station I phoned my parents' house in Azabu and told the maid who answered to summon my mother.

'How's grandmother?', I asked her.

'She's well but it's still a little early for her to go out, so I went to visit the grave this morning by myself', mother answered.

'Did you? I'm on my way to the Aoyama Cemetery now too.'

The two of us were quiet for a while.

'Are you planning to visit anywhere else today besides the cemetery?', she asked.

'I thought I might drop in on a friend too.'

'Your father's at home today. . . .' she said, lowering her voice a little, as if it were difficult for her to say it.

'Is he? In that case, I'll drop by again some other time.' I said this as casually as possible but, although no one was there to notice, I could feel that the expression on my face openly betrayed my painful feeling of humiliation.

'I trust that Sadako and Rumeko are well?' Mother was asking about my wife and my second child, born nine days before, who were still in confinement.

'They're fine.'

'No problem with the breast-feeding?'

'No, the milk's flowing nicely.' Then I said: 'Well, then. . . .'

'Listen. He may go out, so please try calling again later,' she said.

I agreed and hung up the phone.

I immediately headed for Aoyama by tram. I got off at Sanchōme and on my way to the cemetery stopped at a flower

176

shop and bought some colourful flowers. I thought it was a little too soon but anyway I borrowed the store phone and phoned mother again. She said father was still at home. Again I was engulfed by a feeling of misery and, simultaneously, of anger.

I very much wanted to see grandmother that day, more even than usual. For one thing, I was convinced that she was longing to see me.

My child of the previous year had been born at a Tokyo hospital, so grandmother had come to see her every two or three days. But my child this year had been born at Abiko and so grandmother had not yet seen her even once. She had wanted to come but, with the hot weather and her own rather poor health, she had never made it. And so now she seemed all the more to want to meet me and ask after the baby's condition. I felt it was rather ridiculous to disappoint her just because of my unhappy relationship with father. My mother and grand-mother had no choice but to go along with his prohibitions. But for me also to be doing so was ridiculous. In the first place, I felt that, sneaking in stealthily to visit grandmother during father's absence, I presented a very unseemly spectacle, and this made me angry.

I went first to visit the graves of my grandfather and of my birth mother. The graves of my grandfather's older brother and his wife were also there. The flower vases were all full of flowers that had been placed there that morning. The flowers I had brought with me were all intended for my own child's grave, so I placed them for the moment along with my hat on a clipped hedge of Chinese hawthorn.

Except in special cases, I was not in the habit of bowing before graves. This was because sixteen or seventeen years earlier I had been a believer in Christianity. But I found that, if I just strolled about in front of the grave, the person lying there would be brought back to my mind with a closeness and a clarity absolutely not possible in any other place.

I walked for a while in front of my grandfather's grave. Presently he appeared before my mind's eye. I felt an urge to talk things over with him, to say something like: 'I want to go see grandmother today.' And grandfather soon answered: 'Go ahead. That's a good idea.' His answer arose of a sudden, too clearly and too naturally to be a product of my own imagina-tion. It was like meeting someone in a dream, it had that kind of objectivity, and to me it certainly seemed to be my grandfather just as he was when he was alive. I felt that the simple words he

177

spoke were charged with his love for his aged wife. And even though, at that time, I clearly blamed my father for the unhappy relationship between us, not the slightest hint of criticism of father came from the grandfather who appeared within that same me.

I went and stood before the grave of my birth mother. She didn't come to mind as clearly as my grandfather and, when I mentioned to her too my desire to visit grandmother, she mumbled something vague and non-committal, just like a timid woman. I walked away, as if not wanting to have anything to do with her.

I decided, after all, to visit my grandmother. I felt sorry for my stepmother, placed as she was in such a difficult predicament. Perhaps I would go around to the back door and go straight to grandmother's room. That way I could say that I did not enter my father's house but just my grandmother's room. But when I thought this over it did not seem like a good idea. Of course, there was a chance that, if I went through the front door and passed through the living room and by the phone-room, I might exchange glances with father through the window of the phone-room. Even so, I hated the idea of sneaking in by the back door.

I had come to Satoko's grave. The flower vase there was also full of flowers. I placed the bouquet I had brought in front of her grave and set off towards the Azabu house and grandmother.

I passed through the garden gate. Entering the house by the front door, I met mother in the hall, giving orders to the maid. She seemed a little taken aback but soon recovered and greeted me in the usual way. Leaving things at that, I went on to my grandmother's room. Grandmother had two fans set up; one wasn't going but she sat alone cooling her back against the other. All bent over, she was spooning up and drinking some ice water.

She asked me various things about my wife and baby. And she promised that, once it had cooled down a little, she would be sure to come visit us at Abiko. Mother, my small sister and some others came in. The maid brought some cakes and cool drinks. I stayed about half an hour and then left. I finished the visit without once meeting father.

Part Two

I had some work which I had to complete by August 19th. I wrote from about ten at night but the subject was somehow difficult to deal with. At first I called the story 'The Visionary' but later I changed this to 'The Dreamer'. I was trying to write about my relations with father before and after I had lived alone at Onomichi six years previously. I had been very unhappy with him. It seemed to me that this was comprised of various mixed-up, complex feelings, inescapable in any parent-child relationship, but the main element was animosity resulting from the increasing discord between us. Whenever I talked about this with anyone, I found it relatively easy to voice my complaints about father quite openly. But for some reason I could not do the same in writing. I concluded that I did not want to seem to be taking out a grudge against him in my written works. That would be unfair to my father but even more terrible was that it would contaminate my writing.

My feelings were complex. As I tried to write about them I gradually came more and more to see their complexity. When I tried to look at the experience accurately and judge it fairly, I found that this was not within my power. I wrote the story out once and failed. I tried writing it once more but again it didn't satisfy me. Finally there were only six days left to the deadline, and no prospect at all that I would be finished. I had no choice but to change my subject. Promising the story for the October issue of the magazine, I changed its subject to one which could be treated with imaginative freedom and therefore, I thought, could be worked into a story by that time. As if suddenly bursting through the barrier which had blocked my way, I wrote the story with a despatch rare for a slow writer like me. I finished the whole thing on the 15th.

On the morning of the 16th. I left my house with the manuscript. I stopped at the post office and sent it off, then boarded the Tokyo train at a few minutes past nine. A friend had sent me a postcard saying he'd like to meet with me after I'd finished writing the story, so I tried phoning him from Ueno Station. But I was told that he'd gone to Kamakura that same day. I knew that, if he'd gone there, he must be at S.'s house. Since I wanted to see S. too, I considered going out to Kamakura. But somehow I felt tired and lacking in will power and this made me feel lazy. I decided to phone the Azabu house instead. When mother came to the phone she said that father had taken all the children to our villa at Hakone, that he was expected home today but that she was alone with grandmother at the moment and so, if I wanted to, I should come right away. I had been told by letter that, for more than a week now, grandmother had been slightly weakened by a cold. Knowing father, I supposed that he would have set off early that morning from Hakone and would certainly arrive home while I was still there, but I decided to go anyway. I hung up the phone and was soon aboard a tram for Azabu.

Grandmother was sitting on her bed. She seemed pretty well recovered and her face was a fairly healthy colour. After I'd spent about an hour with her I could hear the stirrings of people outside. 'So they're all back', I thought to myself.

The maid came running down the hall. 'Everyone has come home', she reported, and then left. Soon Takako, my third sister, and Masako, my fourth, very little, sister, came in.

'We're back', they both said, and bowed. Seeing me, Takako seemed a little surprised. Then, with a rather perplexed expression on her face, she said directly to me: 'Father also came back with us, you know.'

'It's alright, it's alright', I answered.

'Where's Yoshiko and Rokuko?' asked grandmother.

'Rō-chan's with us too.'

'Rō-chan!' called Masako in a loud voice.

'What?' we heard Rokuko's voice ask from outside.

'How about Yoshiko?' asked grandmother again.

'Yokko-chan stayed behind by herself'.

'Why's that?'

'When we said we'd all come back together, father didn't look too happy about it for some reason.'

'Why?'

'You ask why?' said Takako, looking perplexed. 'Really I wanted to stay too. But I ate so many different things that I've had diarrhoea since yesterday, so I decided to come back.'

We never did find out from Takako's chatter why Yoshiko didn't come home with the rest, but grandmother kept repeating over and over: 'She should have come back with you'.

Rokuko, the youngest child, came running in.

'Grandma, grandma, you know what? Father did nothing but play *Go* with his guests every day. I was so bored!' said Masako in a tone of voice which begged for sympathy. Rokuko joined in: 'Father did nothing but play *Go*. I didn't go anywhere.'

'That's a lie', said Takako with a glare. 'Didn't you go to Otomé Pass?'

'Oh well, I suppose so' said Rokuko, shrugging her shoulders and sticking her tongue out a little.

Father came in from the hall. I changed from a cross-legged posture to a slightly more formal one, with my legs placed to the side, bowing my head a little in the process but not enough to make a formal bow. Father didn't seem to recognize me at first. It had been a full two years since we had last met. (It's true that once during this time, beside Tokyo Station, I had passed him by. He was coming from the opposite direction in a cab, but it was such a wide-open street that even my wife, who was walking beside me, didn't notice him. Thus it didn't seem unnatural when I also pretended not to notice.) Out of laziness, I had allowed my beard to grow almost an inch long, so that my face had changed a bit too. But soon father did recognize me, and his face assumed an indescribably displeased expression. It seemed for a moment that he was going to turn about and leave right there and then but, even so, he asked grandmother how she was doing.

'I'm gradually getting better', she answered. That was all. There was a moment of tense silence. My nature is such that at moments like these I am always more acutely conscious of the tension than others, and so become extremely nervous, but on this occasion, for some reason, I was able to look up calmly into father's face. We had often had such face-to-face confrontations before and, each time, the more his face took on a displeased expression, the more mine would do the same. Though I tried not to let this happen, my own stubborn streak would not allow me to respond in any other way. And often, even after the scene of our confrontation was over, the unhappy memory of it would linger on to torment me.

Without saying a word, father turned about and left.

Lunch being ready, everyone was called into the parlor. My food alone was brought into grandmother's room.

A while later I left the Azabu house.

My body felt terribly heavy and tired. Thinking that I might be falling ill, I decided to return immediately to Abiko. But there was a short wait before the train left.

There was a used-book shop in Kanda where I owed some money, so I dropped in there. To kill time I struck up a conversation with the owner, but I found it very tiresome to answer his questions.

I rested for a while in the waiting room of Ueno Station. Once I boarded the train I sat there nodding drowsily until finally, at some point, I fell fast asleep. After waking up at Kitakogané, I forced myself to stay awake for fear of going past my stop – which had happened to me four or five trips previously on my return from Tokyo.

Planning to take a cab home, I exited the station, only to find someone just about to board the one cab parked outside.

When, at long last, I managed to drag myself home and was mounting the stairs up to my house with a feeling of relief, our hired man, who was doing something at the gate above, suddenly came running down and took my bags.

'Is something the matter? You look very pale', he said.

My wife came out from the entrance hall, holding our baby, and said: 'Welcome home!' The light was coming from behind me so she didn't notice the colour of my face.

'Welcome home, papa', she said again in a slightly flippant tone, thrusting the baby towards me as if she wanted me to hold it. I had a kind of queasy feeling. I remained silent and, when I came to the anteroom of the parlor, I collapsed onto the floor. Her high spirits suddenly punctured, my wife came and sat beside me with an uneasy, bewildered expression on her face.

'I'm feeling a little out of sorts – I'm just too tired to move'.

'Shall I massage your back?'

My wife's mood was completely out of tune with my own. Without a word I got up and went to the toilet. I had a slight case of diarrhoea. When I came out my wife was still sitting in the same place, a vacant expression on her face. I lay myself out again on the floor with my back to her, and purposely at a place somewhat removed from where she was. My wife placed the baby down to sleep and approached me. She tried to massage my back but, without saying anything, I brushed away her hands.

'Why?' she asked in a pitiable voice.

'Anyway, just don't touch me.'

'What are you so angry about?'

'It's much more unpleasant to be with someone like you at a time like this than to be alone.'

A moment later my wife began to cry.

At times like these I gradually become more and more bad-tempered. Eventually I lose all self-control. But working against this now was my feeling that it would be very bad if I should upset my wife so much that her milk stopped flowing. Because I felt sometimes that the baby we had the year before didn't just die but was killed by my own carelessness, I was very strongly determined to treat our present child with the greatest possible care. So I made an effort to control my temper.

That night we sent for a doctor.

I slept for more than two days.

Part Three

O nce recovered, I had to start work again on the story I had promised for the October issue of a certain magazine. I decided to change the title to *The Dreamer*.

When I was writing about real life, I was often misled by the temptation to line up at random all sorts of things that had actually happened to me. I remembered so many different things and wanted to write about all of them, not leaving anything out. All of these facts or events had, more or less, causal connections among them. But I couldn't just write about them one after the other. If I tried, then I would feel dissatisfied because, inevitably, I was unable to adequately describe all those interconnections. I had to make an effort to be skillfully selective and leave out certain happenings even though I wanted to write about them.

When I tried to write about the dispute between father and me, I felt this problem all the more keenly. All too many incidents had happened between us.

Then again, as I have already mentioned, my reluctance to use my writing to air my personal grudge against father prevented me from writing with easy fluency. Nevertheless, the fact of the matter was that this feeling of grudge against father did exist within me. But that wasn't all. Another side of me felt sympathy for him.

Eleven years previously I had heard that father had said to someone: 'From now on, no matter what happens, I'll shed no more tears for my son.' And, even before I'd heard about this, I often used to shudder when I thought of the way I sometimes treated him. How many fathers had ever been treated in such a way by their children? I couldn't bear the thought that I too, as a father, might be treated in that way by my own children. And so, when I'd heard what he'd said, it didn't seem unreasonable to me. And I felt very lonely.

But the complaints father now openly voiced about me had nothing to do with that earlier time. It was in the spring of the year before last. I was living in Kyoto and father, seeking to patch up the dispute between us which had occurred a while earlier, came to visit me with my oldest sister. When I received a telegram from him saying: 'Arriving soon', I thought I would pretend I'd left before the telegram arrived – I would head for Tokyo, passing him by on the way. I disliked the idea of hurting him. But I disliked even more the prospect of meeting with him. I couldn't bear the thought of having to conceal the bad feelings I had towards him and talking to him with a straight face, as if nothing were the matter. If by doing so I deceived myself, thus deceiving my father, what good would it do? The end result would be worse than our present discord. It would just add an element of falsity to that discord, making it even worse. I didn't even dream that we could achieve a true reconciliation at that time.

Perhaps father wouldn't believe that my going up to Tokyo and missing him was accidental. But I guessed that he would half believe it, and so I decided to go.

Just around this time my wife was suffering the onset of a nervous breakdown and often felt very weak. Even if this had not been the case, it would undoubtedly have been a big strain for her, married for only about three months and not yet on intimate terms with my father and sister, to have to play hostess to them in my absence. But on top of that she was, as I said, having a nervous breakdown. And on top of that still my marriage to her was one of the recent causes of my dispute with father. When I told my wife what I intended to do, she broke down and cried. I got angry and stomped out of the house.

Once outside, I began to feel sorry for my wife. Considering her present condition, I really had imposed a bit too heavy a burden on her. Before reaching the station, I turned back for home.

I wrote a letter to father. Without any of the usual polite circumlocutions, I expressed my feelings to him honestly and simply, and told him that I didn't want to meet him. But I asked him to please let my sister visit us alone – although I doubted he would consent.

I expected their train to arrive after dark. I sent my wife to the station with my letter. When she was leaving, I told her emphatically again and again that, without fail, she must give the letter to my father at the station. Again she broke down and cried. 'If you come back without having delivered the letter,' I said, 'I'll immediately leave for Tokyo.'

Soon after my wife had left I also went out. I called at an inn where a friend of mine from Osaka was staying.

About ten o'clock I returned to our house in the Kinugasa area of Kyoto. My wife, my sister and a cousin who happened to drop by in my absence came out to meet me. They all had rather lively expressions on their faces. When I looked at my sister whom I hadn't seen for so long, a mellow, happy feeling arose within me also. But soon I asked my wife about the letter. She told me that, no matter how she tried, she just couldn't hand it over at the station; they had gone together to an inn to eat supper and had been there until now, and during that time also she hadn't had the chance to hand it over. She had returned just now with my sister in a rickshaw. She had made the rickshaw man wait and the three of them had talked things over – and finally, just now, she had got him to deliver the letter. She said further that father was waiting to take us all on a walk around Nara and Osaka. I imagined father all by himself in his room at the inn reading my letter with a sinking heart. I began to feel miserable myself. But I thought that it couldn't be helped.

The following day the four of us left the house in the morning and walked from the Temple of the Silver Pavilion to the Temple of the Thousand and One Kannon Statues on the Higashiyama side of Kyoto. On the day after that we went to Mount Arashi. When, in the evening, we had returned from there and were eating supper in a small restaurant on Shijō Street, I had my sister phone to father at his inn. He was absolutely furious and demanded that she return to the inn at once. We bid her goodbye and returned to our house in Kinugasa. A while later the rickshaw man delivered two letters my sister had written from the inn. One she had written in front of father and it asked us to hand over to the rickshaw man the luggage she had left at our house. The other she had written hurriedly in pencil when father wasn't looking and it told us how very angry father was, how he had scolded her and how they were to leave Kyoto the following morning for Osaka.

More then half a year passed by after this incident before I had any further contact with my father. During that time my wife and I left Kyoto and rented a house in Kamakura with the intention of living there. But my wife's nervous exhaustion became somewhat more severe and so, after just a week, we moved on to Mount Akagi in the north of the prefecture where we stayed for over four months. Then we travelled about for a while again until finally, at the beginning of October, we settled down in our present house in the Teganuma area of Abiko. By now my wife had almost completely recovered from her nervous condition. And she had become pregnant.

One day we went up to Tokyo to visit my grandmother who was sick in bed. We decided to stay the night at the Azabu house and I went out by myself to visit some friends of mine, a married couple who were staying at a certain inn in Kōji-machi. I returned to the Azabu house around midnight. Everyone was asleep but mother and my wife got up to welcome me. Grandmother also woke up and talked with me for a while. Soon I also changed into my night-clothes and went to bed. I had just done so when mother, who had returned to her bedroom, came back again and said: 'I'm asking you to do something very hard but – er, please – please come and apologize to father for what happened in Kyoto.'

I was a little puzzled by this. When I had decided to move to Abiko, I had gone to father's room to report this fact, using it as a way of trying to break the ice with him. Father did not give a proper answer but, by going to bid him farewell, I intended to let him know, at least indirectly, that my feelings had changed since Kyōto. By doing so I intended that we should put all that unpleasantness behind us.

'Is father in his room?' I asked.

'He's got up and he's waiting in his room.'

I turned my kimono sash around so the tie was in back and went in to father's room. He was sitting in front of his desk with his back against it.

'I won't stand in the way of your comings and goings in this house – not at all. I'll gladly allow it. But I want to clearly settle what must be settled – so how about it?' said father.

'I think that what I did in Kyoto was unfortunate. My feelings towards you have changed greatly since then. But even now I don't think that what I did then was wrong in any way,' I answered.

'Is that so? Well, then, if that's the case, I don't want you coming here anymore.'

'Is that so?' I stood up, made a bow and left. I was now in a rage.

'I'm leaving', I said to my grandmother and mother – and to my wife: 'If you want to come too, then come.' I got out a *kimono* to change into.

'You don't have to leave right now, do you ?' said my mother and, with tears flowing, she made as if to retie my *kimono sash*, grabbing my hand so that it couldn't move. 'If you leave now you won't find anywhere to stay. Go home early tomorrow morning. I beg you, please do that.'

My wife also joined in, saying something in a tearful voice. I got angry and pushed her away. She fell down onto the bed.

My grandmother, who had been lying quietly in bed, now said in an excited tone: 'Take Sadako with you.'

My mother also was now resigned to our leaving.

I waited for my wife to get ready, then left the Azabu house.

It was past one o'clock and the streets outside were empty. My wife followed one step behind me without saying a word. Planning to go stay at the inn in Kōji-machi which I had visited about two hours before, I walked in that direction.

'If you have even a slight feeling of criticism for what I've done, then you too don't belong with me', I said suddenly. My wife remained silent.

'If I was such a yes-man to my father, I never would have married you,' I said in an intimidating tone.

Everyone was asleep at the inn. When I knocked at the gate, a maid came in her nightclothes to open it.

She led us to a small room on the second floor.

The next morning my wife was angered when the maid addressed her in an over-familiar, unexpectedly rough manner.

'I brought you here so late last night that she probably thought you were just a woman of the streets', I said. My wife got more angry and wanted to leave right away.

Part Four

My wife was expecting a baby in June of the following year. Because there was no midwife where we were, we decided to go down to Tokyo for the birth. There was a maternity hospital in the city my wife's aunt knew of, so I expected to send her there. But then we heard that father had recommended that she go to a gynecologist who was a close friend of his. At the beginning of June my wife went down to Tokyo and stayed at the Azabu house. When her time was drawing near she entered the hospital father had recommended and soon had an easy delivery of a baby girl.

Father visited the hospital once to see his first grandchild. But he didn't come a second time, perhaps out of fear of running into me. Later my wife often told me that, when the baby was taken to stay at the Azabu house three weeks after its birth, father would sometimes come to see it in the room where it was sleeping alone. She spoke of this with evident joy. But since I had developed a strangely deep distrust towards father, I did not want to hear about her innocent joy.

When grandmother, my wife and others reported that father had said he would pay all the expenses of the birth, they were overjoyed by this demonstration of his good will. But I reacted against this too. In the end, though, I accepted father's payment. My grandmother urged me many times: 'Just go and say thanks to your father.' I would answer vaguely, 'yes, yes', and end up not going. And finally I had my wife go say it for me.

I knew that everyone was hoping to take advantage of the baby to effect a reconciliation between father and me. Obviously there was an unspoken agreement to use her as much as possible for this purpose. But the use of such means went very much against my grain.

Because the two children of the gatekeeper at the Azabu house contracted dysentery one after the other, my wife and child came back to Abiko earlier than planned – exactly twenty-four days after the birth. It was still a little too early for the baby to ride on trains. That night she didn't sleep very well, her mind being over-excited by so many new stimuli. But she was better by the following day.

Almost a month later, I got a letter from grandmother asking me to bring the baby in the near future, as father wanted to see her. Somehow I did not want the baby to travel all the way to Tokyo. Besides, I still felt mistrustful. It seemed to me that father wanted the baby there only so that his eighty-one-year-old mother would not have to visit us at Abiko. From long before he had been extremely averse to this – perhaps because he was frightened by the idea that his aged mother might become seriously ill while staying with us, forcing him to break his resolution never to enter my house.

I had sometimes gone to see grandmother. But even if my wife stayed at the Azabu house, I never did. I stayed rather with friends, with my uncle or at an inn.

Before answering grandmother, I sent a letter to the doctor in Tokyo asking him if it was now alright for the baby to travel by train. He answered that it was better to move a baby around as little as possible during about the first hundred days. When I went up to Tokyo I told this to my mother over the phone and asked that grandmother come to visit us instead.

Two or three days later grandmother arrived at Abiko with a group of four people from the Azabu house and a child of our uncle at Akasaka. They all stayed two nights and left on the afternoon of the third day.

When she was leaving grandmother again said that father wanted to see the baby and so she would like to take it back with her. I thought it strange that she would ask this, considering that the doctor had said it was best to move the baby as little as possible right now. But then I thought that the doctor was probably being over-cautious. Actually, I remembered now that, when the baby was moved here to Abiko at twenty-four days, he had been consulted and had said it was alright. Even so, I didn't feel like letting grandmother take the baby. I realized later that she didn't know at this time that the doctor had advised against moving the baby. Whether this was because mother had forgotten to tell her, or because grandmother herself had forgotten what was said, I didn't know. Whichever it was, it obviously wasn't my fault. Still, even though I knew this, and somehow didn't feel like allowing her to take the baby, finally I weakened and gave my consent. The baby was unlucky. If I had repeated then the doctor's words which I had told my mother over the phone, grandmother surely would have desisted from her request. For some reason I didn't do this – but, anyway, it is foolish to brood about it now. Such brooding does not help one decide which branch to take of the forked road leading to happiness or misery.

Outside Ueno Station I put my grandmother, my wife and child into a vacant cab and then went with my two oldest sisters to eat at a place under the Murai Bank. I phoned to the Azabu house from there. I was told that their taxi had got into an accident on the way home and they had changed to another one at Tokyo Station – but they had all arrived home safely.

After a while I said goodbye to my sisters and went to a friend's house. Three other friends also arrived. We sat up all night playing games, and continued to play until about noon of the following day.

I left in the evening and went to my uncle's house in Akasaka. It was a day of violent wind and rain. My uncle and his wife repeatedly urged me to stay with them. But I was tired and longed for my own bed.

I left their house in the midst of the storm, wanting to board the last train. Before I reached the station I was drenched right through. Once aboard the train, I remembered that, on the way home, we would have to cross over the railway bridge without a railing at Nakagawa, and I was suddenly overcome by fear. Even on normal days it felt dangerous to cross over a bridge without a railing. And so, on a stormy night like this, it seemed that the wind could easily blow the train sideways off the bridge – and that would be that.

And so I got off the train early, at Sudachō. Huge drops of rain rebounded off the pavement of the walkway. The telegraph wires gave off a strange sound. A workman who was drenched to the skin stood dejectedly in the rain in front of one of the shops, lifting up a long bamboo pole with a hook on the end and putting it around the cord of an outside lamp. But whenever the wind blew strongly, the cord would rub against something and purple sparks would fall from the parts of the cord where the covering was ripped.

I myself, at any rate, had to seek shelter from the rain. All the shops in the area had already closed. I went to the Mansei Bridge Station. I didn't like the idea of going back to my uncle's house in Akasaka. I bought the evening paper from a newsboy and sat down on a bench to read it. While I sat there the time passed for the last train home. Having no choice now, I resigned myself and boarded the train back to my uncle's house.

Even though I had not had enough sleep, I was strangely agitated that night – and also bitten by fleas – so that I couldn't get to sleep.

At about nine o'clock the next morning I sent someone to the Azabu house to tell my wife that I was in Tokyo again. But word came back from mother that my wife had left with the baby early that morning for Abiko. So I too returned home on the afternoon train.

Part Five

That evening when we had lit some incense to drive away the mosquitoes and settled down for our supper, the baby began to cry in another part of the house.

'The mosquitoes are terrible, you know. Shall we bring baby Sato-bō in here?' asked my wife. And then, still sitting where she was, she called for Ryū, our twelve-year-old nursemaid.

Ryū didn't answer. I also called for her in a loud voice. But no sooner had I called than her shadow appeared on the sliding door and, without answering, she opened it.

'Madame, the baby seemed to throw up just now', she said.

My wife took the baby, laid it on a flat cushion and looked at its diapers. The baby started to cry again.

My wife held the diapers up to the light of the lamp. 'It's a little green.' she said. 'It's mixed with mucus,' she added, and frowned.

'If that's the case, give it some milk tonight. Let's check its temperature.'

'I checked a while ago and there was no fever.'

I put my hand on the baby's forehead but there didn't seem to be any fever.

After changing the baby's diapers, my wife took it in her arms. The baby cried even more than before.

'Oh, who, who' – saying this, my wife rubbed her own cheek and the baby tried to put its open mouth against the cheek she had touched.

'Hey there. That's your mother's cheek', she said.

Laughing, Ryū went down to the maid's room.

The baby just wouldn't stop crying.

'What's the matter, Sato-chan?'

My wife's face took on an uneasy expression.

'Isn't her way of crying a little strange?'

The voice the baby cried in really was abnormal.

'When I was washing her, a little water from the gauze went up her nose – but it wouldn't be that, would it?'

'Not likely. Anyway you'd better put her to bed quickly', I said. 'Have you made up the bed?'

'Not yet'.

'Well then, hadn't you better be quick about it?' For no particular reason I was getting angry.

On top of the headache I had from my prolonged lack of sleep, I had a boil on my thigh from which I hadn't yet had the pus discharged. It throbbed with pain. Thus, all in all, I was feeling rather miserable. When the maid, Tsune, had made up our bed, I immediately changed into my nightwear and went to bed.

For a while my wife paced back and forth in the dark on the porch, singing a lullaby. When the baby was asleep, she came behind the mosquito net and placed the baby in a small bed surrounded by netting.

After massaging my head for a while, my wife went outside the mosquito net.

About fifteen minutes later the baby again opened its eyes and began to cry. My wife got up and came in from the living room; with her forehead pressing against the mosquito net, she looked in on the baby. I spoke to her in a low voice: 'If you fuss about her so much, she'll think you're going to pick her up again and cry all the more – so you'd better let her be'.

'What should I do?'

'She's alright so just stay away from her.'

My wife went outside. The baby didn't cry so violently, but she just wouldn't stop.

'I'm also going to go to sleep', said my wife, getting ready for bed.

I had become a little uneasy. I suppressed that uneasiness for a while and kept silent. But when I could no longer bear it, I got up and picked up the baby and, sitting cross-legged, I rocked her in my arms. The baby slept for a while again.

My wife hung our summer *kimono* on some bamboo hangers, tidied up a bit, went to pray before the Buddha image, and then came behind the mosquito net. Meanwhile we didn't speak to each other, for fear of waking up the baby. I noticed how bad the baby's complexion was. I wondered what to do. Then the baby opened her eyes and began to cry again. While I was holding her, I placed my cheek against the baby's face. My cheek felt chilled. The baby's lips had turned purple.

'I think you'd better get one of the servants to go tell them at the hospital. One would be lonely by herself – so let two of them go.'

My wife went out from the mosquito net and hurried into the kitchen.

'Be quick about it. Alright? Be quick about it. Sato looks a little strange,' I heard her say.

The baby's crying had become markedly strange. It sounded something like 'ahha, ahha.'

'Just throw anything on and go as quickly as you can', I shouted.

My wife came back behind the mosquito net.

'Shall I try giving her some milk?'

'Yes, try it.'

I gave the baby to my wife. But the baby no longer had any desire to drink milk. The colour of her face seemed to change every moment. My wife became agitated. Then, as if to scold the baby, she said in a fierce voice: 'Sato-chan! Sato-chan!' and roughly forced the baby's small purple lips against her nipple.

I took the baby away from my wife, stood up, held it by its legs and tried shaking it upside down. This had no effect. Her face was almost earth-coloured.

'I'd better take her to the hospital myself'.

Holding the baby I went out from the mosquito net and, since the other doors were all locked, I walked barefoot out of the kitchen door.

'Ah, ah', my wife exclaimed in a strange, despairing voice, and seized my arm that was holding the baby.

'What are we going to do?' she asked.

'You can't come with me', I replied.

'I can't stay here alone' she said, shaking her head.

'In that case, go stay with Y.'

I hurried out the front gate and down into the dark road. It had just stopped raining and I got muddy up to my ankles on the country road. I went to wake up the farmers in the house next door.

'Please hurry and light a lantern', I shouted. But even while saying this, I didn't stop walking, because in the distance I could see the lantern of our two servants, Tsune and Ryū, whom we'd just sent out. I tried to hurry as much as I could without shaking the baby too violently. When I had caught up to them, I said: 'Tsune, you come with me quickly to the hospital. And you, Ryū, take my wife to Y.'s house.' Then I noticed the pale white form of my wife twenty or thirty paces behind, and said to her in a loud voice: 'You're to go with Ryū to Y.'s place. Don't follow me.'

The hem of my sleeping *kimono* was wet with muddy water up to my knees, and this became tangled about my legs. I hurried on nonetheless.

The baby was crying,' aaa, aaa', constantly in a feeble voice. And her body seemed somehow lighter than usual. Her muscles had all loosened. I felt that I was carrying a dead rabbit.

'Sato-bō, Sato-bō' – now and then I called the baby's name.

The town headman's small house was at the foot of a low hill away from the road.

When I was passing it by, I said to the maid, 'You can see the road now, so you run on to the doctor's'. Tsune quickened her pace a little but she didn't run.

'Why don't you run?' I was a little angry.

'I can't', she answered. I remembered that she was sick with beriberi. Despite this she was hurrying as fast as she could.

People were cooling off in front of their houses along the street. At last I reached the doctor's house but he was out – he'd gone to a silk mill more than five or six blocks back. I immediately got someone to go fetch him.

Shortly after I got someone else to go too.

The baby's face looked very strange. And there was some slight trembling around her mouth.

I noticed that my wife and Ryū were standing in the darkness of the dirt-floored entrance hall of the house.

'You must go to Y.'s house. If you have a nervous breakdown again it'll be twice the trouble, won't it? Go quickly!'

Walking back and forth, my wife still seemed to be waiting for the doctor. But soon I no longer noticed her.

'Sato-bō, Sato-bō', I said now and then.

I kept looking first at the passersby outside and then back at the baby.

'Please come in', the doctor's wife said to me. I was sitting on a narrow step that led down to the dirt-floor of the entrance-hall.

'My feet are muddy.'

'I'll hold the baby, so you go wash your feet', she said. I passed the baby to her and went and washed my feet in the kitchen into which the dirt floor continued.

On my return, the doctor's wife had folded a mattress in two and put the baby to sleep on top of it. She placed her hand on the baby's forehead and said: 'She doesn't seem to have any fever.'

The doctor came hurrying back.

I told him briefly about the progress of the baby's condition, about how I had taken her to Tokyo two days before, and how we had returned that morning and she had seemed fine until the evening.

Placing a finger behind each side of the baby's head, the doctor lifted it up innumerable times to examine it. I watched his face closely. He bent his head down. I saw no hope in that face.

'She doesn't seem to have a fever, does she? This might give some stimulus to her brain' – and he raised and lowered the baby's head even more.

'We have to do it like this, touching the chin to the chest. She's beginning to have some convulsions.' He looked at her hands. He grasped both of them hard and showed them to me silently.

The doctor went into the next room, brought out a reflex mirror with a hole in the centre of it and looked into the baby's eyes by the light of a candle.

'How is she?' I asked.

'The pupils of her eyes are open.'

'How is her heart?'

The doctor picked up a stethoscope which had been thrown down nearby and listened. 'The heart still seems alright', he said, taking the stethoscope from his ear. Then he became lost in thought, pulling the tip of his drooping mustache into his mouth with the edge of his lower lip – a habit of his.

'Anyway, shall we rub in a bottle of camphor?' he asked. He went and prepared it and was back in a moment. With a piece of cotton soaked in alcohol, he vigorously wiped the area around the baby's small nipples; then he took the nipples between his fingers, raised them up and pierced them deeply from the side with needles more than an inch long. The baby seemed to have not the slightest sensation. The doctor quietly rubbed on the medicine. He withdrew the needles, pressed down on the skin to make a mark, and then put on some rubber plasters that he had stuck to the back of his hand.

'Let's cool off her head', he said while putting his instruments away. He had a member of his household go fetch some ice.

'Let's give her an enema too' – so saying, he stood up and went into the next room again. For some reason I also stood up and went after him.

It seemed to me that the doctor had given up. But I asked him about it anyway. It was difficult for him to answer. Finally, with considerable reluctance, he answered: 'It seems to be very serious.'

I helped him give the enema. Then he sent me to get some ice, but I soon returned, telling him there was none to be found anywhere.

'Did you check at the Hanzaemu place?' he asked.

'There was none in there either. . . . They'll have some at the confectionery store in front of the railway station. I'll borrow your bicycle and go there myself'.

I thought that I should call the Tokyo pediatrician in on this too. I borrowed a brush and paper and wrote telegrams to him and to the Azabu house, then sped towards the station on the doctor's bicycle. I thought to myself that, if one didn't remain calm, it was at just such a time as this, rushing along a dark street without a lamp, that one might have an accident.

There was no ice at the confectionery either. They told me that, because of a storm the day before, the ice that was supposed to come from across the swamp hadn't come, so there was none to be found anywhere that day. I didn't know what to do.

The next train left Ueno at nine o'clock and it was the last. My telegram to the pediatrician said: 'Baby seriously ill. Doctor here says over-stimulation of brain. Please come by car'. Then I added, 'No ice here either', and sent it from the station.

When I arrived back at the doctor's house, Y. had come. His male servant Sanzō was with him. The grandmother from the farmer's house next door had also come. Ryū, who had seen my wife home, was also back.

'There must be some in Yamaichi. You go quickly and see', the doctor was saying to Ikuko. He had Y., Sanzō and the grandmother from next door go to an ice storehouse across the swamp.

The baby's earth-coloured lips began to undergo a strange spasm, quivering faintly. Her whole body had cooled down. And her abdomen had swollen out grotesquely.

Some ice arrived before long. It was cut into small pieces and an ice-pillow was made. The baby's head was cooled off from above too, with an ice-pack. Some hot fomentations were put on her chest. Y. went around to the baby's feet, which were cold, and warmed them with both his hands. We all wanted to do whatever we could. But none of us really had any idea what to do.

The doctor gave her an enema again. Nothing came out which looked like excrement. Only the liquid he had given her emerged again quickly, looking the same as when it went in. The doctor rubbed his finger into what had soaked into the diaper and examined it.

'Just as I thought, a little mucus has come out, hasn't it?' he said.

I also rubbed the tip of my finger into it. It was slimy.

'Isn't it meningitis?' I asked.

'No, not meningitis. It's just that the brain has been over-stimulated.'

I called to Ryū, who was standing out in the dirt-floored lobby looking over at us: 'Ryū, you didn't knock the baby's head against something when you were carrying her before, did you?'

'Honestly, sir, I didn't', she answered quickly.

'If this baby had hit her head she would have immediately cried out in a loud voice, so Ryū would have known, wouldn't she?'.

'So, after all, the train ride was bad for her', I said. I felt a painful regret that I had let her go.

'If the over-stimulation had been caused by her being jolted about on the train, then one would have expected it to have occurred a little earlier', the doctor answered.

'Sadako came back in the morning, didn't she?' asked Y.

'Yes, the baby seemed in extremely good health. I came back in the evening and by that time she was sleeping but I was told that she had been laughing a lot up until just before then'.

I sat down by the baby's pillow and pressed the ice-pack onto her forehead. I couldn't bear to look into the baby's eyes, wide-open, with a vacant expression in them. With the cloth that was spread beneath the ice-pack, I covered them over. I felt that, just by shutting off her power of vision, I would help her save some amount of energy.

The baby cried, 'ahh, ahh', but there was almost no expression of pain on her face. It was unbearable to me to see how she struggled with all her might to resist the disease.

'Perhaps her stomach hurts,' the doctor said.

Y.'s old housekeeper brought a letter from K.-ko-san. She was also carrying a flat bottle of something.

'K.-ko sends to suggest applying a mustard plaster. She says a child in her family was helped that way', said Y. while reading over the letter.

'Shall we try it?' I said, looking over at the doctor.

'Yes, let's do it.'

The doctor emptied some mustard powder out of the flat bottle and mixed it with some water in a dish. While helping with this, Y. said to his housekeeper: 'Tell K.-ko that if she has any other good ideas she should let us know about them immediately.' Then he said to me: 'She says that Sadako shouldn't worry'.

'Thank-you', I said from the bottom of my heart.

The mustard was spread over some paper and applied from the solar plexus to the abdomen, then to the back, then to both legs.

'Well, that should be enough', said the doctor, looking up at the wall-clock.

'Is that all?'

'If we leave it on too long then something like blisters could develop and cause her discomfort.'

I said that a little discomfort was alright and I wanted the plasters to be left on long enough. Y. agreed with me.

My one faint hope now lay in the Tokyo doctor.

'The telegram reached him at nine-thirty so if we add another thirty minutes for his getting ready, then he should arrive an hour and a half after that', the doctor said.

'It should only take him an hour to get here', said Y.

'But he's travelling at night', I said sceptically.

'At the earliest, eleven-thirty then?', said the doctor.

'I wonder if the roads will be flooded after yesterday's storm?', I said again.

The doctor gently peeled off the mustard plaster from the baby's chest. There was a clear outline where the plaster had been and the skin was all red.

'It's had an effect.' So saying he went around again to the top of the bed and, sitting with his knees drawn up, tried raising and lowering the baby's head. 'It bends a little, doesn't it?' He looked at my face.

'There are far fewer convulsions too – although there's still a bit around the mouth.' He opened the baby's palms. 'Her hands seem to open now.'

With my hopes raised I looked around at Y.

'She seems to have gotten a little better, doesn't she?'

'Compared to before she's much better', said Y.

'She's crying a bit now but if this grows into a loud, continuous 'ahh' then she'll probably be alright,' the doctor said.

'Is that right? Sato-bō, cry loudly! Try to cry more loudly!' I urged her with all my power.

'It's fifteen minutes now, so shall we take the plaster off her stomach?', the doctor asked.

'Well, I suppose so'. I felt that I wanted to leave it for a little while longer.

The doctor peeled off the plaster in the area of the solar plexus, showing me the skin underneath. It was a rather violent shade of red. He had his wife wring out a towel in hot water, and with it he wiped the reddened area. I felt that perhaps the skin had all peeled off with the plaster.

'Let's leave just the ones on her back for a while longer', the doctor said.

There was a kind of lull in the tension.

'Any ordinary baby would not have survived those convulsions. She really put up a good fight', the doctor said.

I felt a joy arise from deep within me. With all the gut force I could command, I urged her again: 'Come on now, cry louder!'

It was a hot, humid night. We were all weakened by the mosquitoes biting at our ankles.

Soon Sanzō and the grandmother from next door returned from across the swamp with plenty of ice. I had Sanzō go get the baby's night-clothes and some diapers, a mosquito-net to enclose on eight-*tatami*-mat area, and my own *kimono*.

I noticed that my own headache had at some time gotten better. And I noticed also that the boil which had been throbbing with pain until the early evening no longer gave me any trouble. But every now and then a yawn escaped me.

The baby began to cry loudly a little more often. We were gladdened by this. But the doctor said that she should be crying even more loudly. He said that all would be well if she cried two or three times louder and kept it up.

He examined her eyes again with his reflex mirror.

'How are they?' I asked from beside him.

'They've narrowed considerably', he answered.

'Then she'll survive, won't she?' I said. I could feel my eyes shining.

Sanzō brought in various things. We changed our old clothes for the new ones, and everyone got behind the mosquito net. While the baby's clothes were being changed, the doctor examined her abdomen. It had grown considerably smaller than before. I thought that everything seemed to be gradually getting back to normal.

'If her heart keeps up like this then everything will be fine', said the doctor.

The clock stuck eleven. I thought that it would be only another thirty minutes or an hour. All I was doing now was waiting for the specialist from Tokyo.

The baby cried out 'ahh' now and then in a loud voice. Each time she did so we all looked into each other's faces. But we didn't tell each other that we were praying that she would cry a little louder.

'Can't you cry harder?' I said as if scolding her.

The time passed gradually by. The baby's condition neither improved nor deteriorated. We waited anxiously for the sound of a car. Even at the slightest sound we would say, 'Perhaps he's come', and strain our ears. We were fooled many times by the sound of a freight train.

'It's about time he should get here', we would say now and then, looking up at the wall-clock.

'This time it is him,' said Y., who had gone outside to look.

Four hours had passed by. The baby had by now opened her eyes for good. It was indeed pitiful to watch her struggling like this with all her might against death, a child who, up to now, would become drowsy when she was drinking her milk and soon fall asleep – especially at night, when she always slept soundly except for that one moment when she was woken up for her milk.

'Ahh, ahh, ahh' – for the first time now the baby cried out in a loud voice. I immediately looked at the doctor's face.

'Yes', he said with a nod.

Y. also expressed great joy.

'If this continues then all will be well', said the doctor. I began to weep. I had been looking at the baby's face but now I couldn't see it.

'Should I send for Sadako?' I asked Y.

'Please send for her immediately', he answered. The doctor agreed.

I at once sent Tsune, who was sitting on the narrow step of the dirt-floored entrance hall, off to Y.'s house to get my wife.

Part Six

B ut the baby did not survive after all. The Tokyo doctor, who arrived finally at about one o'clock, did all he could but couldn't save her. As her condition gradually worsened, he gave her camphor injections and salt injections every ten or twenty minutes. The camphor he injected into her chest. Finally he had put so many plasters on where he had injected her that there was no more room left on her small chest for injections. The baby's breath stank of camphor. The salty water was injected into her thigh. Whichever part of her was injected, the baby's body had become completely numb. Even so, it was plain that there was a strong will to live still at work within her, though she was unconscious of everything. At a time like this, the power of medicine becomes a 'trifling thing'.

The only question was whether or not this small baby herself would continue for some time to struggle with all her might against death. The Tokyo doctor himself said so. He said that, if, somewhere along the line, we could come to grips with her, then she would survive.

He gave the baby an enema. With the help of the Abiko doctor, he tried doing it again and again. Although her stomach had deflated to normal size once earlier, it had at some time swollen up again and now, no matter how many times it was cleaned out, it would not grow smaller. Her lips, which had just a little life-blood left in them before, now were the colour of earth, and were continually trembling with cramp.

It was about four o'clock. The Tokyo doctor said he'd better return home in the car waiting for him outside but he'd be back later. We all felt rather unhappy about this. But we thought that, by saying so, he was telling us that the baby had no chance of survival. I didn't feel like saying anything but I said: 'Do you have another patient in a critical condition?'

'No, it's not that,' he answered.

With an obvious expression of displeasure on their faces, Y. and the Abiko doctor asked him to stay longer. Then Y., who just happened to have some business in Tokyo, offered to return there in the waiting car and ask the doctor's friend, another pediatrician, to come. Y. also was a friend of this other doctor.

It was now light outside.

The baby's body had grown gradually colder and colder. This was because her heart had weakened. We tried to warm her with towels that had been dipped in boiling water. K.-ko-san, who had come before and helped a lot with the baby and Sadako, had sent Sanzō to get all the towels from Y.'s house and my own.

Two big towels, each the size of one *tatami* mat, and many small ones were brought from Y.'s house, plus every towel that could be found from my own house. The doctor's wife boiled the water. K.-ko san, Sanzō and Tsune wrung out towels in very hot water. After cooling them off a bit, they put them on the baby's back, chest and feet. They tried with all their might to warm the baby but she wouldn't get warm. Nonetheless, her condition improved a little. But this didn't last even twenty minutes. Her heart weakened again. The eight people there could do nothing but try to warm up the baby – so they did this with all their might. The Tokyo doctor also worked as hard as he could. I was deeply impressed with all of them. But I felt sorry for the baby that there were no close relatives here from the Azabu house to tend to her. And I also felt that something was missing.

Although the towels were untouchably hot, still the baby didn't warm up. No matter what happened to the baby later, even if she were crippled, still I didn't want her to die.

Her belly kept swelling up more and more. I didn't know what was in her stomach but I thought if I could take it out now she might improve. The Tokyo doctor put a rubber tube up her anus as far as possible to wash out her stomach.

The baby grew weaker and weaker. But she was still struggling to live with all her small energy.

The Tokyo doctor sucked on the tube to try to suck out everything from the baby's stomach. He spat out into a basin but almost nothing came out. While he was doing this the baby stopped breathing. A black murky fluid came out of her nose and mouth. It spread over her cheeks which had become blue and flowed down the nape of her neck. The doctor quickly wiped that up and gave her artificial respiration. But that was just to console those of us standing around. My wife cried violently and collapsed. K.-ko-san lifted her up and put her head against her chest: 'Sadako, be brave, be brave,' she said. K.-ko also cried.

I wept. I wept as when my real mother died.

Part Seven

I had someone bring a good *kimono* for the baby from my house. We left the doctor's house with Sanzō's wife carrying the baby. It was daylight and the weather was fine. My wife carefully put a new handkerchief over the baby's face. We returned to our house along the same road we had stumbled along the night before with a lantern, now in morning sunlight. Sanzō's wife walked about fifty meters ahead of us with the baby. Looking down, my wife followed five or six meters behind me.

Having received the telegram we sent the night before, my mother came from Azabu. A telegram was sent to my wife's parents and they also came. My father's cousin's husband, T.-san, also arrived.

'A terrible thing has happened', said T. 'I saw the telegram just a while ago and immediately phoned your father at the Hakone villa and asked what we should do. He ordered that Satoko be buried at an Abiko temple.'

Upon hearing this I became nauseous with anger.

'I don't know how long we'll be living in Abiko, you see. So I plan to bury her in Tokyo.'

'Oh, are you opposed?' T. answered simply.

I felt displeased with all the people at Azabu – both my grandmother and my mother too. I had told them in last night's telegram that the baby's condition was serious but I hadn't asked them to come – nevertheless, I told them the Tokyo doctor was coming by car, hinting that they could come with him.

But I felt even more displeased when I heard that mother and grandmother thought I was over-reacting. Once before I had sent them a telegram because I was shocked when the baby had had a little spasm. But this was different. Although I had written that she was 'dangerously ill', they had chosen to ignore this and take it lightly. I was especially angry at grandmother, who had wanted me to bring the baby to Tokyo. I would also have expected T. to know that I wasn't the sort of person to take orders – he shouldn't have repeated the order so directly. Before he had said that I had been in a rather sentimental mood. I had been thinking, for the baby's sake and for the sake of my real mother, that I would bury her at Aoyama, next to my real mother, as she was her first grandchild (and my mother had died at a younger age than I was now). But I didn't want to say this myself. Besides, I hadn't said I wanted to bury her in Tokyo before with the idea of burying her next to my real mother. I asked T. to buy for me two or three square meters of land in the Aoyama Cemetery, and to make arrangements for the burial the next day. Instead of having *sutras* read by a monk 'with bones like a horse', I asked him to get my uncle's teacher, the abbot of Kenchoji, to give her a Buddhist name and offer up *sutras* for her at Kamakura on the same day.

The painter S.K. came to see me from Tokyo. We sat up with the baby all night. We put various things in the coffin, including our photos and all my wife's Sashiro dolls. Also a *kimono* with my wife's family crest on it.

Next morning a car came from Tokyo and S.K., Y. and myself went in it together. My carpenter and gardener carried the coffin to the temple. While we were going up a road between rice-fields towards town, an old woman we knew came out with an arm-full of wild flowers to see us off. She put the flowers on the coffin. My wife stayed at home, since it wasn't yet seventy-five days after she'd given birth. That morning a telegram had arrived from my Akasaka uncle saying we could bring the coffin to Akasaka. Father had forbidden our taking the coffin to the Azabu house. I felt deeply angry about this. It seemed to me that, if everyone had not tried to use the baby to improve my relations with father, she would still be alive. From the beginning I didn't want to let the baby go to Tokyo but I suppressed this feeling and agreed to let her go – I felt I couldn't repent enough for this, but now it was too late. Nonetheless, because of this I now wanted to do all I could for the deceased. Furthermore, when I heard that father, on top of refusing to allow the coffin to come to the Azabu house, had forbidden the baby's young aunts and great-grandmother from going to its funeral in Akasaka, I became even more furious. I would never forget my disgust towards him for transferring his anger from me to the baby, the baby whom I had watched steadily from two nights before to yesterday morning struggling with all her might against an unnatural death that was encroaching upon her little by little.

Everything had gone wrong because of my unsatisfactory relations with the Azabu house. This was extremely frustrating. But, in order to improve those relations, I had to send the baby for grandmother to see. This made me angry, but the discord in our relations always came from such anger. And such anger also interfered with my writing. I didn't know how many times, in the past five or six years, I had planned to write about my dispute with father. But it always ended in failure. I might say that one reason was my lack of perseverance, and another was that I didn't want to write out of a personal grudge against father. The main reason, though, was that, when I considered the prospect of such a book actually being published, I felt depressed – and especially I couldn't bear the thought of how its publication would throw a dark shadow over my relations with grandmother. When I was living in Matsue more than three years before, out of my desire to get around that 'tragedy' I planned the following outline for a novel: a certain miserable-faced youth comes to visit me. This youth has been writing a serial story in a Matsue newspaper and brings it for me to read. It is about a discord with his father. Before long the series suddenly disappears from the paper, though it has not yet come to an end. The youth comes to visit me in an excited state. Even though he had used a pseudonym in writing of his father, his father had nonetheless discovered who was being written about and had sent someone down from Tokyo to pay off the newspaper not to publish the series anymore. Afterwards various unpleasant incidents had occurred between father and son. I wrote of these from a third-person point of view. The near-desperate youth, in his anger, had very unpleasant negotiations with his father. His father told him never to come home again. Besides this, I wrote about various other such unpleasant incidents which could have really happened between father and myself, thinking that, if I wrote about them openly, I might prevent them really happening. And I thought that I would put the greatest tragedy of all as the climax at the end, to occur during the grandmother's dying scene. Imagining how the excited youth would barge in against all opposition and how perhaps he would have a wild fight with his father, something more than just a fist-fight, I wondered whether to have the father kill the son or the son kill the father. But, while I was imagining the most intense moment of this fight, there suddenly arose within me a different twist to the scene: the father and son suddenly stopped fighting, hugged each others and wept violently. This scene, which spontaneously leapt into my mind, was unexpected even to myself. As I imagined it, I had to fight back the tears.

Anyway I postponed the decision about whether to write the catastrophe into my novella. Since I couldn't make up my mind about it, I would have to actually write the story up to that point before deciding how it would turn out. But what a good thing it would be if the story had turned out to have that happy outcome.

I wrote some of this story but found I couldn't continue with it. My relations with father had begun to grow worse over the issue of my marriage. It seemed to me that the 'catastrophe' scene I had imagined spontaneously might actually occur sometime between father and me. At a very tragic moment in our relationship it might indeed happen. Or it might not necessarily happen. Even though I wouldn't know how it would turn out until it actually happened, I felt, nonetheless, that there was still something remaining in both father and me which might make for a sudden turnaround of a catastrophe. I talked about this with my wife and some friends.

Part Eight

After the baby's death our house was very lonely. I would bring a chair out to the garden at night to cool off and when I heard the birds crying 'ahh, ahh' in the forest beyond the swamp I couldn't bear it.

I could no longer stand living in Abiko. We talked about moving to the suburbs of Kyoto around the end of the year.

After about ten days Y. left on a trip for Korea and China and Abiko became even more lonely. Just about that time my oldest and closest friend M. came with his wife to stay with us.

M. said the doctor had told him his chest was bad. When I heard this somehow my own body also felt as if it were out of sorts for a moment. I asked him if he wouldn't like to stay at Abiko. I had forgotten for a moment about my plans for moving to Kyoto. I was sure that area beside the swamp with its many pine trees, its moist air even in winter and its relatively warm temperature was good for someone with respiratory disease.

M. and his wife didn't stay on at Abiko but they built a new house at a place which had taken their fancy in a neighboring village on a hill surrounded in the rear by pine woods. A while after they had decided on this, M. discovered that the doctor had been mistaken in diagnosing his T.B.

We wanted to travel in order to recover as soon as possible from the heartbreak of having lost our child. We decided to leave on the twentieth of August, seventy-five days after my wife had given birth.

Just a while earlier the painter S.K. had gone with his family to the Kanbayashi hotspring in Shinshu, so we decided to go there too. We left Abiko on the morning of August 20th. and my wife visited the child's grave for the first time. After that I visited my friend's house. My wife went by herself to my family's house in Azabu. We decided to meet later at the Roppongi Station in Azabu, from where we planned on going to Ueno. But the appointed hour came and went and my wife didn't show up. I walked a little towards the Azabu house, becoming more and more irritated. Finally my wife came towards me with a tired face but hurrying all the same. On top of the fact that she was late for our appointment, the humiliation of my being unable to enter the Azabu house made me all the more angry, and I scolded her quite severely.

On the train she told me, weeping, how when she had gone to my father's room he had suddenly asked her angrily why she had brought the baby's corpse to Tokyo. On that day my grandmother, mother and little sisters were not there, having gone to our Hakone villa. Only my second-oldest sister, Yoshiko, and my father were there. My wife had become so emotionally sensitive at this time that she would feel an urge to cry whenever she met anyone. When she was about to enter my father's room, the tears already began to fall. Undoubtedly she had unconsciously expected my father to say sympathetically: 'It's a great shame about Satoko, isn't it?' But he suddenly got angry. My wife was shocked. While speaking of this she began to cry. Although I felt a deep anger arise towards father, I spoke to her in a tone half-consoling and half-scolding. I noticed that the other passengers were giving us strange looks but I was so angry that I didn't get embarrassed.

From Ueno we took the Kobe-bound night-train on the Shinetsu line. On the train I couldn't help but feel that we were going to have an accident. I borrowed my wife's cotton sash and placed it between the train wall and my head. I thought this would help somewhat when my head hit the wall after the train crashed. The train was so crowded I hardly slept at all but, despite my anxieties, we arrived safely at our destination. Nevertheless, from the night we arrived at Kanbayashi, I was menaced by other obsessions. Every now and then I'd hear a great thud and the earth would tremble. On the evening of the third day I finally couldn't stand it any longer. It puzzled me that no one else was bothered by it. I repeatedly asked S.K. to go away with me. But he felt he could do enough work there and, at that moment, in fact, he was in the middle of painting a number-twelve-sized canvas. I felt uneasy staying there for even a minute. But for anyone else it would be unthinkable to leave like this: since it was already evening, we would have to pack lots of luggage, and S.K. would have to take his children, who were a little sick, five or six miles by rickshaw.

We left the next day, carrying all the luggage we had brought when planning to stay about two months. The landlord and maids of the inn all had a good laugh.

Though I regret the inconvenience I caused S.K., at the time I thought that the laughing landlord and maids were reckless idiots for staying there. After we left, the rumbling of the mountain gradually got worse and worse and, a while after we had arrived at the Yamanaka hotspring in Koga, we read in the newspaper that prefectural officials had gone to examine the mountain, Mount Kasahōshi.

After about a month we parted from S.K. and went to Kyoto. We hiked around Nara, Hōryūji and the Ishiyama area and then, at the beginning of October, we went back to Abiko. Three or four carpenters from Tokyo were hard at work on M.'s property.

When we had started on our trip, my wife became upset whenever she saw a baby about the same age as her own who had died. Compared with her, I was not so sensitive. When we were together sometimes she would wander off somewhere by herself. Often, at these times, there would be someone holding a baby where she went. But these incidents gradually grew more rare.

One day in November my oldest sister, who had married a naval officer, gave birth to a baby girl. A message came from my grandmother saying she was going to visit her with a young group the following Sunday and asking if I'd like to go too. My wife, although feeling it might be dangerous for her to see someone else's baby, wanted to go also.

That day we left Abiko early and met grandmother and the others at Shinbashi Station. First we went to visit uncle's house. Uncle had been practicing Zen at Kenchōji for perhaps ten years or more but, because of an eye disease, he had rented a house in Akasaka and gone to see a doctor from there for more than a year. About the beginning of September, though, his eyes had finally improved a little and he had returned to Kamakura.

My sister and her baby were both well. Before I had a baby all babies looked the same but, when I looked at my sister's baby, she was completely different from my baby who had died. I remembered my baby a little but not very much. My sister was born on New Year's day when I was fifteen. I talked about the evening when she was born. I, who had had no brother or sister until then, was waiting very delightedly in the living room when my Kamakura uncle's grandmother came in holding the baby. It was a strange bright red thing with a ridiculously long head. I remarked that that baby had now given birth to this baby.

My youngest sister, Rokuko, put her face near the baby and made as if to smell it, then suddenly said: 'When Satoko-chan died she had a nice smell'. We had sprinkled some perfume around the coffin. She remembered that. My startled wife pushed Rokuko in the back.

A while later my wife made a strange face, stood up quickly and went out towards the entrance hall. Shortly afterwards I too went out and found her in tears. 'Please excuse me to everyone. I don't know what came over me', she said. And she repeated 'excuse me' over and over again.

'It's good that you're so calm, isn't it?' she added sarcastically.

I sent my wife back to uncle's house right away. A while after I also returned to his house with grandmother and the kids.

Whenever my wife looked into my face, she would immediately take me where no-one could see us and say: 'What should I do? I came determined not to cry because its bad for everyone. . . .'

'It can't be helped. It's alright. No-one takes it badly' – even though I reassured her in this way, still she just wouldn't stop saying this. I left her and went to where grandmother was.

I talked with grandmother. Bent over as if to cover her own knees, she sat smoking. Sadako came in with her eyes all red. She came and sat before grandmother, suddenly bowed and said in a quivering voice: 'Grandmother, please forgive me.' Still maintaining her bent posture and looking down with the mouth of her pipe between her lips, grandmother remained silent. Her lips trembled.

I felt ashamed at that moment that I had felt a grudge towards grandmother because of my child's death.

Part Nine

A while after we had returned from Kamakura, we discovered that my wife was pregnant again. I felt it was a little too soon. Even if she was already capable of having another baby, it seemed better to wait a while longer. But my wife was happy. Grandmother was also pleased. And considering that before I had blamed grandmother, even a little, for my child's death, for her sake I also was happy that another child was coming so soon.

Towards the end of the year M. moved to a neighboring village, so that Abiko also became quite lively. Since I had been moving from one place to another over the past five or six years and hadn't seen M. for a long time, we now visited each other frequently. And, as the days and months passed by, I felt that something new was added to the love I had always felt for him. This was a happy thing. And it had a good effect on my emotional life. Really he possessed the strange power to bring out the good in other people. Also, he understood so well the subtle beauty of the direct communion of heart to heart. He had never been disappointed by this. I began to feel mellow inside and none of our days were dull.

It was now going on four years since I had lived in Matsue. As I have already mentioned, I had found myself unable to get beyond the planning stages of a novel and, after that, I decided not to do any creative writing for a while. I thought that it was a mistake from the beginning because my frame of mind at that time was too bad, my mood was too gloomy, too miserable, to attempt to do spontaneous creative work. And so, until just recently, I had not written much at all. Those few times when I tried to write something, I failed. I had no intention of giving up writing but, the few times I tried to write, I didn't feel the kind of excitement I had felt six or seven years before and this made me rather uneasy.

Around February I started to put together a circulating magazine every Saturday with a certain close friend of mine who had also stopped writing for a while because of ill health. We did it half in jest. But we both felt that something real would come out of that joke. Steadfastly I started on my novel again. I published three parts of it, then stopped midway and published a short story. The next thing I published was also another short story. But while we were doing all this, my friend was told some bad news about his health by an unsparing doctor. Before we knew it, our circulating magazine was no more. But, by force of habit, I wrote another short piece. I didn't show it to anybody. And I had no confidence in those things I had scribbled hastily one or two nights before the Saturday deadline, nor any wish to publish them.

Just at that time word came from a certain bookstore that they wanted to publish my previous writings as one volume of a series. At first the bookstore had gone to M. asking to publish his work and, at the same time, they had told him they wanted to publish my work too. M. had answered that I'd probably refuse and hadn't said anything about it to me but, when his wife happened to mention it, I thought I might as well let them publish. I felt that such a publication might give me the impetus to write something new. And I did still want to write.

One day I showed M. two stories I had printed in the circulating magazine. He said he thought one of them was well written. Of the other he said that it expressed well an atmosphere of profound and quiet sadness. And he suggested that I publish them. When M. returned home I walked with him along the country road. As we walked together, he gave a pleasing and perceptive analysis of my works. I published one of them in the following month's issue of the *White Birch* magazine.

It was two or three days later. Perhaps by chance, a representative of a certain magazine company came to per-suade me to publish something in his magazine. I had him publish the other story two months later. Soon another magazine asked me for a story. I still had another short story left but I wrote a new one for them. I wrote about something I had spontaneously imagined during the free time I had the summer before when my wife had visited the Tokyo hospital because of her pregnancy.

This was a story about a husband one could describe as honest but not as habitually well-behaved. His wife leaves the house for a while on some business. During this time the maid becomes pregnant. But the husband is not responsible. Even though his conscience is clear, he's the type of person one can't help but have suspicions about. One day, though, when it becomes clear that the maid is pregnant, he says to his wife: 'I had nothing to do with it'. His wife just says: 'Oh, is that so?', and believes him. I wanted to write just that. Both the husband and the wife were intelligent. So, until the end, I couldn't put in any tragedy. I wanted to express the idea in this way. Now that I was gradually being restored to a peaceful frame of mind, I thought that it would be unfortunate if, in my real life, out of stupidity, I should harbour suspicions about people I should believe in and so cause any number of tragedies which didn't have to happen. And, of course, this idea did not necessarily relate to anyone else.

Anyway, the story was a failure. If I hadn't promised it by a certain date, I would have been able to revise it and perhaps would have captured the feeling I wanted a little more. But the deadline date arrived and I had to send it off in an unsatisfactory state.

A while later I received a request from a newspaper for about ten pages of diary or essay. I sent a two-and-a-half-page story called, *A Certain Father and His Son*. This was different from what they had ordered, so I sent a letter saying that if they didn't want it they should send it right back and I wouldn't complain. This wasn't something I had written myself – I had taken it, without permission, from a work of almost two hundred pages written by a postal clerk I had met in a certain city, and I had just changed some of the sentences a little. I informed the newspaper of this fact also.

The hero of the story worked at a telephone company and, because of his relationship with a beautiful operator there, was severely reprimanded by the boss: 'You have done something ugly and shameful'. Shortly afterwards he and the girl were fired but, just before that, the man had told his parents everything and asked their permission to marry. It was just this latter conversational scene that I sent to the publishers. It told how the father soon gave his consent and the mother too, gladly, with tears flowing. Even so, I myself was suffering the tragedy of a break with my father because something strangely warped within us prevented us from achieving the harmony that could easily be achieved – thus I was attracted to the opposite of this situation as expressed in the piece I had copied. I was thinking also of my own relationship with my father when I gave it the title, *A Certain Father and His Son*, but I realized that, just by this title alone, a very few close friends would know that I was referring to the fact that I had quarreled with my own father over my marriage four times, before and after my wedding.

Gradually I settled into a more and more peaceful frame of mind. I began to question myself a little as to whether everything was fine left as it was. But I thought that, compared to my uneasiness before, I was at least becoming more peaceful. And I also thought that I couldn't go on forever writing about only the good fortune of good people.

My peaceful frame of mind gradually began to influence my feelings towards my father. Of course, there were still some slight upsets. One time, for instance, when I went up to Tokyo with my wife and phoned my parents' house to ask after grandmother's health, father just happened to be out so mother asked us to come over quickly. We immediately headed for Azabu by tram. Just as we were about to enter the front gate, however, Takako, who was standing there waiting for us, came running up and said in a low voice: 'Father is back'. Although we had just entered the gate and had not yet met anyone, we immediately turned around and left. At times like this, as might be expected, my peaceful frame of mind was disturbed for a while. Then again, sometimes when I heard rumours that father kept saying irritable, demanding things to my sisters, I couldn't help thinking that this irritability was caused by his rift with me, and I felt guilty that now only I was enjoying a peaceful frame of mind. I felt a deep sympathy for his unhappiness, especially because he was gradually getting old.

Part Ten

The day of my wife's delivery drew closer and closer. This time she was going to have it at Abiko. If she gave birth at a Tokyo hospital she'd have to take the chance of coming back by train after three or four weeks. Rather than that it was better by far to be cautious and have the baby at home. But sometimes it occurred to me that there was one chance in ten thousand that it might be a difficult delivery. And I thought that, because of what had happened last year, I had become a little too much of a coward. On the other hand it was good to be very careful. Nonetheless, it also occurred to me that by being too neurotically careful I could make something go wrong. I tried as much as possible to get rid of my uneasiness.

For a midwife I decided to ask the same woman as the year before and for a doctor I decided on a local one. For a nurse I asked a woman living with the midwife who, although old, was also qualified to practice midwifery. That nurse came on July thirteenth.

About a week passed but the baby gave no sign at all of being born. I planned to go stay at Y.'s place when it looked like the baby was about to come and to return after the birth.

One day the midwife came from Tokyo on an intuition that the baby was about to be born – but her intuition was wrong and she returned the following morning.

Again, K.-kun, who I'd met about two years before, came to visit me one day. He had recently become a father. The way he talked, he seemed to get nervous at every little bad smell his baby might have.

K.'s baby was delivered at a Tokyo hospital. When he was told by phone that the birth was near, he was strangely unsettled, and even though he was at home he didn't know what to do with himself until finally he got word that it was a safe delivery. He went quickly to the hospital and found the new-born baby lying beside his wife under a small *futon*. Seeing this, he said: 'Just so!' There was somehow a lot of feeling in this 'just so!' and we all laughed heartily.

K. knew a lot about how to raise babies so he and the nurse had a lot to talk about. While they were talking, my wife suddenly said that the baby inside her felt a little strange. After inquiring about her feelings in more detail, the nurse then asked K.: 'What do you think – will it be soon?' K. replied: 'It might be about two o'clock tomorrow afternoon. Somehow I feel it will be.' When we asked him about this, we discovered that K.'s baby had been born about two in the afternoon. Soon he went home. I took him to the station and asked him to give a call to the Azabu house anyway when he got back to Tokyo. But my wife's stomach got better.

It was the evening of the twenty-second. I put a chair out in the garden and, while I was enjoying the cool breeze that blew off the marsh, my wife said: 'My belly feels a little tight.' If I called the midwife, it would already be too late for her to catch the final train. The nurse said that the midwife would come by car anyway, so we could wait a while to see how things would develop. 'The baby won't come out until tomorrow morning or afternoon anyway,' she said.

I went to sleep. My wife wasn't in much pain so everyone else also followed my example. But I was awakened about one-thirty by my wife's voice. I got up and woke up the nurse. I also woke up Tsune and Hisa and told them to hurry up and boil some water. Then, carrying a lamp, I went to the station. Teru the dog tagged along behind me.

At Abiko they wouldn't send a telegram after hours. I had to depend on the kindness of the station master to allow me, against the rules, to use his phone. After my baby had died the year before, the assistant station-master who was there then had kindly told me I could use the phone any time in an emergency. That person had since been transferred but I asked the man who'd replaced him. He cheerfully agreed – but no-one answered at Ueno Station for a long while. When they finally answered it took them a long time to understand what we wanted. Meanwhile a freight train arrived from Tokyo and the assistant had to go out to the platform to hand over the tablet. Another station employee whose face was familiar phoned instead and finally my message got through.

I hurried back home.

The nurse was busily going about her work, all the while saying: 'It won't come out with just that little effort.'

I wanted to use the eight-mat living room as the delivery room. The nurse wanted to use the six-mat room beside it. She was a kind woman of good character but rather stubborn, and she wouldn't listen to me. I got angry and, all by myself, pulled the maternity bed she'd made up into the living room.

Outside it was still pitch dark. I couldn't escape to Y's place, since he'd still be asleep.

'When the time's come I'll go out into the garden', I said. It seemed to me there was a good reason for the traditional belief that a husband should not witness his wife giving birth. And I felt that the husband should be considerate towards his wife's feeling that she didn't want him to see her face and body in the unsightly agony of giving birth – as long as he knew it was a safe birth, that was enough. Besides, it would be painful for me to have to sit and watch her suffering.

The pain in her belly came on strong sometimes and then went away again. But the periods of rest gradually grew shorter and shorter. I sent Hisa to Sanzō's house to tell him to go fetch the doctor from town.

Outside it had grown lighter. I heard the sound of beating wings as some pigeons flew out of the eaves of the entrance hall.

My wife's pain gradually got more severe. I too became strangely restless and walked aimlessly in and out of the room and around the house. There was really no one to help. I didn't feel like going off by myself into the garden and leaving everything to our maids, who were still so young. But what should I do? There didn't seem to be anything particularly I could do.

'Sir, sir', the nurse called out. I went.

'Hold tightly onto both your wife's shoulders'.

I immediately sat near the pillow and held down her shoulders with a firm grip. My wife pressed her two hands tightly against her chest, putting strength into her whole body. Her slightly pale face grimaced and, with her eyeteeth, she bit with all her might into a piece of gauze which had been folded many times over. Expressing as it did her enormous effort and determination, her face seemed more beautiful than usual.

'Will the baby be first, or our doctor from Tokyo, or the local doctor? It's a race', the nurse said, putting on a calm front. But I knew very well that she was nervous.

My wife stopped breathing and closed her eyes tightly. I tensed up along with her, clenching my fists.

'The baby has won the race! It's won the race!'

Water spurted up about a foot, a bit like a fountain. At the same time the baby's black head protruded out. And then, just as when a small stream which has been dammed up suddenly breaks through, the whole tiny body came flowing smoothly out between its mother's wide-open knees. The baby immediately gave out its first big cry. I was deeply moved, almost to the point of tears. Not caring that the nurse was looking on, I kissed my wife on her pale forehead.

'That's excellent, excellent! The baby has won, it's won!' With beads of sweat standing all over her face, the nurse said this while quickly cleaning up the afterbirth. She then stood up and left, letting the baby lie as it was. The baby began to cry all the more fiercely, kicking the inside of its mother's thighs with its tiny feet.

Breathing deeply, my wife looked up into my eyes with a tired but peaceful smile.

'Good, good', I nodded, fighting back the tears. I felt a strong need to express gratitude to something, and my heart searched for an appropriate object.

I didn't have an especially parental feeling towards the new-born baby – indeed, I had no particular desire to become more closely acquainted with that bawling infant who was kicking and struggling there. And I didn't want to find out quickly whether it was a boy or girl. The only thing I felt was the afterglow of the joyful and tearful excitement awakened in my heart by the baby's birth.

There had been nothing ugly in the process of birth. One reason was that it had been a very natural birth. There had been nothing at all unsightly expressed in my wife's face or body. It had all been beautiful.

After the birth too everything had gone smoothly. The town doctor arrived, then the Tokyo midwife, and then, a while later, mother from Tokyo.

I asked my wife to ask grandmother to choose a name for the baby.

To officially register the birth, I went up to Tokyo two or three days later with my seal. Grandmother could not think of a particularly good name so she suggested her own, 'Rume'. My second sister laughed and said it was a funny name – perhaps because there were no girls with that name in her school. But I liked grandmother's name, and my mother also approved of it.

Thinking, though, that it might cause problems to have two people of the same sex with exactly the same name in our family, I added the character 'ko' to make it 'Rumeko'.

Part Eleven

All that happened more than four weeks ago now.

Shortly afterwards, when I saw a review in the newspaper of *Danshichi Kurobee*, a play at the *kabuki* theatre, I felt that I wanted to go to the theatre for the first time in a long while.

I invited M. to come along, and we decided to go on the twenty-third of the month. Any other day would have been inconvenient for me – however, it turned out that the play closed before the twenty-third. Nevertheless, we thought there would be a good play on somewhere else that day or, if not, we could go see a film. I would settle all my business before then, and I'd meet M. at twelve-thirty on the second floor of

Maruzen Book Store or, if I came later, at the Takashimaya Department Store, where his wife bought her *kimono.*

On rising that day I left immediately, without even eating breakfast. I had some business with a friend in Hashiba, so I got off the train at Minamisenju and visited him for over an hour, then went on to the Mitsui Bank in Nihonbashi. I'd planned to be there no more than fifteen minutes but even after two hours my business still wasn't finished. I couldn't stand the irritation of waiting impatiently while they called out number after number, but never mine. It wouldn't have been so bad if I had brought along something to read. But just to stand there so long breathing in that foul air was enough to put me in a very bad mood. I was surrounded by complete strangers. Among them I felt like oil dropped into water.

Finally I couldn't stand it anymore and left the bank without getting any money. I concluded that, although it was a large building with many employees, it wasn't a place where much work got done. During the time they'd kept me waiting on the bench I could have gone as far as Kouzu by express train – it was terrible that I'd had to wait that long without even getting my business done. I thought it was unkind of them not to warn a customer who was waiting patiently without knowing the situation about how long it was going to take.

After crossing the Nihon Bridge, I dropped in at the Morimura Bank, then went to the Kuroeya store across the street and, as my wife had requested, bought a nest of boxes for red bean rice. These were to take along with us the following day when we visited a Shintō shrine. I borrowed the store's phone and tried calling the Azabu house. Mother answered.

'Grandmother's jaw has gotten out of joint', she said.

She then told me that, when Yoshiko had gone to grandmother's room that morning, she had found her sitting on the bed in an absent-minded daze, her mouth wide open. Even when Yoshiko said something to her, grandmother had simply nodded and, with her mouth still wide open, gasped, 'ah, ah'. I'd heard that once before too, though I hadn't known about it at the time, when grandmother had been standing out on the veranda and someone had remarked to her that the moon was out, she had looked up suddenly and by that movement dislocated one side of her jaw. Because Yoshiko remembered this, she had immediately summoned mother and phoned one of our relatives who was a doctor. But he himself had been sick. Then she'd phoned another of our doctor relatives but he was away on a trip. In desperation, she'd phoned back the first doctor and asked him to recommend someone else. Feeling sorry for her, he'd suppressed his own sickness and came over right away. Mother told me that one side of the jaw had been relocated easily but the other side took a long time and caused grandmother much pain.

'She's sleeping very well at the moment but she does seem to have a little fever', she said.

'What's her temperature?'

'When I measured it a while ago it was thirty-eight point three.'

'Quite high, isn't it? Well, I have a little business to do, but as soon as I'm finished I'll be over there.'

'Yes', mother answered. I thought to myself that father must be home.

I left the store, weighed down with the huge package containing the nest of lacquered boxes. I concluded my business at the Morimura Bank in a satisfactory way and then returned to the Mitsui Bank for one more try. No luck again.

I was worried about grandmother. Until now I hadn't known about her dislocated jaw. I supposed that a dislocated jaw was not something one should be particularly concerned about. But somehow the sense I had that her body was becoming more and more fragile gave me a forlorn feeling.

It was already a little past the time I was supposed to meet my friends at Maruzen Bookstore, so I went directly to the Takashimaya Department Store. I couldn't see them at first, but soon they came walking up the stairs. They told me they'd missed the express train.

The three of us lunched together at the store restaurant. The depressing news about grandmother's health coming on top of my frustrating experience at the bank had put me in a thoroughly bad mood. When we'd finished eating, M. and I left by ourselves. I didn't feel like going back to the bank. It closed at four so I thought if I went just before then I could get everything settled quickly. After arranging to meet M. at five o'clock at a small cinema in Asakusa, I headed for Azabu. M. headed for the Maruzen Bookstore where, I suspected, he would meet up with his wife again after she'd finished her business at the *kimono* store.

I was suffering from an unpleasant sense of both physical and emotional exhaustion. On top of that, it made me feel even worse to have to walk along weighed down by a terribly bulky package filled with lacquered boxes.

Alighting from the train, I hurried to the Azabu house. I left my package in the entrance hall and went directly to grandmother's room. Mother and Takako were there.

Mother immediately moved her face close to grandmother's and said in a slightly raised voice: 'Junkichi has come to visit.'

Grandmother opened her heavy eyelids a little. I looked at her clouded, bloodshot eyes. Right away she closed them again.

Now I moved my face close to hers.

'Grandmother, the baby is fine.'

With her eyes still shut, she nodded imperceptibly. In a voice raised just one degree, I said again: 'A dislocated jaw is nothing to worry about.' She made no answer, as if she found it too troublesome even to nod a little.

'Please put some tobacco in her pipe', mother said.

I filled the long pipe that was lying at grandmother's side. When I passed it to her she still kept her eyes closed but loosened her lips a little, just enough to insert the mouthpiece, and inhaled. But it seemed to me that she wasn't clearly conscious of what she was doing.

Soon grandmother began to move her thighs restlessly. She was soiling herself. The chamber pot was brought from the next room. I picked her up in my arms and held her from behind over the pot.

All this made me feel extremely helpless and disheartened. I felt a pain in my chest. Strong-minded and fastidious as she was, grandmother had been particularly fussy about such things – even when she was seriously ill she hated to use the chamber pot in her bedroom. I had often gotten angry with her about it. But, even so, she had forced herself to stand up and walk to the toilet, saying: 'I have to because if I'm not in the toilet it won't come out.' But gradually even she had stopped saying such unreasonable things. And she didn't complain much when the chamber pot was put in her sick room. Nonetheless, until now I had never known her to relieve herself without knowing what she was doing.

Mother had the maid bring some warm water and with it she carefully cleaned the lower part of grandmother's body. While she was doing that another maid came and said to her: 'The master is calling for you.'

When she'd finished with the cleaning mother stood up and left.

For an eighty-two-year-old, grandmother had a look in her eyes that was unusually strong and lively. Though I had thought that her body had weakened bit by bit over the previous four or five years, whenever I looked at that expression in her eyes I felt relieved, confident that she would last many years more. Her voice too possessed a certain power – as she demonstrated when, without getting up from sitting, she would shout commands to a maid in another room or to her grandchildren. When I heard her do that I always felt a certain pleasure. In reality I was afraid of grandmother's death. And when I imagined the unpleasantness which might occur between father and me at the scene of her death, that was terrible too. But, anyway, what I wanted above all was for grandmother to live longer. When I had written previously a story about a wife giving birth attended by her husband and maid, and had written that the wife's grandmother had gotten very sick, I had made the age of that grandmother two years older than mine and had also written that she had recovered from her grave illness. Somehow I couldn't bear not making the omens auspicious. But now I didn't know where to place my hope in the grandmother who lay before me. Having just been struck by the ease with which her jaw could be dislocated, I now witnessed her lack of self-control. I was overcome by the terrifying feeling that what I had long feared would happen had finally happened.

Mother returned with an unhappy face and beckoned to me from the veranda. I stood up and went to her. In a low voice she said: 'If grandmother goes on like this there's no need to worry about her, so please go home now. Don't take this badly.' But I was offended and said nothing. I couldn't understand how she could say there was nothing to worry about if grandmother continued as she was.

'Because if you should have any kind of clash with your father during this sickness that would be the worst misfortune of all,' she added.

'I think of my relationship with father as completely separate from my relationship with grandmother. Perhaps you will also recognize this fact?' I spoke in a slightly agitated voice.

'Yes, I understand that very well.'

'So let's get father also to recognize it. But even if he doesn't I'll behave in the same way. Anyway, I'll try writing a letter to ask him about it as calmly as possible.'

'That would be good. Calmly and from the heart.'

'In that case I'd rather meet with him right now. Is he in the study?'

'Somehow I don't think now is the right time. Please write him about it calmly when you're feeling more relaxed.'

'Oh? Alright then, that's what I'll do. But there's another thing, something I wanted to ask you. In your letters to me you always write about grandmother as if you don't want to cause me any worry. That makes me worry all the more. So from now on please be honest and tell me the truth. Because if I think you've left out something, my own imagination supplies the details. And since I don't know exactly how many details to supply, this causes me all the more anxiety.'

'I understand. I'll be careful about that', mother said.

'Well, I'll go home then, but please send a telegram to Abiko tomorrow morning. Either way I'll come back here in two or three days, but please send me a telegram anyway.'

'Alright. But in the letter you send to father please don't argue about anything – just be as calm as possible, won't you?'

Five minutes later I left the Azabu house, weighed down again by my huge parcel.

My mood grew worse and worse. I imagined father turning purple with rage as he ordered mother to kick me out of the house right away. I seemed also to actually hear him say: 'No matter what happens, I'll never let that person enter my house again.'

I was unhappy. And angry too. But, reminding myself that nothing had happened there which I had not expected, I was able to prevent my whole emotional being from surrendering to that unhappiness. I consciously resisted that temptation. Even so, grandmother's condition caused me deep distress.

My wife had asked me to buy various 'return gifts' to give to people who had given us gifts of congratulation on the birth of our child. She wanted me to buy them in time for our visit to the shrine the next day. Though I was feeling physically tired and emotionally drained, I went to the bank to get some money for these gifts. Besides the lacquered boxes I acquired two more paper packages.

Just a little before four I went to the Mitsui Bank again. Finally I got my business done. Then I went on to Asakusa.

I met with Mr. and Mrs. M. at the small cinema we'd agreed upon. When one film had finished, M. showed me a big book on Rodin he'd bought at Maruzen that day. Before I'd seen more than three or four photos, the lights went out again. Given the mood I was in, the film didn't interest me at all.

After another thirty minutes or so, the three of us left. Originally we had planned to see two films, but no one mentioned that once we were outside. The M.'s were very considerate of my feelings at that moment. In the mood I was in I wanted to be consoled without words, just by the feelings that passed between us. Although they were carrying quite a few parcels themselves, they offered to carry some of mine too. When we went into a restaurant I phoned mother.

'There hasn't been any particular change so there's nothing to worry about,' she said.

After a while the three of us left the restaurant. As we strolled aimlessly around, I told M. about what had happened when I left my parents' house. I talked about it with a quiet feeling.

'Your father was stubborn as usual', said M. with a slightly forlorn smile.

We still had a little time before the last train left at nine o'clock, so we took a tram from Kaminarimon to Hirokōji in the Ueno area of Tokyo, and from there we walked in the opposite direction towards the train station along a road where night stalls had been set up.

In front of the station the three of us entered an ice shop. From there I tried phoning my parents' house again. I didn't want to keep pestering my mother, so I just asked the maid who answered the phone whether there'd been any change in grandmother's condition. Since she said there hadn't been, I told her there was no need to call anyone and hung up the phone.

My low spirits seemed not to be getting any better. It occurred to me that, if this mood continued even a while longer, I might end up as crazy as the hero of *The Dreamer*, a story I was writing at that time. Even after boarding the train, I sat there for a while in a complete daze.

From about the time the train passed through Kitasenju, I began looking at the pictures in M.'s Rodin book. With so much weighing heavily on my mind, at first it was difficult for me to feel much interest in them. But after a while I gradually became absorbed. I felt with great intensity the eternal quality of Rodin's art. And a feeling of excitement welled up from the depths of my being. In a very pleasurable way, I was liberated from my bad mood. I felt that my heart was searching for Rodin's heart, was trying to take flight to his heart. To a surprising extent, my mood suddenly brightened.

At the Abiko Station Sanzō was waiting for me along with my dog, Teru, and the people who had come from the M.'s house to meet them. Teru was overjoyed and jumped wildly all

over me. I parted from the M.'s in front of the shrine at the end
of the street which led away from the station.

Teru had great fun as he tagged along with us, running on
ahead, stopping by the roadside, then running to catch up with
us -meanwhile urinating all over the place.

I heard from Sanzō that my friend Y. was supposed to go up
to Tokyo early the next morning. As soon as I got home I wrote
a letter asking him to phone my parents and inquire about
grandmother's condition before he came back. I had Sanzō
deliver the letter right away.

Part Twelve

The next day I tried writing a letter to father. I didn't feel
like arguing with him – even to the extent mother had
worried about. If arguments worked then our problems could
have been easily resolved. But I understood that, in reality, it
would be totally useless to argue reasonably about how just
and fair my requests were. If, even though I was aware of this
fact, I persisted in standing upon reason, saying things to
father about his prohibition of my visits that were difficult to
say to him, it was certain that the more I wrote the worse the
result would be. Thus I had no intention whatsoever of writing
that kind of letter. On the other hand, when I tried to write a
letter that would appeal somewhat to his feelings, I quickly
gave that up too. The impure feeling of writing consciously to
try to move someone else seemed so ugly to me that I just
couldn't go on.

After two or three revisions, I understood that it was
impossible for me at this moment to express my feelings in a
letter. The biggest problem was that, while I was writing the
letter, the father who was in my mind did not stay in one spot
even for an instant. In other words, the problem was that my
own feelings towards father were constantly vacillating. Perhaps
I would begin writing in a harmonious mood, the father who
came into my mind had a comparatively calm face, and my
feelings too would grow calm as I wrote about him. But as I was
writing father's face would gradually change and I myself would
actually begin to get argumentative until, suddenly, his face
would take on a stubborn, unhappy expression. I could do
nothing but put down my pen.

I concluded that at present I was incapable of writing a letter
to father. I wrote a letter to mother explaining this and

promising that, instead, I would come up to Tokyo soon and speak to him directly.

A telegram arrived in the afternoon: 'She's better than yesterday. Temperature 37.2. Dr. Ishiguro examined her. Intestinal catarrh. Nurse coming. Don't worry.'

The day before I had been frightened about what might happen to grandmother if she continued as she was for two or three more days. So I felt relieved by this telegram.

While I was eating dinner, a friend from Hashiba whom I'd visited the day before called on me to settle various items of business. When he returned home on the last train at ten twelve, I accompanied him to the station.

The Tokyo-bound train was a little late, so the train coming the other way, from Ueno, arrived before it. Y. got off. He told me in great detail about what he'd heard about grandmother's condition over the phone. The news was so good I thought that, at this rate, the fears I'd had the day before would turn out to be completely groundless. After the Tokyo train left, I returned home with Y.

The following day I read a newspaper article about the serious illness of a certain old man I knew at Waseda University. Although this old man had a big mouth and I had disliked him, now I hoped he would recover. Old people seem to drop off one after the other when there are sudden seasonal changes of temperature. I was worried on behalf of grandmother that now might be such a time.

I started working again on *The Dreamer*, a story I was supposed to publish in the October issue of a certain magazine.

I did not hate father now. But I was worried about whether I would be able to calmly maintain this neutral feeling towards him if he openly expressed his heart-felt hatred towards me. When I was in Kyoto, a cousin who was attending high school sent me a letter saying: 'I hope that some day your great love will embrace your father unconditionally.' This made me very angry. 'A person who has never really experienced great love should not recklessly preach about it to someone else,' I replied. I remembered that incident now. I thought I was somewhat conceited in my belief that I would maintain my calm composure no matter what attitude father adopted towards my present harmonious mood. My feeling that, without knowing what I was doing, I could embrace father unconditionally with a so-called great love, seemed rather silly – since I hadn't even measured the power of my real love.

Nothing would be better than if, no matter what attitude father adopted, I would not be drawn into it, I would be able spontaneously and effortlessly to draw back and maintain a certain composure. But there seemed to be something missing in this way of thinking. Somewhere I had skipped over some stage in thinking that I, at this present moment, would necessarily be able to respond in this way.

Anyway, I concluded that the only thing I could do was meet father and let matters take their own natural course. It was truly foolish to think that one could adopt and make oneself stick to a plan of action in matters of the heart.

August the thirtieth was the twenty-third anniversary of the death of my real mother. I decided that, when I went up to Tokyo to visit my mother's grave on that day, if father was home I would meet with him.

Part Thirteen

On the thirtieth I went up to Tokyo, taking a bicycle with me. S.K. the painter had ridden this bicycle down from Tokyo two days before and left it with us.

From Ueno Station I rode the bicycle towards my parents' house in Azabu.

When I reached the slope that rises from Tanimachi to our Azabu house, I dismounted. As I was pushing the bike up the slope, I imagined that I saw father in Western clothes walking towards me from the opposite direction. In reality this might have happened, because father, if he didn't want to meet me and had left home in order to avoid doing so, might well have taken this road, which was in the opposite direction to the closest way to the train station. I thought that, if father did come, I had better just talk to him, after all. The imagined scene floated up now into my mind. As I approached father with the intention of speaking to him, he quickened his pace and, without a word, tried to pass me by. Muttering something, I stood in his way. Still not speaking a word, he forced his way past me. This scene arose within me. Although it was imaginary, I thought that, of all my imaginings, it was the closest to what might actually happen.

I came to the Azabu house. I noticed that our Kamakura uncle's walking stick was in the doorway. I headed immediately towards grandmother's room. On that day her bed had been made up in the room next door, which was beside the hall. I placed a cushion beside her bed and sat down. Her face seemed much healthier than I'd expected. Her forceful look also had at some time returned to her eyes again. I was overjoyed. Two nurses attended her. Also present in the room were my uncle, my stepmother, and my sisters, who were wearing better *kimono* than usual.

Grandmother asked me why I hadn't come sooner. She said something about it being a shame that I'd missed the Buddhist priest's chanting of the *sutras*, which had just finished.

Uncle said he planned to go to Kyoto within two or three days. Whereupon grandmother said to him: 'Last night I dreamt that you went to get a diploma at a Kyoto temple, and mother doubted that you were ready to get it yet.' Making her face assume a slight frown, she laughed.

'It's rather cruel to put it that way', uncle replied. 'But it's true that I still haven't been able to get a diploma yet.'

'Uncle Masa, are you going to get a diploma?' asked Takako.

'Not at all', he answered with a laugh. 'That's grandmother's dream. I'm going to see the Zen master at Kenninji Temple, who I haven't seen in a long time. Haven't I already told you about my going to Kyoto, mother? Somehow I don't think I have.'

'I seem not to have heard about it', answered grandmother.

My stepmother, who had seemed a little uneasy about something for a while, asked me to go and offer some incense to the Buddha.

I nodded assent, got up and went to the room which contained the Buddha altar.

Stepmother followed right after me.

On the Buddha altar there were candles, flowers and incense and offerings of tea, sweets and fruit. Beside the altar hung a scroll with a badly drawn picture of my late mother, the buddha of that day, holding my older brother, who had died when he was three.

I lit some incense and bowed.

'Father's at home, isn't he?' I asked mother who was sitting beside me.

'Yes, he is', she replied.

'I find it very difficult to express my feelings in a letter so I've decided it would be better to meet with him directly after all'.

'In that case, if you could talk calmly to him, nothing could be better. What about it? Please make yourself really calm and talk with him quietly. Me too – any number of times since this morning I've prayed to your late mother, today's buddha, and asked for her guidance. Please don't let the feelings of the moment get the better of you and make you speak harsh words again. Even one word of apology is enough, so please swallow your pride, admit that the problems between you and him up to now have been your fault, and apologize. Father is growing old, so really he is suffering greatly because of his present relationship with you. And so, if you say just one word of apology, he will be satisfied with that. As a parent, he feels that he should not initiate a dialogue with such a rebellious child – that's not unreasonable, is it? Certainly he is a very stubborn man, but he is not an especially bad person.' Mother said this with tears in her eyes.

'That's true. But this is what I think. The difficulties of my relationship with father up to now could not have been avoided. In fact, it would have been a problem for me if things hadn't turned out this way. But I really do feel sorry for him. And also I do believe that I was wrong in some things. But I think that the present situation could not have been avoided and I cannot regret it. Because if I imagine now that I had actually become the kind of person father wanted me to be, from my present point of view I would find that unbearable'.

'Yes, I understand that. I know very well that the kind of person who has no self-respect and who thinks he must agree with everything his parents say is unbearable to you. Even so, if you just say one word of apology now to your father you won't suddenly lose your self-respect – so please, I beg you, just say that you've been bad up to now and offer one word of apology. Because, if you say even that one word, everybody in this house, beginning with father and grandmother, will cheer up immensely and will be able to live happily from now on. Please swallow your pride somehow and say that word of apology. As a favour to me.' Mother spoke with great emotion, bowing her head any number of times.

'But my feelings don't go that far, so I can't just swallow my pride and say I'm sorry. For me now to do as you say and just go to father and apologize, I would have to jump over a wide moat in a single leap. And even if I were to jump over and apologize, father would notice that moat and realize that my apology was just a formality – so nothing would really be accomplished.

'But anyway I'll try meeting him. It's largely an emotional matter so one cannot plan ahead of time how things will go.

Maybe when I actually meet him my feelings will improve more easily than I presently imagine.'

'That's very true. By all means try to make progress in that calm way.'

'Is father in the study?'

'Probably. If not then he's probably in the interior room.'

I rose and headed for the Western-style room. I felt my heart tremble with agitation. Not wanting to meet father in this state of mind, I tried to calm myself by pacing back and forth in the *tatami*-matted hall. I didn't think at all about what my first words should be. In about two minutes I had calmed down. I went to the door of father's study and knocked. There was no answer. I opened the door and looked within. Father wasn't there. I went to the Japanese-style living room in the interior of the house. He wasn't there either. I returned to grandmother's room again.

'He's not there', I said to mother.

'Perhaps he's in the garden. I'll go call him.' She got up and left.

A while later she hurried back.

'He's in the study now', she said.

I stood up and went.

The study door was open. I saw father's peaceful face as he sat facing towards me in a chair in front of the desk.

'That chair', he said, glancing at a chair placed beside the window and pointing to the floor in front of him.

I carried the chair to where he pointed and sat down facing him. I didn't speak.

'Let's hear what you have to say first', he said. Then: 'Is Masa out there?' The way he said it made a good impression on me.

'He is', I answered.

Father stood up and rang the bell on the wall. Then, after returning to his chair, he looked at the still-silent me and asked: 'Well, then?'

The maid came to ask why he rang.

'Ask the gentleman from Kamakura to come here right away.'

'I think it would be meaningless for our present relationship to continue as it is.'

'Mmm.'

'The way things have gone up to now couldn't be helped. I feel sorry for you because of some of the things I've done. And I think I was wrong sometimes.'

'Mmm', father nodded. Because of nervous excitement, I seemed to say all this in an angry tone of voice. From the outset, I had been unable to maintain the kind of quiet, calm tone I had repeatedly promised mother I would maintain. But it was the most natural tone, born out of the situation, and I felt that, for now, there could be no more appropriate tone for the relationship between father and me.

'But what's past can't be helped. It's just that I think it would be foolish to continue like this forever.'

Uncle came in and sat down in a chair behind me.

'Good. Well, then? Does what you are saying apply only while grandmother is alive, or do you intend it to be more permanent?' asked father.

'Until I met with you today I didn't intend it to be permanent. It would have been enough to get your permission to visit grandmother freely while she was alive. But if I may really hope for something more than that, then that would be ideal.' While saying this I had to fight back the tears.

'Is that so?' said father. He pressed his lips tightly shut and some tears formed in his eyes.

'The truth is I'm gradually getting old, and our relationship really has caused me a great deal of pain. There were times when I hated you from the depths of my heart. When you announced last year that you had decided to leave home, I objected many times but you wouldn't listen. I was really at a loss. Though I agreed to it, not having much choice, I had never had any intention of forcing you out of the house. And the way things have been between us up to now. . . .'

While saying all this father had begun to cry. I also could no longer hold back the tears. Neither of us said anything more. Behind us uncle was trying to say something but soon he too had begun to sob.

In a while father stood up and rang the bell on the wall again. When the maid came he said: 'Call my wife right away.'

Mother entered the room. She sat down in the low chair beside father.

'Junkichi has just said that he too disapproves of the way our relationship has been going, and in future he wants us to relate with each other as father and son again. Is that right?' He stopped and looked over at me.

'Yes', I said, and nodded. Immediately mother rose and rushed over to me, shook my hand vigorously and bowed again and again close to my chest, crying all the while and saying:

'Thank you, Junkichi, thank you.'

I had no choice but to bow over her head and, since she was just on her way up at that moment, my mouth hit against her hairdo.

Mother then went to uncle and said with heart-felt feeling: 'Thank-you, Masa-san. Thank-you.'

'Go tell grandmother now', father said to her. Wiping away her tears, mother hurried out.

My four sisters now came in, including even the six-year-old Rokuko. Though not collecting around anyone in particular, somehow they all gathered together in a group before us and bowed.

When they had all left, father suddenly said: 'Let's visit you in Abiko tomorrow', and looked at me as if asking whether that would be convenient.

'Yes, please come.'

'Alright. I'd like to see your baby, Rumeko, and also what kind of house you're living in.' He said this with a cheerful expression on his face.

'You're very welcome to come', I said.

Part Fourteen

Grandmother's bed had at some time been moved back again from the adjacent room to her own room. While uncle and I were talking there father came in.

'You've heard about what just happened between me and Junkichi?' he asked grandmother.

'Yes, I have.'

Father seemed to be waiting for grandmother to say something more, and I wished that she would show him a little more of the reaction he was hoping for. But grandmother's character was such that she didn't openly reveal all she was feeling. Father began to say something and then stopped. Then, for some reason, he began glancing at the Buddha altar every now and then. As I've already written, next to the altar there hung a poorly drawn picture of my deceased mother holding my deceased older brother.

At lunch-time father drank some saké. Mother, uncle, myself and my sisters also all drank some, one after the other. Those who couldn't drink just pretended to.

No one spoke openly of what we were celebrating. Everyone simply enjoyed the peaceful, happy feeling that flowed from heart to heart, but no one spoke of it. That felt very good. We just talked a little gossip. Even so, father remembered to say: 'Okō, send a telegram to Fusako and tell her about what happened today.'

Fusako was my oldest sister, who lived in Kamakura.

'I'll go and tell her all about it either tonight or early tomorrow', said uncle.

'Oh, in that case, it's alright then', answered father. 'Who's going to Abiko tomorrow?' Saying that, he ran his eyes inquiringly over the whole group of us.

'I'm going!' shouted Rokuko.

'Me too!' said Masako.

'Oh, really? How about those big sisters over there?' Father laughed as he looked over at them.

'We're all going', said Yoshiko.

I'd left home that morning without eating much, but I didn't feel like eating anything for lunch either. I mixed the wine father had ordered for me with a little water and drank that.

That afternoon seven of us went together to the Aoyama Cemetery, leaving grandmother and father behind. He was a little drunk from the saké and wanted to sober up a bit and take a bath, but promised to join us later. Pushing my bicycle, I walked beside uncle along a road that had no trams. We didn't mention anything about the day's events. Mother also said nothing about it.

I parted from everyone at the grave of my child who had died the year before, and went by bike to S.K.'s house in Yotsuya.

S.K. was watering his garden. While he was finishing that off and washing his feet, I wrote a thank-you letter to mother. I was grateful for the fact that, even though she was caught on the horns of a painful dilemma for so long, she had never given up hope for a reconciliation between father and me, though we had failed to achieve it many times. And I also wrote that I believed this present reconciliation would never be broken, because, to a greater extent than I'd expected, it was achieved calmly, without any forced emotions, and without the kind of leaping over moats I had mentioned earlier.

I told S.K. about what had happened. He was extremely happy for me, and showed me even more kindness than usual.

'Why don't you send a telegram to Sadako? She'll be overjoyed', he said.

'She probably doesn't know I met father today, so I don't think she's worrying about it particularly', I answered.

A while later two of the friends who were supposed to meet us there that day showed up.

Since arriving at S.K.'s house I had begun to feel both physically and emotionally tired. But it wasn't an unpleasant kind of tiredness. Rather it was a gentle fatigue that brought with it a sense of slightly detached tranquility, like that of a small lake shrouded by heavy mist in the depths of the mountains. It was also like the tiredness of a traveller who has finally reached home after a tediously long and unpleasant journey.

I parted from my friends and headed for Ueno in time to catch the last train home.

Sanzō was waiting for me at Abiko Station, holding a paper lantern. As we were walking home he said to me from behind: 'I hear that the master is coming to visit us tomorrow from Azabu.'

'Did a telegram come?'

'Yes, at about three o'clock.'

'Quite a little group is coming, you know. We'll go clam-picking if the weather's fine, so bring the boat around to the front of the house tomorrow morning.'

'Certainly, sir. Earlier today I ordered chicken for tomorrow from the butcher.'

'Good. And, by the way, if you can come tomorrow come as early as possible and sweep a little around the outside of the house.'

'I've already completely finished all the cleaning, under your wife's direction, both inside and outside the house.'

As I was about to ascend the slope up to my house, I noticed my wife standing there. She approached me without saying a word, took my hands in hers and squeezed them tightly.

'Congratulations', she said.

Part Fifteen

The following morning I went alone to meet them at the station. My wife wanted to come but our baby's body was twitching strangely so I wouldn't let her.

The train arrived. Takako got off first, followed by Rokuko and Masako. Then father got off. I bowed. Without any expression on his face, he bowed his head slightly and said 'ahh'.

I didn't speak with him much until we'd left the station. We both felt somewhat constrained. I trusted that he would soon remove that constraint. But I also felt that it would be wrong for us to try to remove it by forcing ourselves to make small talk. Father also did not try to force himself to speak.

Everyone rode to my house by rickshaw. My wife came out from the front gate, holding our baby. When she saw my father's face tears began to flow from her eyes. Father looked at the baby.

That day I felt good all day. The constraint between father and me soon vanished. We talked mainly of paintings and pottery. I got out the few old pieces of china and the few old scraps of hand-woven fabric I possessed and showed them to him. He talked about some of the picture scrolls he had recently acquired. We no longer felt any constraint at all. But we didn't say anything about what had happened the day before. Nevertheless, when the small group had all gone outside, father said to my wife: 'Junkichi says he hopes that from now on we can relate to each other as father and son, and truly this is also my own wish, so I would like you too to act as if all the unpleasantness between us had never happened.'

Unable to answer, my wife simply nodded and wiped the tears away from her eyes. When father had begun to speak, I expected him to say to my wife exactly what he'd said to mother the day before. And I'd been confident that, even if he said only that, I would certainly not be dissatisfied. But he hadn't just repeated himself, and I felt very good about this – and also was grateful to him.

'I wonder what happened with your baby, Satoko', said father. We couldn't answer. But I sensed that now I felt no resentment towards him, even because of Satoko.

They all decided to return home on the three o'clock train.

Just as he was leaving, father said to my wife again: 'From now on I'll visit you every now and then.'

'Please do. By all means please do come', she answered. And simultaneously I also said: 'Please do.'

I accompanied them to the train station. The train was late. I said to my little sister, Yoshiko: 'Your older brother's going to be a little busy from now on so he won't be able to come to Tokyo for a while.' Masako looked up from the side and said: 'But, older brother, you'll come this year, won't you? Be sure to come. That would be good. Be sure to come.' The older sisters laughed. Masako seemed to have something in mind, because she kept repeating that I should be sure to come. I thought to myself that undoubtedly this reconciliation was not a minor event, even in the small heart of Masako, who was not yet eight.

Father seemed a little tired. A while later the train arrived. Everyone boarded. Father sat beside the window opposite to the platform where I stood. My sisters gathered on the near side and lined up their faces at the window.

When the whistle blew, everyone said: 'Sayonara.'

Father was looking in my direction. Meeting his gaze, I put my hand to my hat and bowed. He nodded a little and said 'ahh', but somehow that didn't satisfy me. I looked into his eyes again, with a strange expression on my face somewhere between crying and frowning. Whereupon suddenly a certain expression came into his eyes. It was what I'd been searching for. I'd been searching for it unconsciously. With all the pleasure and excitement of our heart-to-heart communion, my face began to assume even more an expression between crying and frowning. The train began to move. My sisters couldn't stop waving. They waved until the train had moved beyond the long platform and curved around to the right and out of sight. I suddenly noticed that I'd been standing for a long time all by myself on the empty platform holding up my umbrella. After leaving the station I hurried home. I didn't know why I was hurrying. I thought to myself that my present reconciliation with father would certainly not be broken. I felt love for him now from the depths of my heart. And I felt that all the various bad feelings of the past were melting in that love.

Part Sixteen

I no longer felt like continuing to write along the same lines my story, *The Dreamer*, which was based on my fight with father. I had to search for some other theme. There were other possibilities but I needed time to become emotionally involved in them. Even if I were given that time, I still might not become sufficiently absorbed. If I forced myself to write at such times, the result would be a lifeless fabrication. It would be a failure. I wondered if I'd find something worth writing about by the mid-month deadline.

While I was worrying about this, it occurred to me that at some time I would feel like reliving the experience I'd had with father. Recently I'd begun to want to see him again. I also felt that it would actually be better if I met him again now rather than two or three weeks later. Wishing in some way to express my good will towards him, I hit upon the idea of using some of the money I'd made by my own work to commission S.K. to

234

paint father's portrait, which I would then present to him. It seemed particularly appropriate to me that S.K. would paint it, since he'd been so genuinely happy about our reconciliation. I immediately wrote him a letter.

After mailing the letter the next morning, September 2nd., I decided that I'd better go up to Tokyo and settle my business with both S.K. and father immediately.

On the way to the train station I stopped by at the post office to pick up my mail. There was a letter from my sister in Kamakura. I read it while walking:

> Early this morning, while I was still sleeping, Uncle
> Masa arrived with such happy, happy news. As he
> was telling me all about it, I broke down and cried.

The letter was addressed to both me and my wife. On reading it, I myself was moved to tears.

Upon arriving in Tokyo I went directly to our house in Azabu, then directly to father's study. He wasn't there. Masako, who came from the interior of the house to see what I wanted, suggested that he was probably in the garden. She went out on the living-room veranda and called to him in a loud voice. Father came rushing out of the eastern wing of the house. He seemed to think he was wanted on the phone.

I slipped my feet into some clogs and stepped down into the garden.

Just as on the morning two days earlier, we again felt a little stiff and constrained with each other. This seemed unavoidable. I just went ahead and talked about my idea for a portrait and asked him if he'd sit for one. He gladly agreed.

When I stepped back onto the veranda and was about to reenter the house, father stood up and seemed to be thinking about something. Then suddenly he turned in my direction and seemed on the point of saying something. I moved back towards him a little. But he only mumbled 'uhh', then looked down and walked away.

When I headed next to grandmother's room, I found mother at rest in one of the rooms I passed through. She told me her stomach was bad. Because she had diarrhea, she hadn't eaten anything at all, so she felt completely exhausted.

'Since our long-lasting troubles have finally come to an end, I suppose my tiredness is also partly psychological', she said.

'I understand. You've heard about father's visit to us in Abiko the other day from Yoshiko, I suppose?'

'Yes. And I also received a letter from Sadako. Really I felt such a great relief.'

After staying with mother for a while, I went on to grandmother's room. Grandmother's face looked healthy. Even so, her sick-bed was still laid out on the floor, although she was sitting on some cushions off to the side.

'Because this time I didn't force my feelings at all, I think it'll be alright.'

'Yes, it really is a good thing.' Unlike three days earlier, she now showed a heart-felt pleasure on her face.

'My sister Otaka went back to our home town and told everybody she visited about it. She said they all had a good cry together. She tells me about it in one of those letters she sent to me.' She pointed to a pile of letters on her bed.

'Oh, really?' I didn't look at the letters.

Grandmother then told me that father had spoken well of Abiko, saying that it was a better place than he'd expected, and had also praised my house and garden. After saying this she fell silent.

I casually introduced some other topics of conversation. Grandmother looked down and didn't answer. It seemed to me that, all of a sudden, she had felt deeply moved by something she was thinking about. Or, if not that, perhaps she had dislocated her jaw again. I was a little worried. But her mouth was tightly closed.

A maid came in and said something. Grandmother immediately answered her.

My Kamakura sister came in with her baby. Soon father came in too.

'It's too bad Masa isn't here, but since everyone else is today let's go out somewhere to eat', he said.

We decided on the Sannōdai Restaurant. So that I'd have enough time to catch the train home later, we decided to go there at four o'clock. I made the reservation.

I left the Azabu house for a while and went to visit S.K. He was out, having gone to play tennis at Nagatachō. I headed there next. At the tennis court I found S.K., dripping with sweat, playing singles with H. After watching them play for about thirty minutes, I left with them. S.K. already had two commissions which he had to finish some time in October. He promised to paint my father's portrait afterwards, if that was alright with me. I agreed.

Along with H., I dropped in at S.K.'s house. I left there around two o'clock and returned to Azabu. In a while my

Kamakura sister's husband also arrived. There were eight of us now, but my younger brother Junzō still hadn't shown up. Father kept fretting about this and ordering us to try to reach him on the phone at any place we guessed him to be.

Unable to wait any longer, we all left. Since it had begun to rain a little, the ladies rode in a rickshaw. Father, me and my sister's husband went on foot.

Even after we arrived at the restaurant, Junzō still didn't show up. Father got into such a state about this that it was almost laughable. He justified himself by saying: 'Somehow I just can't stand it when people don't show up for their appointments.'

He was in a good mood, nonetheless. But certainly, as the host, he had sufficient reason to be irritated or even enraged by the fact that Junzō didn't come at the appointed hour and everyone was kept waiting while the food that was already prepared went unserved. I only hoped that Junzō would show up before father's mood turned sour. But, even though he was so obviously worried, he was being very patient and didn't give way to anger. I thought that perhaps he was controlling himself so as not to disturb with any anger the peaceful mood of the past few days. But perhaps more than that he was unable to get angry because of the harmony which now prevailed in his heart.

'Let's wait a little while longer, then start eating if he doesn't come', father said to me.

About three and a half years before, I had felt unhappy with him about something. But he seemed not to realize how unhappy I was. The following day he suddenly invited everyone in the house to come to the restaurant where we now were. He had phoned to make a reservation and told them how many people to expect, including me. Because of my mood at that moment, though, I had felt that it was absolutely impossible for me to go with them. I had told this to mother and gone off somewhere by myself at around noon.

Grandmother had told me later that, once they had arrived at the restaurant, father had repeatedly asked why I hadn't come. I remembered all of this now. I could have acted in no other way. Nevertheless, I felt sorry for father now for the unhappiness he had suffered.

Junzō arrived soon after we had started eating. Father's mood recovered completely.

We all left the restaurant at around seven o'clock. I still had two hours until the last train back to Abiko. Father said that, since he felt drunk and a little sleepy, he would go straight home, but he suggested that, after we saw him off, the rest of us should take a walk along the Ginza.

He boarded a rickshaw with a deep sigh. Just as he was going, I saw that the day's events had lit a light of love in his eyes – quite naturally and in a delightfully free way. I no longer felt any doubt about the permanence of our reconciliation.

I parted with everyone on the Ginza.

I was worried that there were getting to be fewer and fewer days left for work. I decided, after all, to write about what most preoccupied my mind at that moment: my reconciliation with father.

About half a month went by. A letter arrived from my uncle, who had returned to Kamakura from Kyoto. It was an answer to the thank-you letter I had sent at the beginning of the month:

> Your recent reconciliation with your father seemed to me a completely unexpected blessing – as if it were caused by the sudden change of season. I feel this very deeply. Your father has confided to me his conviction that this time it will last. In your letter you also tell me that you are sure it is not merely a temporary phenomenon. I agree with both of you. Indeed, I feel much as the old poem says:

> *Though we wander the world over*
> *So far from each other,*
> *In the depths of the night*
> *We both catch sight*
> *Of the same starlit snow. . . .*
> *Setting the peak of Thousand Rocks aglow.*

NOTES TO PART ONE

Introduction: The Importance of Shiga Naoya

1 The term is often literally translated as 'I-novel' – and, indeed, was apparently first coined by Mori Ōgai as a literal translation of the German, '*Ich-Roman*' – but now this is rather misleading, because the *shi-shôsetsu* is not necessarily written in the first person, and may be of any length. Unlike some other recent writers on this genre, however, I see no great objection to calling it a 'novel' if it is of novel length, or a short story or novella if shorter, because it seems to me that these terms as used now in English are mere terms of convenience which refer to nothing more than the length of anything resembling a piece of prose narrative fiction (and, regardless of how ambiguously fictional *shi-shōsetsu* are, few scholars would argue that they are autobiography pure and simple). Nevertheless, I would prefer that the term *shi-shōsetsu* be left untranslated and incorporated into English, as with the terms for older genres of Japanese literature such as *haiku*, *renga* and *nō*, and that it be regarded as a distinct national variety or genre of world fiction.

2 See Nakamura Mitsuo, *Shiga Naoya ron* (Tokyo: Chikuma shobō, 1966), p.5.

3 Shiga Naoya, *The Paper Door and Other Stories*, translated by Lane Dunlop (San Francisco: North Point Press, 1987). Shiga Naoya, *Le Samourai*, translated by Marc Mécréant (Paris: Marabout, 1970). Includes twenty-two Shiga stories.

4 Edward Seidensticker, 'Strangely Shaped Novels', in *Studies in Japanese Culture*, ed. Joseph Roggendorf (Tokyo: Sophia Univ. Press, 1963), p.217.

5 ibid.

6 Mishima Yukio, Introduction to *New Writing in Japan*, ed. Mlshima Yukio and Geoffrey Bownas (Harmondsworth, Middlesex: Penguin Books, 1972), p.20.

7 Shin'ichi Hisamatsu, *Zen and the Fine Arts* (Tokyo: Kodansha, 1971), especially the chapter on *Zen Aesthetics*, pp.28-40.

8 Literally, 'theories about the Japanese people'. A genre of scholarly and pseudo-scholarly works concerning the Japanese national character, very popular in Japan itself, and often characterized by wild and groundless generalizations.

9 Donald Keene, *Appreciations of Japanese Culture* (Tokyo: Kodansha, 1971), pp.11-25.

Chapter One: The Logic of Everyday Life

1 See Makoto Ueda, *Modern Japanese Writers and the Nature of Literature* (Stanford Univ. Press, 1976), p.106, footnote.
2 Francis Mathy, *Shiga Naoya* (New York: Twayne, 1974).
3 ibid., p.41.
4 ibid., p.42.
5 Shiga Naoya, *Aru asa*, in *Seibei to hyōtan* (Tokyo: Shinchōsha, 1968), p.17. My translation.
6 ibid., p.18.
7 As, for instance, analyzed by the psychiatrist Takeo Doi in *The Anatomy of Dependence*, translated by John Bester (Tokyo: Kodansha, 1973).
8 Tanizaki Junichirō, 'Bunshō Tokuhon', *Tanizaki Junichirō Zenshū* (Tokyo: Chūo Kōronsha, 1958), xxi. pp. 84-90.
9 Both writers, for instance, generally restrict themselves to only the most simple adjectives descriptive of subjective judgements: 'good', 'nice', 'pleasant', 'bad', etc.
10 Shiga Naoya, 'Rhythm', translated by William Sibley in *The Shiga Hero* (Univ. of Chicago Ph.D. dissertation, 1971), p.257.
11 ibid., p.257.
12 ibid.
13 ibid., p.260.
14 Mathy, *Shiga*, p.45.
15 ibid.
16 Jay Rubin, 'Sōseki on Individualism', in *Monumenta Nipponica*, vol. xxxiv, no.1 (1979), p.21.
17 ibid., p.25.
18 ibid., p.21.
19 Natsume Sōseki, *Watakushi no kojinshugi* (My Individualism), translated by Jay Rubin in *Monumenta Nipponica*, vol.xxxiv, no.1 (1979), p.43.
20 On Ōgai's reactions to this issue, see Richard Bowring, *Mori Ōgai and the Modernization of Japanese Culture* (Cambridge Univ. Press, 1979).
21 For an account of this episode in Shiga's life, see Mathy, p.23.
22 Akutagawa Ryūnosuke, *Isho* (Suicide Note), reprinted in Howard Hibbett and Gen Itasaka, *Modern Japanese* (Cambridge: Harvard Univ. Press, 1965), pp.188-193.
23 *Kobayashi Hideo Zenshū* (Shinchōsha, 1955-57), vol. vi, pp.34-35. This translation by Edward Seidensticker in his essay, 'Kobayashi Hideo' in *Tradition and Modernization in Japanese Culture*, edited by Donald Shively (Princeton Univ. Press, 1971) p.433.
24 Nakamura Hajime, *Ways of Thinking of Eastern Peoples*, translated by Philip Wiener (Honolulu: East-West Center Press, 1964).

25 Quoted in Sibley, *Shiga Hero*, p.89.
26 Seidensticker, 'Strangely Shaped Novels', in *Studies in Japanese Culture*, p.219.
27 Sibley, *Shiga Hero*, p.126.
28 ibid.
29 ibid.
30 See Ueda, *Modern Japanese Writers*, p.104. Ironically, Akutagawa himself later became an apologist of the Shigaesque 'plotless story' and ended his career with some *shi-shōsetsu* which describe in harrowing detail his own descent into madness and suicide.
31 Kobayashi, vol.vi, pp.117-19. Quoted in Seidensticker, 'Kobayashi Hideo' in *This Country, Japan* (Kodansha, 1979), p.181.
32 Ueda, *Modern Japanese Writers*, p.99.
33 ibid.
34 See Stephen Kohl, *Shiga Naoya: a Critical Biography* (Univ. of Washington Ph.D. dissertation, 1974), p.21.
35 ibid., p.20.
36 Traditional Japanese literature is replete with works of mixed fictional/autobiographical status.
37 Seidensticker, *Studies in Japanese Culture*, p.217.
38 Mathy, *Shiga*, p.44.
39 Ibid., p.41.
40 Ibid.
41 Nakamura Mitsuo, *Shiga Naoya ron* (Tokyo: Chikuma Shobō, 1966), p.91.
42 Seidensticker, *Japan Quarterly*, vol. xi, no.1, 1964.
43 Seidensticker, *This Country, Japan*, p.100.
44 See Ueda, p.131.
45 Herbert Franke, Introduction, *The Golden Casket: Chinese Novellas of Two Millenia*, translated by Christopher Levenson (New York: Harcourt, Brace and World, 1964), p.3.
46 Plato, *Republic*, Book X.
47 Franke, *Novellas of Two Millenia*, p.16.
48 Murasaki Shikibu, *The Tale of Genji*, translated by Edward Seidensticker, (New York: Alfred Knopf, 1977), pp.437-38.
49 Donald Keene, *World Within Walls* (New York: Holt, Rinehart and Winston, 1976), p.211.
50 ibid.
51 Sibley, *Shiga Hero*, p.260.
52 Keene, *World Within Walls*, p.392.
53 ibid.
54 ibid., p.371.
55 ibid., p.573.
56 Ivan Morris, *Modern Japanese Stories* (Rutland, Vermont: Charles Tuttle, 1962), pp.12-13.
57 ibid., p.13.

58 Tsubouchi Shōyō, 'The Essence of the Novel', translated by Donald Keene in *Modern Japanese Literature* (New York: Grove Press, 1956), pp.57-58.
59 Morris, *Modern Japanese Stories*, p.15.
60 ibid., p.16.
61 Itō Sei, 'Natsume Sōseki - His Personality and Works', in *Essays on Natsume Sōseki's Works* (Tokyo: Ministry of Education, 1970), p.5. Itō was an important theorist and practitioner of the *shi-shōsetsu* of a later generation than Shiga.
62 ibid., pp.15-16.
63 Quoted by Kinya Tsuruta in 'Akutagawa Ryūnosuke and I-Novelists', *Monumenta Nipponica*, vol.xxv, nos.1-2 (1970), p.14.
64 ibid., p.20.
65 Seidensticker, 'The "Pure" and the "In-Between" in Modern Japanese Theories of the Novel', in *This Country, Japan*, pp.98-111.
66 Seidensticker, *Studies in Japanese Culture*, p.212.
67 Quoted in Seidensticker, *This Country, Japan*, p.102.
68 Seidensticker, *Studies in Japanese Culture*, p.217.
69 Makoto Ueda, *Literary and Art Theories in Japan* (Cleveland: Press of Western Reserve Univ., 1967), pp.224-25.
70 Quoted in Sibley, *Shiga Hero*, p.1.
71 Aristotle, *Poetics*, Chapter 7.
72 On the principles of *renga*, see Earl Miner's *Japanese Linked Poetry* (Princeton Univ. Press, 1979).
73 Quoted in Seidensticker, *Tradition and Modernization in Japanese Culture*, p.426.
74 Quoted in Sibley, *Shiga Hero*, p.1.
75 ibid.
76 Ueda, *Modern Japanese Writers*, p.106.

Chapter Two: The Natural Way of Death

1 See, for instance, Tanikawa Tetsuzō's fulsome praise in his *Shiga Naoya no sakuhin* (vol.2), (Tokyo: Mikasa Shobō, 1942), p.92.
2 Shiga, *At Kinosaki*. My translation, p.121 of this book.
3 *Tanizaki Junichirō Zenshū* (Tokyo: Chuō Kōronsha, 1958), xxi, p.90.
4 *At Kinosaki*, p.122-3 of this book.
5 ibid., p.123
6 ibid.
7 ibid.
8 ibid.
9 ibid.
10 ibid., p.124
11 ibid., pp.123-4.
12 ibid., p.124.
13 ibid.

14 ibid.
15 ibid., pp.124-5.
16 ibid., p.125.
17 ibid., p.126.
18 ibid.
19 ibid., p.126-7.
20 ibid., p.127.
21 ibid.
22 ibid.
23 ibid.
24 ibid.
25 ibid.
26 Tanikawa, *Shiga no sakuhin*, p.92.
27 ibid.
28 Mathy, *Shiga*, p.173.
29 Leo Tolstoy, *What is Art?* (Oxford Univ. Press, 1929), p.228.
30 Mathy, *Shiga*, pp.64-65.
31 F.R. Leavis, *Reality and Sincerity*, in his *A Selection from Scrutiny* (Cambridge Univ. Press, 1968) p.252.
32 ibid.
33 ibid.
34 ibid., p.276.
35 Quoted in William Barry, *Heralds of Revolt* (Port Washington, New York: Kennikat Press, 1971), p.237.
36 ibid.
37 *Kobayashi Zenshū* I, pp.12-13. Translated by Seidensticker in *This Country, Japan*, p.156.
38 Fowler, *The Rhetoric of Confession*, pp.187-247.
39 ibid., p.241.
40 Yoshida Sei-ichi, *Shōsetsu no bunshō*, in *Bunshō to buntai* (Tokyo: Meiji Shoin, 1963) p.46. My translation.
41 ibid.
42 ibid., p.47.
43 ibid.
44 p.124 of this book.
45 Yoshida, p.47.
46 For an account of Tanizaki's debate with Akutagawa on this subject, see Ueda, *Modern Japanese Writers*, pp.71-72.
47 Tanizaki, *Zenshū*, xxi, p.18.
48 ibid.
49 ibid.
50 ibid.
51 p.122 of this book.
52 Tanizaki, ibid.
53 Tanikawa, *Shiga no sakuhin*, p.92. My translation.
54 The entire 'Shirakaba group' are sometimes characterized as

'Tolstoyan idealists'. At any rate, Shiga had a lifelong admiration for the works of the Russian master.
55 Leo Tolstoy, *Three Deaths* (1859) in *Nine Stories* translated by Louise and Aylmer Maude (London: Oxford Univ. Press), pp.305-306.
56 ibid., p.307.
57 ibid., p.308.
58 ibid., p.291.
59 ibid., p.viii.
60 I use the term 'Shiga hero' in the same sense that one may speak of Nick Adams as the 'Hemingway hero': as a protagonist who is an obvious fictional projection of the author's own self, though by no means to be as closely identified with that self as in a pure autobiography, and whose experiences and development we may follow through a whole series of fictional works.
61 Quoted in Mathy, *Shiga*, p.161.
62 ibid., p.160.
63 Tolstoy, *Nine Stories*, p.307.
64 Wayne Booth, *The Rhetoric of Fiction* (Univ. of Chicago Press, 1966), p.3.
65 See p.121 of this book.
66 ibid., p.125.
67 ibid., pp.125-6.
68 ibid., p.126.
69 E.M. Forster, *Aspects of the Novel* (London: Edward Arnold, 1927), pp.73-80.
70 Edward Fowler, *Shishōsetsu in Modern Japanese Literature* (Durham, N.C.: Center for International Studies, Duke University, 1986), p.4.
71 Barry, *Revolt*, p.237.
72 For a useful discussion of the Western confessional novel, see Peter M. Axthelm, *The Modern Confessional Novel* (New Haven: Yale University Press, 1967).
73 Karatani Kōjin, *Origins of Modern Japanese Literature*, edited by Brett de Bary (Durham, N.C.: Duke University Press, 1993), p.76.
74 See pp.43-5 of this book.
75 ibid., p.123.
76 ibid., p.124.
77 ibid., p.127.
78 Sibley, *Shiga Hero*, p.227.
79 Ueda, *Literary and Art Theories in Japan*, p.150.
80 ibid.
81 ibid.
82 ibid., p.151.
83 p.123 of this book.
84 ibid., p.125.
85 ibid., p.127.
86 ibid.

87 Ueda, *Literary and Art Theories*, p.150.
88 Mathy, *Shiga*, p.28.
89 Sibley, *Shiga Hero*, p.231.
90 Shiga Naoya, *A Dark Night's Passing*, translated by Edwin McClellan (Tokyo: Kodansha, 1976), p.375.
91 p.127 of this book.
92 Shiga, *Dark Night's Passing*, pp.400-401.
93 For Kobayashi's view on this, see Seidensticker's article on him in *Tradition and Modernization in Japanese Culture*, p.427.

Chapter Three: A Fire in the Heart

1 Quoted in Beongcheon Yu, *Akutagawa: An Introduction* (Detroit: Wayne State University Press, 1972), p.79.
2 ibid.
3 ibid.
4 ibid.
5 ibid.
6 Shiga Naoya, *Takibi*, in *Kozō no kamisama* (Tokyo: Iwanami Shoten, 1928), p.173. My translation, p.128 in this book.
7 ibid.
8 Quoted in Ueda, *Modern Japanese Writers*, p.86.
9 *Kozō no kamisama*, p.175. p.129 of this book.
10 ibid.
11 ibid., p.176. p.130 of this book.
12 ibid.
13 ibid., p.179. p.132 of this book.
14 ibid.
15 ibid., p.180. pp.132-133 of this book.
16 ibid., p.181. p.133 of this book.
17 Shiga, *A Dark Night's Passing*, p.290.
18 See, for example, D.C. Holtom's account of the role of fire in Shintō ritual in his *The National Faith of Japan* (New York: Paragon Book Reprint Corp., 1965), p.29.
19 Norman Friedman, 'Symbol', in *Princeton Encyclopedia of Poetry and Poetics*, edited by Alex Preminger (Princeton University Press, 1974), p.834.
20 Shiga, *Kozō no kamisama*, p.182. p.134 of this book.
21 ibid., p.183. p.134 of this book.
22 ibid., pp.183-84. pp.134-135 of this book.
23 ibid., p.184. p.135 of this book.
24 ibid., p.185. p.136 of this book.
25 ibid., p.187. pp.136–137.
26 ibid., p.137 of this book.
27 ibid., p.188. pp.137-138 of this book.
28 ibid., p.138 of this book.

29 See Mathy, *Shiga*, p.161.

30 Shiga, *Kozō no kamisama*, p.188. p.138 of this book.

31 *Oxford English Dictionary*, (Oxford University Press, 1971), p.2210. Quoting Lewis, *Meth. Reason. Politics* v.118: 'In every narrative, there is a certain connexion of events, which in a work of fiction, is called a plot.'

32 See p.18 of this book.

33 For repetition as a 'non-logical' use of language, see Elizabeth Wells, *Statistical Analysis of the Prose Style of 'Big Two-Hearted River'*, in Jackson Benson, *The Short Stories of Ernest Hemingway: Critical Essays* (Durham: Duke University Press, 1975) p.131: 'It is most often considered to be the language of those incapable of cause-and-effect reasoning....'

34 See above, p.41.

35 Quoted in Edmund Wilson, *Eight Essays*, (New York: Doubleday, 1954), pp.93-94.

36 Comte de Buffon, *Discours sur le style* (1753).

37 M.H. Abrams, *A Glossary of Literary Terms* (New York: Holt, Rinehart and Winston, 1971), p.137.

38 Quoted in A.E. Hotchner, *Papa Hemingway* (New York: Random House, 1966) p.199.

39 See Benson, *Hemingway*, p.xi.

40 Scott Donaldson, *By Force of Will: the Life and Art of Ernest Hemingway* (New York: Viking Press, 1977), p.242.

41 Hemingway, *Green Hills of Africa* (New York: Scribner's, 1935), p.70.

42 See Earl Miner, *The Japanese Tradition in British and American Literature* (Princeton University Press, 1958), especially chapters v-vi.

43 Benson, *Hemingway*, p.307.

44 ibid.

45 Quoted in Donaldson, *Will*, p.247.

46 Benson, *Hemingway*, p.309.

47 See above, p.62.

48 Quoted in Benson, *Hemingway*, p.307.

49 Ralph Freedman, *The Lyrical Novel* (Princeton, New Jersey: Princeton University Press, 1963).

50 Benson, *Hemingway*, p.157.

51 Hemingway, *Africa*, Foreword.

52 Hemingway, *A Moveable Feast* (New York: Scribner's, 1964), *Preface*.

53 Fraser Sutherland, *The Style of Innocence* (Toronto: Clarke, Irwin, 1972), p.83.

54 Benson, *Hemingway*, p.275.

55 ibid.

56 Robert Weeks, editor, *Hemingway: a Collection of Critical Essays* (Englewood Cliffs N.J.: Prentice-Hall, 1962).

57 Benson, *Hemingway*, p.309.

58 ibid.

59 See Julian Smith's article, *Hemingway and the Thing Left Out*, in Benson, *Hemingway*, p.136.
60 Donaldson, *Will*, p.245.
61 Benson, *Hemingway*, p.39.
62 ibid., p.131.
63 ibid., p.297.
64 Weeks, *Hemingway*, p.106.
65 Hemingway, *Cross-Country Snow*, in *In Our Time* (New York: Scribner's, 1925), p.107.
66 Benson, *Hemingway*, p.154.
67 p.127 of this book.
68 Hemingway, *Big Two-Hearted River*, in *In Our Time*, p.142.
69 ibid., p.156.
70 Mathy, *Shiga*, pp.29-30.
71 Shiga, *Kozō no kamisama*, p.176. p.130 of this book.
72 On Hemingway's obsession with death, see Donaldson, *Will* p.282.

Chapter Four: An Artless Art, A Selfless Self

1 Quoted in Mathy, *Shiga*, p.83.
2 ibid.
3 ibid., p.92. While I am not arguing here that we should accept the author's word as the 'last word' on his own work, nor would I argue, as seems to be the critical fashion in some quarters these days, that his views should be completely discounted. One must, of course, weigh the author's views along with all other available evidence.
4 ibid., p.101.
5 ibid., pp.91 and 157.
6 ibid., p.157.
7 Shiga Naoya, *A Dark Night's Passing*, translated by Edwin McClellan (Tokyo: Kodansha, 1976), p.16.
8 ibid., p.17.
9 ibid., p.18.
10 ibid.
11 ibid., pp.19-20.
12 The literal meaning of *shi-shōsetsu* but, as I said in the Introduction, it seems better to me to use the Japanese generic term even in English.
13 Fowler, *Rhetoric of Confession*, pp.4-6, 238-41.
14 Shiga, *A Dark Night's Passing*, p.25.
15 ibid.
16 ibid., p.26.
17 ibid.
18 ibid., pp.26-27.
19 ibid., p.27.
20 ibid.
21 ibid., p.28.

22 ibid., p.30.
23 ibid., p.26.
24 ibid.
25 ibid., p.29.
26 ibid., p.30.
27 ibid.
28 ibid., p.81.
29 ibid., p.101.
30 ibid., p.104.
31 ibid., p.115.
32 ibid., p.123.
33 See Mathy, *Shiga*, p.43.
34 Shiga, *A Dark Night's Passing*, p.125.
35 ibid.
36 ibid.
37 ibid., p.146.
38 ibid.
39 ibid., p.148.
40 ibid.
41 ibid., p.150.
42 ibid., p.158.
43 ibid., p.172.
44 ibid.
45 ibid., p.186.
46 ibid., p.375.
47 ibid., pp.186-7.
48 For further discussion of this issue, see my *Deadly Dialectics: Sex, Violence and Nihilism in the World of Yukio Mishima* (Japan Library/Curzon Press and the University of Hawaii Press, 1994) and my *Soundings in Time: The Fictive Art of Kawabata Yasunari* (Japan Library/Curzon Press and the University of Hawaii Press, 1998).
49 Shiga, *A Dark Night's Passing*, p.184.
50 ibid., p.193.
51 ibid., p.194.
52 ibid., p.181.
53 ibid., p.174.
54 ibid., p.178.
55 On this point, see Ueda, *Modern Japanese Writers*, p.87.
56 Shiga, *A Dark Night's Passing*, p.178.
57 ibid., p.185.
58 ibid.
59 Shiga, *A Dark Night's Passing*, the latter two stories are translated in this book, pp.144-175.
60 Shiga, *A Dark Night's Passing*, p.201.
61 ibid., p.202.
62 ibid., p.271.

63 ibid., p.312.
64 ibid., pp.311-2.
65 ibid., p.337.
66 ibid., p.338.
67 ibid.
68 ibid., p.341.
69 ibid.
70 ibid.
71 ibid., p.251.
72 ibid.
73 ibid.
74 ibid., p.352.
75 ibid., pp.354-5.
76 ibid., p.356.
77 ibid.
78 ibid.
79 ibid., p.357.
80 ibid., p.358.
81 ibid.
82 ibid., p.357.
83 ibid., p.364.
84 ibid., p.369.
85 ibid., p.381.
86 ibid., p.392.
87 ibid., pp.383-4.
88 ibid., p.399.
89 ibid.
90 ibid., p.398.
91 ibid., p.400.
92 ibid., pp.400-1.
93 Daisetz Teitaro Suzuki, *Essays in Zen Buddhism*, in 3 volumes, (New York: Samuel Weiser, 1971).
94 Shiga, A *Dark Night's Passing*, p.401.
95 ibid.
96 ibid., p.407.
97 ibid., p.400.
98 ibid., p.407.
99 Percy Lubbock, *The Craft of Fiction* (London: Johnathan Cape, 1939).
100 Shiga, *A Dark Night's Passing*, p.408.
101 See Mathy, p.102.
102 See, for instance, Mathy, p.102, and Edwin McClellan's essay in the *Nihon Bungaku Kenkyū Shiryō Sōsho* series (Tokyo: Yuseido, 1970), pp.300-01.
103 For concise definitions of Zen aesthetics, see Shin'ichi Hisamatsu, *Zen and the Fine Arts*, especially pp.28-40, and Donald Keene, 'Japanese Aesthetics', in *Appreciations of Japanese Culture*, pp.11-25.

104 See above, pp.84-85.
105 See Mathy, *Shiga*, p.28.
106 See this book, pp. 57-59.
107 Karatani Kōjin, *Origins of Modern Japanese Literature*, edited by Brett de Bary (Durham, N.C.: Duke University Press, 1993), p.164.
108 Seidensticker, in *Studies in Japanese Culture*, p.210.

BIBLIOGRAPHY

Arima, Tatsuo, *The Failure of Freedom: A Portrait of Modern Japanese Intellectuals*. Cambridge, Mass.: Harvard University Press, 1969.

Axthelm, Peter M., *The Modern Confessional Novel*. New Haven: Yale University Press, 1967.

Benson, Jackson, editor, *The Short Stories of Ernest Hemingway: Critical Essays*. Durham: Duke University Press, 1975.

Booth, Wayne, *The Rhetoric of Fiction*. Chicago University Press, 1966.

Bradbury, Malcolm, *The Modern British Novel*. London: Penguin Books, 1994.

Doi Takeo, *The Anatomy of Dependence*. Tokyo: Kodansha, 1973.

Donaldson, Scott, *By Force of Will: the Life and Art of Ernest Hemingway*. New York: Viking Press, 1977.

Forster, E.M., *Aspects of the Novel*. London: Edward Arnold, 1927.

Fowler, Edward, *Shishōsetsu in Modern Japanese Literature*. Durham, N.C.: Center for International Studies, Duke University, 1986.

Fowler, Edward, *The Rhetoric of Confession: Shishōsetsu in Early Twentieth-Century Japanese Fiction*. Berkeley: University of California Press, 1988.

Freedman, Ralph, *The Lyrical Novel*. Princeton University Press, 1963.

Fujii, James A., *Complicit Fictions: The Subject in Modern Japanese Prose Narrative*. Berkeley: University of California Press, 1993.

Gessel, Van C., *The Sting of Life: Four Contemporary Japanese Novelists*. New York: Columbia University Press, 1989.

Gessel, Van C., *Three Modern Novelists: Sōseki, Tanizaki, Kawabata*. Tokyo: Kodansha, 1993.

Goossen, Theodore, 'Instinct and Harmony in the Animal Stories of Charles G.D. Roberts and Naoya Shiga.' In *Nature and Identity in Canadian and Japanese Literature*. Edited by Kinya Tsuruta and Theodore Goossen. Toronto: University of Toronto-York University Joint Centre for Asia Pacific Studies, 1988.

Hagiwara Takao, 'Man and Nature in Sinclair Ross' *As for Me and My House* and Naoya Shiga's *A Dark Night's Passing*.' In *Nature and Identity in Canadian and Japanese Literature*. Edited by Kinya Tsuruta and Theodore Goossen. Toronto: University of Toronto-York University Joint Centre for Asia Pacific Studies, 1988.

Hemingway, Ernest, *In Our Time*. New York: Scribner's, 1925.

Hijiya-Kirschnereit, Irmela, *Rituals of Self-Revelation: Shi-Shōsetsu as*

Literary Genre and Socio-cultural Phenomenon. Cambridge: Harvard University Press, 1996.

Hijiya-Kirschnereit, Irmela, *Shishōsetsu - Gattungsgeschichte und Gattungstheorie einer autobiographischen Romanliteratur des modernen Japan.* Bochum: Ruuhr-Universität, 1980.

Hisamatsu Shin'ichi, *Zen and the Fine Arts.* Tokyo: Kodansha, 1971.

Ito, Ken, *Visions of Desire: Tanizaki's Fictional Worlds.* Stanford: Stanford University Press, 1991.

Itō Sei, *Essays on Natsume Sōseki's Works.* Tokyo: Ministry of Education, 1970.

Jackson, Earl, 'Elaboration of the Moment: The Lyric Tradition in Modern Japanese Literature.' In *Literary History, Narrative, and Culture,* edited by Wimal Dissanayake and Steven Bradbury. Honolulu: The College of Languages, Linguistics and Literature University of Hawaii and the East-West Center, 1989.

Karatani Kōjin, *Origins of Modern Japanese Literature.* Translation edited by Brett de Bary. Durham, N.C.: Duke University Press, 1993.

Katō Shūichi, *A History of Japanese Literature, Volume 3, The Modern Years.* Translated by Don Sanderson. Tokyo: Kodansha International, 1990.

Keene, Donald, *Appreciations of Japanese Culture.* Tokyo: Kodansha, 1971.

Keene, Donald, *Dawn to the West: Japanese Literature in the Modern Era (Fiction).* New York: Holt, Rinehart and Winston, 1984.

Keene, Donald, editor, *Modern Japanese Literature.* New York: Grove Press, 1956.

Keene, Donald, *World Within Walls: Japanese Literature of the Pre-Modern Era, 1600-1867.* New York: Holt, Rinehart, Winston, 1976.

Keene, Donald, editor, *Modern Japanese Literature.* New York: Grove Press, 1956.

Kenmochi Takehiko et al, editors. *Nihonjin to ma.* Tokyo: Kōdansha, 1981.

Kobayashi, Hideo, *Kobayashi Hideo Zenshū.* Tokyo: Shinchōsha, 1955.

Leavis, F.R., *A Selection from Scrutiny.* Cambridge: Cambridge University Press, 1968.

Kōno Toshirō, Miyoshi Yukio, Takemori Tenyū and Hiraoka Toshio, editors. *Taishō no bungaku.* Tokyo: Yūhikaku, 1972.

Leavis, F.R., *A Selection from Scrutiny.* Cambridge: Cambridge University Press, 1968.

Lodge, David, *After Bakhtin: Essays on Fiction and Criticism.* London: Routledge, 1990.

Lubbock, Percy, *The Craft of Fiction.* London: Johnathan Cape, 1939.

Marcus, Marvin. *Paragons of the Ordinary: The Biographical Literature of Mori Ōgai.* Honolulu: University of Hawaii Press, 1993.

Mathy, Francis, *Shiga Naoya.* New York: Twayne Publishers, 1974.

Miner, Earl, *The Japanese Tradition in British and American Literature.* Princeton University Press, 1958.

Miyoshi, Masao, *Accomplices of Silence*. Berkeley: Univ. of Calif. Press, 1974.

Miyoshi Masao, 'Against the Grain.' In *Postmodernism and Japan*. Edited by Masao Miyoshi and H.D. Harootunian. Durham: Duke University Press, 1988.

Miyoshi, Masao, *Off Center: Power and Culture Relations between Japan and the United States*. Cambridge: Harvard University Press, 1991.

Morris, Ivan, editor, *Modern Japanese Stories*. Rutland, Vermont: Charles E. Tuttle, 1962.

Mishima Yukio and Bownas, Geoffrey, *New Writing in Japan*. Harmondsworth, Middlesex: Penguin Books, 1972.

Napier, Susan J., *The Fantastic in Modern Japanese Literature: The Subversion of Modernity*. London and New York: Routledge, 1996.

Petersen, Gwenn Boardman, *The Moon in the Water*. Honolulu: The University Press of Hawaii, 1979.

Pollack, David, *Reading against Culture: Ideology and Narrative in the Japanese Novel*. Ithaca: Cornell University Press, 1992.

Rimer, J. Thomas, editor. *Culture and Identity: Japanese Intellectuals During the Interwar Years*. Princeton: Princeton University Press, 1990.

Roggendorf, Joseph, *Studies in Japanese Culture*. Tokyo: Sophia University Press, 1963.

Rosenberger, Nancy R., *Japanese Sense of Self*. Cambridge: Cambridge University Press, 1992.

Satō, Tadao, *Currents in Japanese Cinema*. Tokyo: Kodansha, 1982.

Seidensticker, Edward, *This Country, Japan*. Tokyo: Kodansha, 1979.

Shiga Naoya, *Shiga Naoya Zenshū*. Tokyo: Iwanami Shoten, 1955-56.

Shiga Naoya, *Seibei to hyōtan*. Tokyo: Shinchosha, 1968.

Shiga Naoya, *Kozō no kamisama*. Tokyo, Iwanami Shoten, 1928.

Shiga Naoya, *A Dark Night's Passing*. A translation of *An'ya kōro* by Edwin McClellan. Tokyo: Kodansha, 1976.

Shively, Donald, *Tradition and Modernization in Japanese Culture*. Princeton University Press, 1971.

Shirane, Haruo, *The Bridge of Dreams: Poetics in the Tale of Genji*. Stanford: Stanford University Press, 1987.

Sibley, William, *The Shiga Hero*. University of Chicago Ph.D. dissertation, 1971.

Silverberg, Miriam, *Changing Song: The Marxist Manifestos of Nakano Shigeharu*. Princeton: Princeton University Press, 1990.

Starrs, Roy, *Deadly Dialectics: Sex, Violence and Nihilism in the World of Yukio Mishima*. Honolulu: University of Hawaii Press and Folkestone, England: Japan Library, 1994.

Starrs, Roy, 'Modernism and Tradition in Kawabata's Art of Fiction.' In *Cultural Encounters: China, Japan, and the West*. Edited by Søren Clausen, Roy Starrs and Anne Wedell-Wedellsborg. Aarhus, Denmark: Aarhus University Press, 1995.

Starrs, Roy, *Soundings in Time: The Fictive Art of Kawabata Yasunari*. Honolulu: University of Hawaii Press and Folkestone, England: Japan Library, 1998.

Steiner, George, *Language and Silence*. London: Faber and Faber, 1967.

Steiner, George, *What Is Comparative Literature?* Oxford: Clarendon Press, 1995.

Suzuki Daisetsu, *Zen and Japanese Culture*. Princeton University Press, 1959.

Tanizaki Jun'ichirō, *Tanizaki Jun'ichirō Zenshū*. Tokyo: Chūō Kōronsha, 1958.

Tanizaki Jun'ichirō, *In Praise of Shadows*. New Haven: Leete's Island Books, 1977.

Tanikawa Tetsuzō, *Shiga Naoya no sakuhin*. Tokyo: Mikasa shobō, 1942.

Tolstoy, Leo, *Nine Stories*. Translated by Louise and Aylmer Maude. London: Oxford University Press, 1934.

Tolstoy, Leo, *What Is Art?* Translated by Aylmer Maude. Oxford University Press, 1929.

Tsuruta, Kinya and Goossen, Theodore, editors. *Nature and Identity in Canadian and Japanese Literature*. Toronto: University of Toronto-York University Joint Centre for Asia Pacific Studies, 1988.

Ueda Makoto, *Modern Japanese Writers and the Nature of Literature*. Stanford University Press, 1976.

Ueda Makoto, *Literary and Art Theories in Japan*. Cleveland: Western Reserve University, 1957.

Washburn, Dennis C., *The Dilemma of the Modern in Japanese Fiction*. New Haven: Yale University Press, 1995.

Weeks, Robert, *Hemingway: a Collection of Critical Essays*. Englewood Cliffs, N.J.: Prentice-Hall, 1962.

Wilson, Edmund, *Eight Essays*. New York: Doubleday, 1954.

Yanagida Izumi, Katsumoto Seiichirō and Ino Kenji, editors. *Zadankai: Taishō bungaku shi*. Tokyo: Iwanami shoten, 1965.

Yoshida Sei-ichi, *Bunshō to buntai*. Tokyo: Meiji Shoin, 1963.

Zweig, Paul, *The Heresy of Self-Love*. Princeton: Princeton University Press, 1980.

INDEX